Work Hard, Be Hard

Work Hard, Be Hard

*Journeys Through
"No Excuses" Teaching*

Jim Horn

ROWMAN & LITTLEFIELD
Lanham • Boulder • New York • London

Published by Rowman & Littlefield
A wholly owned subsidiary of The Rowman & Littlefield Publishing Group, Inc.
4501 Forbes Boulevard, Suite 200, Lanham, Maryland 20706
www.rowman.com

Unit A, Whitacre Mews, 26-34 Stannary Street, London SE11 4AB

British Library Cataloguing in Publication Information Available

Library of Congress Cataloging-in-Publication Data

ISBN 978-1-4758-2579-4 (cloth : alk. paper) -- ISBN 978-1-4758-2580-0 (pbk. : alk. paper) -- ISBN
978-1-4758-2581-7 (electronic)

♾ ™ The paper used in this publication meets the minimum requirements of American
National Standard for Information Sciences Permanence of Paper for Printed Library
Materials, ANSI/NISO Z39.48-1992.

Printed in the United States of America

Contents

List of Figures

Preface

KIPP [Knowledge Is Power Program] is the way the white and powerful want the poor of color to be educated.
—Ira Socol (2010)

It is interesting to speculate as to what direction education for black and brown children in the segregated South might have taken if separate schools based on race had not been declared unconstitutional by *Brown v. Board* in 1954. Would policy elites have continued to ignore the plight of black children in the absence of the *Brown* ruling, or would they have tried other educational interventions besides desegregation and resource transfusions to raise achievement levels of black children stranded by generations of poverty, racism, and separation?

What if black parents during the late Jim Crow era before *Brown v. Board* had been offered something other than neglected public schools with old textbooks and worn-out band instruments and leaky roofs? What if the philanthropic community and government had come together to offer a different kind of school as a tax-supported alternative to the grossly inequitable public schools for black children during the late Jim Crow era? What if it were, in fact,

- a school that would be based on a non-negotiable philosophy and instructional model that accepted No Excuses for any shortcomings in expected behaviors, attitudes, or academic performance?
- a school where privileged, beginning teachers with little or no professional training would replace most of the credentialed black teachers with years of experience in working with black children?

- a school that focused principally on reading and math, with little interest, time, or resources expended for athletics, drama, art, libraries, vocational skills, or even textbooks?
- a school that required children to attend school for ten hours a day and on Saturdays, plus three weeks during the summer?
- a school where a school uniform and even a desk to sit in would have to be earned?
- a school where children would be forced to be silent most of the day and made to march silently in single file from class to class?
- a school that would demand total compliance with instant punishment for any infraction, using methods that would include isolation, shaming, humiliation, and screaming at them?
- a school that would be open to white, middle-class children, even if none chose to attend?
- a school that would remain, in fact, segregated, even though the stated goal of the school would be to prepare children for college and careers in the wider world?
- a school that would require parents and children to sign contracts if they were to be admitted and remain enrolled, contracts that guaranteed support for rules, policies, and methods that parents would have no direct or indirect role in deciding?
- a school that would use public school tax dollars without public oversight to pay a nonprofit corporation to run the school?
- a school receiving millions of dollars in support from the largest corporations and corporate foundations in America?
- a school that required children to sacrifice much of their childhood just to survive in the school?

Would black parents of the Jim Crow era choose such a new kind of school for their children, or would they, in fact, continue to prefer the run-down public schools in their neighborhoods where their children at least would be taught by professional, empathetic teachers who believe children deserve dignity and respect? Somehow I think that black parents of the 1950s would wonder how such a new "choice" could represent an educational improvement over what they were accustomed to.

After all, their children in the old Jim Crow era public schools had a curriculum that emphasized social studies and science, health and art, along with reading and math, even if their textbooks were discards from the white schools. And their children certainly were less stressed, tired, and guilt-ridden for not living up to white adult expectations and demands of the new "choice" school. Their children could, at least, remain children.

I believe black parents of the 1950s would denounce such new schools, much the same way that black intellectuals, leaders, journalists, and parents, too, rejected the methods and ideology of the industrial education schools so popular among white Northern philanthropists in the post-Civil War era South (Anderson, 1988). In those schools of that earlier era, teaching focused on the "dignity of labor," rudimentary academic skills, character traits, and social skills required for second-class citizenship, continued racial separation, and total compliance to white economic demands.

Though largely uneducated, the majority of black parents, even then, wanted the same educational rights for their children that were provided for white children of the late nineteenth and early twentieth centuries. In most cases, of course, black parents never came close to that kind of educational equality, but they remained insistent upon control of their schools, even if public support was meager at best. The majority of black parents and leaders rejected the spread of schools, either public or private, developed on the "industrial education model" (Anderson, 1988), as it came to be known.

If black parents of the Jim Crow era, whether in 1890 or 1950, would have rejected the alternative "choice" described above, then we may wonder how long it will take parents of this era to reject the new No Excuses schools that have all the qualities described above and that are now proliferating in the early twenty-first century. When will black and white citizens, alike, demand what most former slave parents and their children asked for over a hundred years ago, which was an equal education in nonsegregated schools?

And why have they not done so already, when we might expect rage from parents as a suitable response to such second-class schools? Part of the answer, I believe, is attributable to a widespread hopelessness among urban parents for anything better than what is being offered as the only choice to another generation of schools characterized by malignant neglect. As Hannah Arendt (1969) noted, it is only where "there is some reason to suspect that conditions could be changed and are not [that we see] rage arise." The absence of rage or resistance or demands for humanizing educational alternatives among urban parents may offer "the clearest sign of dehumanization" (p. 63).

Another part of the answer to these questions has much to do with how little parents, children, teachers, and other citizens know about the No Excuses KIPP (Knowledge Is Power Program) charter school model. Most of what they do know has been provided to them by corporate think tanks, sponsored research reports, corporate foundations, public relations and marketing specialists, charter school organizations, spokesmen for the education industry, and print and nonprint mass media outlets and social media that can be counted on to report the talking points of corporate education reformers and their wealthy benefactors.

This book represents a modest effort, then, to provide information that most parents and teachers, college presidents, or local politicians have not heard or read before. As such, it represents a departure from the official story of the No Excuses school model presented in Jay Mathews's (2009a) paean to the KIPP school founders, *Work Hard, Be Nice: How Two Inspired Teachers Created the Most Promising Schools in America*. Unlike Mathews's *Work Hard, Be Nice*, however, this is not a book designed to celebrate the KIPP Model or KIPP's founders, David Levin and Mike Feinberg.

Work Hard, Be Hard: Journeys Through "No Excuses" Teaching is not a book that ignores or downplays the uncomfortable facts, sad ironies, and tough questions surrounding the widely supported, segregated No Excuses model for educating urban poor children in punishing, total-compliance environments. My purpose in writing this book was to closely examine and interrogate the practices and ideology of the No Excuses charter schools that have become synonymous with the KIPP Model.

Unlike Jay Mathews, I did not visit any KIPP schools during the years of writing this book—even though I tried. In fact, when my repeated requests to visit the KIPP schools in Memphis in 2013 and 2014 were denied, I contacted Jay, with whom I have maintained a prickly relationship over the past ten years by writing from contrasting perspectives about corporate education issues and education reform schools. His interventions did not help, however, and his queries to KIPP's director of public affairs, Steve Mancini, brought a finalizing negative response that indicated that the content of my previous writing and speaking about KIPP had disqualified me from visiting any of KIPP's campuses. And so it goes.

The principal source materials for this book, then, are from public documents and first-person published and unpublished accounts. The book's core is based on in-depth interviews with twenty-five former charter school teachers, twenty-three of whom are former KIPP teachers and two who are teachers from charter chains based on the KIPP No Excuses model. All the interviews were conducted between 2011 and 2014, and each was recorded and transcribed verbatim. All former KIPP teachers who contacted me wanting to share their stories were included, and all of the individual interview excerpts were selected with an eye to remaining true to the tone of the individual accounts.

Because former teachers expressed anxiety or fear of potential repercussions as a result of sharing their experiences, all information has been carefully edited to eliminate the possibility of breaching anonymity. Along with some descriptive thematic groupings and some limited interpretation and contextualizing of participant accounts, I have used many direct quotes from former teachers, preferring the profundity of participant accounts to my commentary on them. Each excerpt is identifiable by a number designated by the data analysis tool HyperQual (Padilla, 2011), which can be linked back to individual interview transcripts. All original recordings have been retained.

While two teachers were still teaching at KIPP when they were interviewed, all of the teachers interviewed had already made the decision to leave KIPP. I was most interested to know what it was like inside the KIPP bubble from the perspectives of those who were no longer inside it, either psychologically or physically. The majority of participants had had some time to recover and to reflect on their experiences prior to their interviews, even though all these teachers felt working in No Excuses environments had indelibly influenced them.

Seven of the KIPP teachers interviewed (see figure 0.1) had less than two years of experience when they began at KIPP, and five of them began teaching at KIPP without teaching experience. Seventeen of the teachers had less than four years of experience. Seventeen interview participants were women, and eight were men. Twenty-two were Caucasian, and three were African American. Eight of the teachers worked at KIPP between two and four years, and ten lasted less than a year at KIPP.

Seven worked between one and two years at KIPP. Five had degrees in education with professional certification. Nineteen had bachelor's degrees, and six had advanced degrees. Sixteen of the teachers taught at KIPP middle schools, and four taught at KIPP high schools. Seven KIPP teachers had previously taught for two-year stints for Teach for America before coming to KIPP, and none had been assigned to KIPP to fulfill a TFA commitment.

Using hundreds of pages of transcribed data based on firsthand accounts of life inside No Excuses schools, the goal has been to achieve a new level of public understanding of the KIPP Model. While the stories of former KIPP Model teachers provide the core of this work, the book offers, too, a brief historical perspective on previous efforts to provide paternalistic educational interventions directed toward marginalized and economically disadvantaged populations.

Joining me in this effort with their own individual contributions in chapter 3 and chapter 9, respectively, are Scott Ellison and Barbara Veltri. Professor Ellison provides a cultural studies orientation to examining the KIPP organization as exemplifying the convergence of neoliberal politics and the assertive activities of the business and philanthropic communities.

Teacher educator, professor Barbara Veltri, examines key elements of KIPP's sister organization, Teach for America. Professor Veltri, author of *Learning on Other People's Kids: Becoming a Teach for America Teacher*, examines the role of Teach for America in providing the manpower and ideological complements required to counter very high levels of teacher attrition in No Excuses schools.

As an antidote to the KIPP Foundation's marketing and public relations outreach, which can be found in any number of examples from both print and nonprint media, this book offers a critical eye and raises serious questions related to public culpability for a punitive type of tax-supported segregated

Gender	Race	Degree	Prior Teaching Experience	No Excuses teaching level	Time at No Excuses School	TFA
F	AA	Sociology	0	Middle	5 months	
M	AA	ECE	0	Middle	6 months	
F	W	Psychology	14 years	Middle	2 years	
F	W	History	2 years	HS	2 years	x
F	W	Science	.5 years	Middle	1 year	x
F	W	Music	Several years	Middle	½ year	
M	W	Physiology	0	Middle	3 years	
M	W	Liberal Arts	2 years	Middle	4 years	x
M	W	Psychology	20	Middle	2.5 years	
F	W	Art	3 years	Middle	2 years	
M	W	History	1 year	Middle	3 months	
F	W	English	6 years	Middle	1 year	
M	W	Political Science	2 years	Middle	2 years	x
M	W	Humanities	2 years	Middle	1 year	x
F	W	Greek	0	High	1 year	
F	W	English	2 years	Middle	4 months	
F	W	Special Ed	2.5 years	Middle	1.5 years	
F	W	Art Ed	1 year	Middle	2 year	
F	AA	English Ed	6 years	High	1 year	
F	W	Social Studies Ed	10 years	Middle	3 months	
M	W	History	13 years	High	3 months	
F	W	Literature	2 years	Middle	6 months	
F	W	English	15 years	Middle	1 year	
F	W	Political Science	2 years	Middle	4 months	x
F	W	English	2	Middle	4 months	x

Figure 0.1. No Excuses teacher interview participants

schooling that our dominant culture celebrates *only* for children who are disenfranchised by poverty and discrimination.

As one former KIPP teacher wondered aloud near the end of our interview, would such schooling practices that we see at KIPP be allowed for the children of white philanthropists who fund these schools? Or would KIPP practices be allowed in the private schools attended by the supportive politicians' children, or for the KIPP administrators and teachers who would never allow their own offspring to be subjected to a harsh, total-compliance charter school like KIPP?

Readers are asked to keep in mind this central question that I try to answer throughout this book: As a result of the spread of the No Excuses charter school teaching model exemplified by KIPP, "Who wins and who loses, and by what mechanisms of power?" (Flyvbjerg, 2001) In addition to trying to answer that core question, this book attempts to unravel a number of conundrums and apparent paradoxes:

1. How did the spread of an unsustainable boutique education intervention like KIPP reach its exemplary status among the advocates of education reform?
2. How did high achievement expectations become exemplified by total-compliance enforcements that are applied only to the segregated and economically disadvantaged children?
3. How did economic and social advantages and resources become insignificant factors to school achievement only for those who don't have such advantages and resources?
4. What rationale is used for insisting that children who are handicapped by poverty and all its attendant problems will achieve equally on standardized measures with children who have every economic and social advantage?
5. How do the grim and punitive environments of No Excuses schools remain underreported by the media and, otherwise, ignored by policymakers and child welfare advocates?
6. What may serve as more humane, sustainable, diverse, and democratic alternatives to the No Excuses charter school teaching model?

By presenting the firsthand facts about teaching within total-compliance No Excuses schools, this book goes beyond accounts offered in news features, articles, and interviews that focus only on the KIPP Model's test scores and its goals for expanding college opportunities among economically disadvantaged children. In short, this book offers a naturalistic palliative to the naïve and misleading portrayals of No Excuses schooling that have garnered support among political and economic elites.

From discipline that crosses over from rigorous intent to abusive practice, and from teacher expectations that go beyond the upper reaches of possibility into the stratosphere of the absurd, this book presents accounts by former teachers who forthrightly share experiences in total-compliance schools that have not been heard before and that are not likely to be soon forgotten.

Finally, *Work Hard, Be Hard* examines new developments in No Excuses schooling practices that, in addition to academic remediation, now focus on psychological interventions intended to alter children's neurological schemas in order to effect changes in their emotional and sociocultural values and behaviors. Fraught with potential for abuse by nonprofessionals who remain laser focused on test performance and grades for "performance character," these latest developments are explicated and then contrasted with other orientations and practices that acknowledge both the sociological and psychological sides of children's experiences. In doing so, I hope to reawaken the virtues of teaching and learning within the expansive boundaries of the science and art of humane pedagogy applied to children who require the most caring, qualified, and experienced teachers.

REFERENCES

Anderson, J. (1988). *The education of Blacks in the South, 1860–1935.* Chapel Hill, NC: University of North Carolina Press.

Arendt, H. (1969). *On violence.* New York: Harcourt, Brace & World.

Flyvbjerg, B. (2001). *Making social science matter: Why social inquiry fails and how it can succeed again.* Cambridge: Cambridge University Press.

Horn, J. (2010). Corporatism, KIPP, and cultural eugenics. In *The Gates Foundation and the future of U.S. "public" schools.* Edited by P. Kovacs. New York: Routledge.

Mathews, J. (2009a). *Work hard, be nice: How two inspired teachers created the most promising schools in America.* New York: Algonquin Books.

Padilla, R. (2011). HyperQualLite version 1.0. Computer software. Boerne, TX: Author. https://sites.google.com/site/hyperqual.

Socol, I. (2010, September 1). Irrepressible ed blogger beats me up, again. http://voices.washingtonpost.com/class-struggle/2010/09/irrepessible_ed_blogger_beats.html .

Acknowledgements

This book has been a long time coming, and it would not have been possible without the patient and articulate teachers who sat for the extended interviews that became the heart of this book. I am so appreciative of their insights, candor, and courage in sharing their experiences in "No Excuses" schools.

I want to thank, too, Professor Scott Ellison and Professor Barbara Veltri for their contributed chapters, which so enrich the theoretical and policy contexts for the book. I extend my deep gratitude to Jan Allen for her invaluable help in cover design.

Many thanks, too, to my patient readers who offered so many constructive remarks: Janeene Larkin Horn, S. D. Wilburn, Susan Ohanian, and Stephen Krashen. Both Stephen and Susan were generous enough to write advance reviews of the book, as did scholar and activist Julian Vasquez Heilig, who posted his review at *Cloaking Inequity*.

Finally, I want to thank Tom Koerner at Rowman & Littlefield for believing in this book.

Introduction

"Negro Problems" and Philanthropic Solutions

The past is never dead. It's not even past.
—William Faulkner (1951)

Shortly after the end the Civil War, a decommissioned Yankee general who was also the son of a former missionary superintendent for the Hawaiian plantation schools opened the Hampton Normal and Agricultural Institute in Hampton, Virginia. When named as Hampton's first superintendent in 1868, Samuel Chapman Armstrong's mission was to rigorously indoctrinate young freedmen to become workers and teachers who would fan out across the South to teach basic literacy to black children and to instill a lifelong devotion to the "dignity of labor" (Anderson, 1988, p. 34).

Armstrong, along with a couple of male assistant administrators and a faculty composed of white female missionaries, taught the future teachers of Southern black children that hard toil and compliant behavior were the habits that could build character and, thus, help to mitigate the moral defects that had been passed down to them as a result of their uniquely inferior race (Anderson, 1988). Armstrong's vision to instill in the children of freed slaves a lasting dedication to labor and self-sacrifice attracted the financial support of wealthy Northern politicians and philanthropists who were eagerly looking for a solution to what they termed the "Negro problem" (Anderson, 1988, p. 72). With almost four million former slaves that outnumbered whites in some regions of the South, it was of paramount importance that African Americans appreciate their role in rebuilding the Southern economy, while understanding the utter folly of aspirations for social equality. Armstrong and his white philanthropist backers hoped that black children would grow up and help rebuild the cotton and tobacco industries that had been destroyed in the war of Emancipation.

With "Negrophobia" (Anderson, 1988, p. 68) at a high point following the end of the war, it was essential, Armstrong believed, that African American youngsters learn the appropriate work behaviors and character habits that would make them assets in reestablishing the Southern agricultural economy, which supplied materials for the textile industries and manufacturing economies of the North.

The education that black students received at Hampton and the schools that came to emulate Hampton celebrated the dignity of hard toil as the most viable way students could overcome their moral inferiority, which black students were taught to accept as the unalterable clasp that bound them together as children of African lineage. Only 20 percent of students that began school at Hampton worked hard enough and remained compliant enough to earn a certificate at the end of the two-to-three-year rigidly controlled program that focused more on work habits than on book learning.

The new black teachers who had survived their Hampton preparation became the carriers of industrial education ideology that espoused the belief that responsible black citizens must shun civic involvement such as voting and race mixing, as their cultural backgrounds and moral failings had left them unprepared and unfit to do either. Many left Hampton believing, as they were told by their social studies teacher, Thomas J. Jones, that slavery had, indeed, provided the basis for their salvation, for without it, they could never have been converted to Christianity or been educated properly, for that matter.

Armstrong's Hampton Model of industrial education came to embody a systematic method to indoctrinate and pacify the freed black population, which was clamoring for that magical thing called education. Freed slaves, educated according to the Hampton Model, offered a renewable stream of cheap and dependable laborers who could be counted upon to embrace their destiny to "plow, hoe, ditch, and grub" (Anderson, 1988, p. 48) without protest, agitation, or workplace demands.

Black workers trained to embrace the "dignity of labor" would humbly seek redemption and acceptance for their shortcomings through their unwavering commitment to achieve what powerful white men determined as the necessary knowledge that would purportedly serve to liberate those who remained steadfast in their efforts. In short, Hampton students were taught everything that was necessary to make them entirely complicit in their own subjugation (Anderson, 1988).

Despite rejection by many black citizens, the black press, and leading intellectuals such as W. E. B. Du Bois, Henry Morehouse, and Malcolm MacVicar, the Hampton Model was fully embraced by a who's who of leading politicians and Northern philanthropists. Rutherford B. Hayes, James

Eastman, Theodore Roosevelt, and Andrew Carnegie were just a few of the progressives who viewed the Hampton Model as the solution to the "Negro problem" (Anderson, 1988, p. 72), and growing political and financial support for Hampton led to the subsequent founding of the Tuskegee Institute, headed by the Hampton-educated former slave Booker T. Washington.

By the end of the nineteenth century, industrial training schools were promoted among white elites as the most suitable education for African American, Hispanic, and Native American students in the South and the North. Hampton's most famous alumnus, Booker T. Washington, became the leading black educator and proponent for the Hampton Model after he was put in charge of the new Tuskegee Institute in 1881. By 1895 Washington was the leading black spokesman for continuing social apartheid and an incremental approach to civil rights, social concepts that reflected what Washington had learned at Hampton from white Northern teachers.

Having been taught that African Americans had centuries to make up in terms of moral and cultural development before they could ever expect social or political equality, Washington argued that racial discrimination could only be remedied by earning the respect that would surely come to those blacks who 1) persisted in working hard at whatever job was offered, and 2) exhibited character traits that would eventually overcome a host of moral and character weaknesses. The story of this largely ignored and dark chapter of our educational history is chronicled in James Anderson's compelling book, *The Education of Blacks in the South: 1860–1935.*

When Samuel Armstrong died in 1893, Hampton chaplain and Yale graduate Hollis Frissell was named principal and remained so until his death in 1917. With the backing of philanthropist and head of Hampton's Board of Trustees Robert Ogden, Frissell widely promoted industrial education based on character training and hard, manual labor. Ogden and other philanthropists such as George Peabody believed that the health of the economy, particularly in the South, depended upon the labor of black men and women, and they sought to promote an educational model that would "attach the Negro to the [Southern] soil and prevent his exodus from the country to the city" (Anderson, quoting Ogden, 1988, p. 89).

The *New York Times* reported November 14, 1898, that Dr. Frissell, accompanied by Ogden, had been in Manhattan raising money for Hampton scholarships. Accompanied by a black student quartet singing "old plantation melodies with pleasing effect," Frissell shared his new stereopticon presentation of life among Hampton students learning to become compliant teachers who would take the industrial education philosophy and practices to black communities across the South: "Most of our pupils prefer to do missionary work among their own people. They do not go north to seek their own fortunes, but go out through the South to help uplift their friends. The work is often attended with great difficulty to them, but they endure it willingly for the sake of the good they can do" (*New York Times*, 1898).

Had it not been for staunch resistance from black intellectuals and religious leaders, the industrial training school model would have had an even deeper impact than it did on the education of African Americans in the decades just before and after the turn of the twentieth century. In a 1903 essay titled "Of Mr. Booker T. Washington and Others," W. E. B. Du Bois (1903) offered this damning assessment of the industrial education model:

> Mr. Washington represents in Negro thought the old attitude of adjustment and submission; but adjustment at such a peculiar time as to make his programme unique. This is an age of unusual economic development, and Mr. Washington's programme naturally takes an economic cast, becoming a gospel of Work and Money to such an extent as apparently almost completely to overshadow the higher aims of life. (chapter 3, para. 15)

By 1905, white Northern neoabolitionists were finally awakened to the ugly realities of the black industrial education model (Anderson, 1988), and resistance to it grew so that Hampton's methods and curriculum were finally updated after Frissell's death in 1917. As it turned out, the philanthropists' public relations machine and the white press could not contain the public debate between Hampton acolyte Booker T. Washington and Harvard sociologist W. E. B. Du Bois.

Du Bois's stinging critique of the Hampton Model became a rallying cry that reminded black and white citizens, alike, how black men and women might interact with the world when they are not trained for subservience and compliance. As it turned out, however, it was Booker T. Washington's racial accommodationist philosophy that prevailed for the first half of the twentieth century. Trained as he was at Hampton to remain dependable, compliant, hardworking, and of sound character, Washington represented the apotheosis of blackness for the vast majority of white elites and policymakers for generations that extended beyond the Civil Rights era that began with *Brown v. Board of Education*.

While Du Bois's insistence on equal educational opportunity for black citizens carried a great deal of weight among African American intellectuals and the black press, we need to remember that it was the dogged determination of local educators and black parents that led to the successful resistance against the white philanthropists' educational solution to the "Negro problem." And even though educational equality remained elusive, the curriculum and instructional methods used in the black schools that black citizens helped build and fund focused most often on the same knowledge and values dominant in the white schools.

By the second decade of the twentieth century, the industrial schooling of the Hampton Model that white philanthropists envisioned for black children came to be understood for what it was: an exploitative and racist indoctrination that served principally the needs of white landowners, Northern industrialists, and politicians determined to maintain racial segregation.

REFERENCES

Anderson, J. (1988). *The education of Blacks in the South, 1860–1935.* Chapel Hill, NC: University of North Carolina Press.

Du Bois, W. E. B. (1903). *The souls of black folk.* Chicago: A. C. McClurg & Co.; Bartleby.com, 1999. www.bartleby.com/114/.

Faulkner, W. (1951). *Requiem for a nun.* New York: Random House.

New York Times. (1898, November 14). To aid Hampton Institute: Dr. Frissell, the principal, explains the work for colored people and Indians at a church meeting. *New York Times.* http://timesmachine.nytimes.com/timesmachine/1898/11/14/102127757.html?pageNumber=2 .

Chapter One

The New Gospel of "Work and Money"

The danger of the past was that men became slaves. The danger of the future is that men may become robots.
—Erich Fromm (1955)

Just over a hundred years after Du Bois's withering criticism of the educational indoctrination that Washington absorbed at Hampton, the evidence that "work and money" have supplanted other "higher aims of life" is even more compelling than it was during America's first Gilded Age. In no venue is it more evident than in the No Excuses KIPP schools that many other charter schools and urban public schools have come to imitate.

The KIPP Model offers a mixture of academic and character education, which KIPP cofounder Mike Feinberg explained to a Tulane University audience in 2011: "KIPP teachers believe their job is to teach 49 percent academics and 51 percent character" (Morris, 2011). KIPP schools operate within total-compliance environments that are intensely segregated, with inexperienced and mostly white, middle-class teachers exacting a brand of strict discipline, long school hours, and more hours of homework.

We can only wonder what resistors of the Hampton Model such as Du Bois, MacVicar, and Morgan would say today about the KIPP Model, which purports to prepare all of its students for college, even though just half of fifth-graders who begin at KIPP schools finish eighth grade there (Miron, Urschel, & Saxton, 2011; Horn, 2010)—and only a third of eighth-grade completers graduate from college.

The Hampton Model died a slow death, with Northern philanthropists clinging to it up through the 1930s by repeated attempts to impose school programs that focused on producing black workers with basic literacy com-

1

petencies and strict character training (Anderson, 1988). We are not suggesting in this book that the KIPP Model and the Hampton Model are on the
same level in terms of severity, outcomes, or overt racism. To do so would be
to ignore the progress in the area of civil rights since the late nineteenth
century.

We do, however, find distinct vestiges of the Hampton Model in KIPP's
ideological grounding, rationale, punitive methods, teacher characteristics,
and financial support structure. Indeed, the tenacious enthusiasms among
white power elites and the mass media today harken back to days when the
Hampton Model was viewed as the solution to the "Negro problem." Echoes
of the Hampton message that can still be heard in schools that use the KIPP
Model will become clearer in the coming chapters.

PRIVATE AND PUBLIC SUPPORT FOR THE KIPP MODEL

KIPP's corporate chain of charter schools has been touted by the Philanthropy Roundtable as "the most recognizable brand name in contemporary
American schooling" (Levenick, 2010), thanks in large part to the deep and
ongoing financial support from federal grants, corporate foundation sources,
and venture philanthropists (Horn & Libby, 2010) that provide financial
advantages to KIPP and other charters that public schools are unable to
match. For instance, researchers (Miron, Urschel, & Saxton, 2011) found that
KIPP schools collected over a third more in revenue from public and private
sources than public schools in the same districts: "Combining public and
private sources of revenue, KIPP received, on average, $18,491 per pupil in
2007–08. . . . $6,500 more per pupil than what the local school districts
received in revenues" (p. ii).

The floodgates of corporate donations for charter construction, renova-
tion, and program funding opened in 2000, when a little-understood law
sailed through Congress in December 2000 and was signed by President Bill
Clinton before leaving office. The Community Renewal Tax Relief Act included a provision known as the New Markets Tax Credit, and it incentivized
new levels of giving (Rawls, 2013) for businesses, both nonprofit and for-
profit, in high-poverty areas:

> Banks and equity funds that invest in charter schools and other projects in
> underserved areas can take advantage of a very generous tax credit—as much
> as 39%—to help offset their expenditure in such projects. In essence, that
> credit amounts to doubling the amount of money they have invested within
> just seven years. Moreover, they are allowed to combinethat tax credit with job
> creation credits and other types of credit, as well as collect interest payments
> on the money they are lending out—all of which can add up to far more than
> double in returns. (para. 11)

Since 2001, then, billions of dollars have passed from venture philanthropists and philanthrocapitalists through equity bundlers, bond investors, and hedge funds into charter management organizations. Hundreds of millions of those dollars have made KIPP the most prominent and well-funded corporate education solution (Horn & Libby, 2010) for the disenfranchised urban poor. The Doris and Donald Fisher Fund, alone, gave over $90 million to the KIPP Foundation between 2001 and 2013, while investing heavily, as well, in KIPP's corporate feeder system for teachers and principals, Teach for America (TFA) (Levenick, 2010).

The financial backing from the Fisher family is emblematic of the philosophy of support for KIPP by its largest corporate foundation donors. The Walton Foundation has provided more than $60 million in grants, and the Gates Foundation has given over $20 million in grants to the KIPP Foundation and to individual KIPP schools. The Gates Foundation, too, has underwritten over $60 million in KIPP loan guarantees to various KIPP school networks (Banjo, 2009).

Clothing magnate and GAP founder, Don Fisher, who was chairman of the board of the KIPP Foundation when he died in 2009, expressed his conviction that "education is a business" and a school is "not much different from a GAP store" (Duxbury, 2008). Scott Hamilton, Fisher's point man for his educational venture philanthropy and the person responsible for bringing KIPP to Fisher's attention as the kind of "scalable" education project he was looking for, told *Philanthropy Magazine* (Levenick, 2010) that "Don treated KIPP and his philanthropic efforts the same creative and rigorous way he did his clothing business . . . and during our years of working together, KIPP in particular became like his second GAP" (para. 12).

With Fisher's $15 million initial donation in 2000 to establish the KIPP Foundation, KIPP gained the resources to become a prominent national player in the growing charter school market. That same year, the Republican National Committee provided national attention, when KIPP students (KIPPsters) performed a skit during TV prime time at the RNC Convention.

Until then, founders David Levin and Mike Feinberg had parlayed financial support from wherever they could find it, including an eccentric Houston furniture dealer, Jim McIngvale, who was widely known from his TV commercials as "Mattress Mack" (Mathews, 2008). Since 2000, however, KIPP has enjoyed lavish support from philanthropists, corporate foundations, the federal government, and Wall Street hedge funds (Gabriel & Medina, 2010).

Vast investments are funneled each year through nonprofit entities to carry out a persistent public relations campaign and to provide the monetary infrastructure for sustaining and growing the KIPP enterprise. In 2015, KIPP had 183 schools and seventy thousand students in twenty states, with plans to double the number of students by 2019. Below is a list of the largest KIPP Foundation (2015a) donors from 2000 to 2014:

$60,000,000 and Above
Doris & Donald Fisher Fund
Walton Family Foundation

$10,000,000–$24,999,999
Atlantic Philanthropies
Broad Foundation
Michael and Susan Dell Foundation
Robertson Foundation

$5,000,000–$9,999,999
Anonymous
Accenture
Bill and Melinda Gates Foundation
Citi Foundation
Thomas and Susan Dunn
Jack Kent Cooke Foundation
Karsh Family Foundation
New Profit, Inc.
Rainwater Charitable Foundation
Arthur Rock and Toni Rembe

$1,000,000–$4,999,999
Anonymous (2)
Akin Gump Strauss Hauer & Feld LLP[*]
Bain & Company[*]
Bezos Family Foundation
Charles and Helen Schwab Foundation
Charles and Lynn Schusterman Family Foundation
Credit Suisse Americas Foundation
Philippe and Debbie Dauman
Ewing Marion Kauffman Foundation
Reed Hastings and Patty Quillin
Laura and John Arnold Foundation
The Louis Calder Foundation
Marcus Foundation
Miles Family Foundation
The Wallace Foundation
William R. Kenan Jr. Charitable Trust

$500,000–999,999
Anonymous (2)
CityBridge Foundation
John and Laura Fisher
Morgridge Family Foundation
Maximilian Stone
U.S. Department of Education

$100,000–$499,999
Abrams Foundation
All Stars Helping Kids
Annenberg Foundation
The Annie E. Casey Foundation
Gordon T. Bell
The Big D. Foundation
The Carlson Family Foundation
Steven and Marilyn Casper
Chamberlin Family Foundation
Ben Chereskin
Kelly Coffey
Robert and Elizabeth Fisher
William and Sakurako Fisher
Goldman Sachs Foundation
Google
The G. R. Harsh IV & M. C. Whitman Charitable Foundation
Kinder Foundation
Leon Lowenstein Foundation
The McCance Foundation Trust
John and Hee-Jung Moon
National Geographic Education Foundation
New Schools Venture Fund
Peter B. and Adeline W. Ruffin Foundation
Prudential Foundation
Raikes Foundation
The Robin Hood Foundation
SAP America, Inc.
Seed the Dream Foundation
Select Equity Group, Inc.
State Farm Companies Foundation
Stephen Jr. and Susan Mandel
Susquehanna Foundation
The Todd Wagner Family Foundation
The William and Flora Hewlett Foundation

$50,000–$99,999
Anonymous
Mr. and Mrs. John D. Baker, II
Jim and Connie Calaway
Gary Chartrand
Congregation Emanu-El of the City of New York
David Goldberg and Sheryl Sandberg
Gurley Family Fund
Hellman Family Foundation
JaMel and Tom Perkins Family Foundation
The Jay Pritzker Foundation
The JPMorgan Chase Foundation
The Katzman Family Fund
Jeffrey and Linda Kofsky
Heidi Lynch and Daniel Greenstone
The Lynde and Harry Bradley Foundation
Elizabeth McLaughlin
NFL Charities
Orinoco
Palm, Inc. Corporate Headquarters
Stephen and Deborah Quazzo
Rose Community Foundation
Thompson Family Foundation

Federal support for KIPP increased dramatically after the election of President Barack Obama and his appointment of Arne Duncan as Secretary of Education. Between 2009 and 2012, the federal portion of KIPP's funding increased from 2 percent to 21 percent. With experience as Chicago Public Schools' CEO from 2001 to 2008, Arne Duncan's energetic support of corporate education reform initiatives was already well established when he arrived in Washington. In September 2010, KIPP received grants worth $10 million from the U.S. Department of Education, and in December 2010 KIPP and TFA each was awarded $50 million (Dillon, 2010) in "Investing in Innovation" grants.

KIPP DC received a Race to the Top district grant of $10 million in 2012 (Brown, 2012). The U.S. DOE gave another $9.4 million in 2011 (U.S. Department of Education, 2011), and in October 2014, the KIPP Foundation and KIPP regional networks received $13.8 million from the U.S. Department of Education's Charter School Program (CSP). The KIPP Foundation's IRS filings in 2011 show federal grants totaled almost $50 million, even though 70 percent of KIPP's income in 2011 came from private contributions.

This represented for the KIPP Foundation a 100.5 percent increase in revenue in a single year and a 288% increase over the 2008 total. During the four-year span (2008–2011), KIPP Foundation receipts went from $17.5 million to $49.2 million per year. Between 2007 and 2011, the KIPP Foundation reported to the IRS that it took in $157,948,811 in donations and philanthropic investments.

These impressive totals do not take into account the money received in public per-pupil state education funds. In 2015, KIPP had seventy thousand students in 183 schools. Based on a conservative estimate of $8,000 per student from state funds, KIPP schools would take in $560 million each year in state funding, alone. With generous support from both corporate and governmental sources, evidence abounds that the KIPP Foundation is flush a decade after its founding. The venture philanthropists' newsletter, *Nonprofit Investor*, rated KIPP a "Buy" in 2012 for individual and corporate funders looking for a good bet on their philanthropic investments.

The philanthropic investments by corporations and their foundations in the KIPP Model schools serve a number of important functions for givers, some of which are more visible than others. Beyond the obvious and substantial reductions in individual and corporate tax obligations that accompanies charitable giving, there is the public relations benefit that accrues for philanthrocapitalists who embark on ventures that are viewed as public minded and generous to the oppressed and disadvantaged. This remains true for the Walton, Gates, and Broad foundations, among others, as well as for Fisher family enterprises.

Less obvious are the benefits emanating from the ongoing corporate crusade to spread business efficiencies that will drive down the cost of public services. The spread of the long-held belief that market models will improve educational and behavioral outcomes while saving money remains a prime motivator for corporate support of KIPP Model schools. In addition, the entrepreneurial rationale and methods undergirding charters translates into the reduction of public oversight, an increase in private management, and the shrinkage of employee protections/benefits.

These less obvious corporate benefits were not invisible to some of the former KIPP teachers interviewed for this book. At the end of our conversation, one teacher expressed her concern that the civil and human rights rhetoric by KIPP's corporate supporters was being used to mask exploitative management and labor practices:

> I guess the one thing that kind of just rubbed me the wrong way and maybe I'm too idealistic about the whole thing—but for an organization [KIPP] supposedly committed to addressing some of the negative effects of poverty, I always found it curious that the organization relied so much on The GAP organization. GAP has a pretty atrocious record when it comes to sweatshop

labor and human rights violations around the world. And they [the Fishers] all sit on the Board, and so to me it seems like there's a definite corporate agenda behind the organization. That's okay for sort of the bandage wound that they're putting on educational inequality and poverty in general, but there's no addressing of the system as a whole and some of the systematic failures that exist in urban education. Because frankly and honestly, for our school to have functioned well we probably would have needed at least six trained counselors. And plenty of other social services for these children, but no one wants to talk about that.

Even if KIPP's original corporate patron, Donald Fisher, viewed schools as "not much different from a GAP store," former teachers interviewed for this book view the sweatshop conditions at KIPP as unsustainable for any significant duration:

It [teaching at KIPP] was ultimately unsustainable. It felt like sprinting a marathon for two years. I probably worked somewhere between 80 and 100 hours every single week for two years and that's unsustainable, even for somebody who didn't have a family. . . . The money was fine. I had no chance to spend it. I was literally at school from 6:00 in the morning until 9:00 at night six days a week, and then working on Sundays as well. It was extremely unsustainable from the time perspective. The second piece, the second part of that answer I think, comes not just from the hours, but the intensity of the hours. It wasn't just working on being at the office or something like that. It was we had to create and own an environment that was difficult to manage, and had to do that over a very long period.

PILLARS, UNDERPINNINGS, AND IDEOLOGICAL LOAD

While KIPP's financial foundation was solidified after 2000 with grants that yielded large tax breaks for donors, the charter chain had already captured the attention of power elites some years earlier. We find out from Jay Mathews's (2009a) *Work Hard, Be Nice* that KIPP's media coming-out party took the form of a 2,799-word story in 1994 on the front page of the *Houston Post*. Mathews offers no details as to how an obscure little program in its first year with forty-seven students was chosen for such coverage, but we know that KIPP's sister organization, Teach for America (TFA), had built an impressive network of corporate funders by 1994. We know, in fact, that TFA's first big media splash in 1990 had resulted after corporate donors wrote to media outlets requesting that reporters be sent out to do a story on Wendy Kopp's new venture (Kopp, 2003).

Nor does the Mathews's book tell us how KIPP cofounder, David Levin, who in 1995 was a third-year teacher from TFA without credentials, found support from the Giuliani administration for opening the second KIPP school in New York City. How did this unknown and uncertified educational neophyte land a New York City teaching position with multiple classrooms and support staff in a public school building in the Bronx? There, Levin would work out the kinks of the KIPP School Model, as Mike Feinberg was doing the same at the original KIPP Academy Middle School in Houston.

Mike Feinberg and David Levin were recent graduates of Yale and the University of Pennsylvania, respectively, when they launched KIPP near the end of their two-year stint with Teach for America (TFA) (Horn, 2010; Ellison, 2012). The story of KIPP's founders has been frequently repeated in popular media and chronicled in Jay Mathews's (2009a) celebratory book, and it has now entered into the canon of entrepreneurial folktales with other famous business success stories, such as Google's genesis in a garage in Silicon Valley (Ellison, 2012).

In the Mathews's account of the KIPP founders (Horn, 2009), Levin and Feinberg returned to their apartment one evening in 1994, following an inspirational speech by famed teacher Rafe Esquith, whose classroom mottoes of "be nice, work hard" and "there are no shortcuts" would subsequently find prominent placement among the festoons and placards in KIPP classrooms. Borrowing from Esquith's "no shortcuts" approach but leaving behind his casual warmth and humane connectedness, Feinberg and Levin created a total-compliance version of the traditional classroom.

The KIPP Model applies a psychological/character intervention program that is sustained by pedagogical machismo mixed with No Excuses authoritarianism. The young founders also borrowed heavily from the inimitable Harriett Ball from Houston, whose teaching style offered a culturally sensitive mash-up of gospel, hip-hop, and rhyming that, one suspects, loses some of its charm in the hands of the white, middle-class TFA enlistees that KIPP depends upon for 30 to 40 percent of its teachers.

It was one of Harriett Ball's chants, as Mathews (2009a) recalls, that inspired the name Knowledge Is Power Program:

> You gotta read, baby, read.
> You gotta read, baby, read.
> The more you read, the more you know,
> Cause knowledge is power,
> Power is money, and
> I want it. (p. 62)

Despite the many hours that Jay Mathews (2009a) spent visiting the No Excuses KIPP schools during the writing of *Work Hard, Be Nice*, there were most likely some disturbing realities of which Mathews remained unaware, such as problem children being sent to the school basement when important visitors were on campus (see chapter 8). Nor was he likely aware of the practice of forcing one hundred new fifth-graders to sit on the floor for days until they learned to follow orders and respect the rules (see chapter 2).

Other troubling facts he does report in his book, and whether of minor of major significance, Mathews recounts them with neither concern nor apparent alarm. As for incidents that may simply raise eyebrows, perhaps, we learn from Mathews that KIPP principals, or "school leaders," view school recess as a "prime distraction," and that field trips are commonly referred to as "field lessons" aimed to produce more grist for the learning mill that grinds on when recreation might, otherwise, intrude.

And then there are the scarier events that Mathews reports with no evident concern, including the time when KIPP founders David Levin and Mike Feinberg loaded schoolchildren into a closed, windowless U-Haul trailer to take them on a local "field lesson" in Houston. More troubling, still, is the incident that Mathews recalls in a tone more appropriate for reporting on a youthful prank, when Feinberg once smashed a plate glass school window with a chair while in a rage that his Houston KIPP students did not show the proper contrition for the admitted offense of having talked during a video lesson (Horn, 2010).

According to the often-repeated story by Levin and Feinberg, the founding pair had stayed up the entire night after the Rafe Esquith presentation, listening to a repeating loop of U2's *Achtung Baby*, while collaborating on what came to be the Five Pillars of the KIPP Model school: high expectations, choice and commitment, more time, power to lead, and focus on results (KIPP, 2015b). Levin and Feinberg had been sent to Houston during their TFA assignments, where they experienced many of the same frustrations of beginning teachers in urban schools with high levels of poverty and low levels of achievement on standardized tests.

The Five Pillars were meant to address four issues plaguing public schools. The first issue Levin and Feinberg identified was a *lack of time* for the intensive instruction that they felt struggling students require to catch up to their peers (Ellison, 2012). They believed that longer school days and school years were first necessary steps to raising academic achievement. The second issue relates to the academic malaise common in poor urban schools that Feinberg and Levin attributed to *low expectations*. For Levin and Feinberg, the low expectations of both teachers and administrators for their students become self-fulfilling prophecies that foster an institutional culture of academic failure.

The third issue stems from the *bureaucratic* nature of large public school systems. Based on their TFA indoctrination, Feinberg and Levin believed that teachers' unions put the interests of their adults before the needs of students and that the university teacher preparation programs block talented young people from entering the teaching profession. Feinberg and Levin became convinced that institutional constraints placed on school principals and teachers made public schools structurally unable to bring about the kind of reforms necessary to raise student test scores and close the achievement gap.

The fourth issue, which Feinberg and Levin identify as _compulsion_ to attend public schools, is due, they contend, to a lack of educational choices available to students and parents. Levin and Feinberg came to believe that these four issues create a situation whereby academic failure becomes a predictable conclusion, and they developed the non-negotiable pillars to support an ideological blueprint they had acquired as Teach for America enlistees: entrepreneurship, commitment, innovation, and leadership can overcome the achievement gap when applied in environments where issues of time, low expectations, bureaucracy, and compulsion have been neutralized (Ellison, 2012).

The KIPP Model holds students to high expectations, and it requires teachers to foster high expectations in their classrooms. KIPP emphasizes that KIPP stakeholders (students, parents, and teachers) are there by choice and must make a commitment to meeting the high expectations of the school, with each party required to sign a non-negotiable contract to that effect. The KIPP Model extends the school day, week, and year.

The typical KIPP school day begins instruction at 7:30 and ends at 5:00, and two to three hours of homework are added on top of that. KIPP students are also expected to attend school every other Saturday from 8:00 to 12:30 and to attend three weeks of full instruction during the summer. Altogether, the average KIPP student spends around 60 percent more time in school than do their peers in traditional public schools (Mathews, 2009a).

Principals, who are known as CEOs or "school leaders," are expected to embody an entrepreneurial spirit while maintaining total control over budgetary, program, and personnel decisions. Finally, the KIPP Model is built around a commitment to producing high scores on standardized tests and "other objective measures" as the way for KIPP students "to succeed at the nation's best high schools and colleges." According to KIPP's website, twenty years after that fateful evening in 1994 the KIPP Model now, as then, is intended to foster a school "culture of high expectations" based on "clearly defined and measurable high expectations for academic achievement and conduct that makes no excuses based on the students' background" (KIPP, 2015b).

The effects of operationalizing the No Excuses ideology for students and teachers within the KIPP schools comes out clearly in the accounts of former KIPP teachers interviewed for this book. Their accounts are interspersed throughout the book, for reasons that include consideration for readers' capacities to absorb the psychological brutality and physical stresses that characterize KIPP teacher experiences. One teacher who was able to revisit some of her painful personal sacrifices during her years at KIPP offered some disturbing insights regarding the repercussions of the No Excuses credo in practice.

When asked why she stayed at KIPP, this teacher pointed to how school leaders had convinced her and many of her fellow teachers of their unique importance to the children and how their work at KIPP was saving children who, otherwise, would be lost to the public bureaucracies that operated for the benefit of adults, not children. As a result, she committed herself to carrying out the mission, regardless of what it took and regardless of personal consequences.

She noted that a mutual lifeboat mentality among the teachers helps create a camaraderie among "team and family," which enables levels of self-sacrifice that remain somewhat mysterious to those who are on the outside. The following teacher's understanding of the phenomenon only took hold when her life was put in jeopardy by refusing to accept her own physical limits in upholding the demand imposed by the No Excuses code:

> I think that there is an expectation where you don't want to let anyone down at KIPP. They [KIPP leaders] are constantly telling you how important you are and how important this work is, and how you're saving all these children. And then you do find yourself thinking, oh my God, what am I doing? You're watching teachers drop left and right. I mean I'm stronger than most because I was experienced, but I'm sitting there watching new teachers literally have— I've seen about four teachers have complete nervous breakdowns.
>
> And then you find yourself asking, why am I doing this? And it's basically because I think something kicks in where you don't want to disappoint. You become almost catatonic. You just keep doing it over and over and over, and it's like you keep telling yourself I've got to stop. I've got to stop this. I got to stop this.
>
> And then before you know it, you're in there a year, you're in there two years. And after two years you're considered like a veteran teacher at KIPP. Then, finally, I just had to stop. I mean you become physically ill. Your body breaks down—you can't take it anymore. I fell asleep one day driving home from work, and I hit a car in front of me. That's when I woke up, and I was like, okay, this is enough. My family's begging me to quit. They're begging me to stop. Why are you doing this? Why are you doing this? So finally you have to start answering to other people because they notice, and that's when I decided to stop. It's enough.

Predictably, this kind of distress contributes to many teachers like this one eventually leaving KIPP. When I asked her what it was like when she left KIPP, she had this to say:

> Heaven, if there is one. It was like for the first time I got to sleep. My body started to repair itself. I noticed that my mind was clearing up. I was being able to communicate effectively. I can't explain what your body does. It shuts down—your body shuts down. You just become like a robot. It took me a good

six months . . . to recover from that experience. And after six months I found myself like enjoying life again because it was absolutely miserable for two years. I was not a happy person.

When I asked another teacher how she understood the KIPP concept of unity expressed in "team and family," she said that she had been encouraged to use "that terminology, even though she said her experiences at KIPP were more akin to being 'part of a very abusive, dysfunctional family.'"

FANCIFUL GOALS AND DANGEROUS ASSUMPTIONS

A significant component of the ideological mortar that built the Five Pillars is based on a late twentieth-century education reform assumption that schools and teachers could "reduce inequality in educational achievement if disadvantaged students were held to the same high standards as everybody else" (Cohen, 1996, p. 101). This belief was foundational to the testing accountability movement that took hold in the United States following the publication of *A Nation at Risk (ANAR)* in 1983.

The language adopted by *ANAR* initiated the media meme that the urban public schools do not promote learning and that children's achievement is low because public school teachers in poor urban schools believe that children living in poverty cannot perform at the same levels as privileged children. The prior focus on education funding initiatives to mitigate poverty during the 1960s and 1970s was transformed by the late 1980s to a focus on school and teacher quality and accountability as keys to student achievement.

Two privileged and ambitious young men like Feinberg and Levin who came of age during an era that accepted President Reagan's belief that "government is not the solution to our problem; government is the problem" were surely not immune to the rhetorical jiu-jitsu by reformist policymakers in education focused on "choice." These advocates for privatization enjoyed success in shifting attention from the tangible effects of child poverty and discrimination in schooling to a kind of brutal, alarmist rhetoric that blamed society's shortcomings on the public institutions that had been previously established and maintained to mitigate some of those problems.

If the kinds of market-based solutions to which education reformers and the KIPP founders subscribed were to gain any traction, then the perception of the problem had to be altered so that the preferred market solutions could fit. The result was the beginning of an education policy era that culminated in the creation of public policy that would assure the widespread public failure required for market solutions to gain some degree of public acceptance. The fact that three-quarters of American children (Anderson, 2011) failed to achieve the fanciful No Child Left Behind mandate of 100 percent reading and math proficiency ten years after NCLB passage has not deterred continuing enthusiasms for similarly unachievable targets among the corporate foundations that determine federal and state education policies.

Billed as an antidote to No Child Left Behind's impossible proficiency targets (100 percent proficiency by 2014), a federal waiver program was devised in 2011 that demanded what some states, including Vermont, considered equally onerous accountability demands for seeking relief from the NCLB proficiency sword. Rather than trade one monstrous system for another that offered more punishing sanctions for low-scoring, high-poverty schools, Vermont stuck with the impossible NCLB mandates.

As predicted by every testing authority in the United States, the state's Secretary of Education, Rebecca Holcombe (Holcombe, 2014), announced in a memorandum to parents and caregivers in August 2014 that, based on federal accountability rules, *all* Vermont public schools in the state were "low performing," with the exception of eight schools that did not take the state tests in 2014. To draw attention to the ludicrous nature of the manufactured dilemma, Holcombe's memo also noted that a national media firm had ranked Vermont schools third in the nation in overall quality the same week that the federal failure was formally acknowledged. Earlier in 2014, *Education Week*'s annual report card had ranked Vermont schools seventh in the nation for overall quality (Education Week, 2014).

While there remains some question as to the percentage of public school personnel who still share in the fanciful myth that all children, regardless of conditions, will achieve the same results on standardized tests, there is less uncertainty about the important role of factors *outside the school* that influence the academic performance of children in school. We know that

> teacher effectiveness constitutes the most important school-based factor to variations in test score achievement (Goldhaber, Liddle, Theobald, & Walch, 2010), with the exact percentage dependent upon the methodology used. Goldhaber (2002), for instance, found that teacher characteristics account for 8.5% of the "variation in student achievement" (para. 8), while analyses by Nye and her colleagues (Nye, Konstantopoulos, & Hedges, 2004) found among 17 studies that "7% to 21% of the variance in achievement gains is associated with variation in teacher effectiveness" (p. 240). What we know, too, is that that other factors have much more influence on student achievement variations than do teachers. Goldhaber and his colleagues (Goldhaber, 2002) have found that additional factors involving family background, peer composition, and other social capital influences make up 60% of the variance in student test scores. (Horn & Wilburn, 2013, p. 77)

Since James Coleman et al.'s (1966) groundbreaking research findings were presented and largely ignored, we have known that "most of the variability in student achievement overall . . . is associated with students (and their families and communities), not the schools they attend" (Rumberger &

Palardy, 2005, p. 2023). Even so, there are certain characteristics of schools that may further hinder the limited influence that schools and teachers do have on student achievement. For instance, Coleman scholar Gerald Grant (2009) has noted that class and racial isolation negatively affect student achievement:

> Coleman found that the achievement of both poor and rich children was depressed by attending a school where most children came from low-income families. More important to the goal of achieving equal educational opportunity, he found that the achievement of poor children was raised by attending a predominantly middle-class school, while the achievement of affluent children in the school was not harmed. This was true even if per-pupil expenditures were the same at both schools. No research over the past 40 years has overturned Coleman's finding.(p. 159)

Some factors that influence student achievement are attributable to both school and community influences. Pupil attitude is an example of this. Of all the school influences, in fact, James Coleman et al. (1966) found pupil attitude to have the strongest relationship to student achievement: "A pupil attitude factor, which appears to have a stronger relationship to achievement than do all the "school" factors together, is the extent to which an individual feels that he has some control over his own destiny" (p. 23).

A sense of individual autonomy, then, is linked to a sense of individual power to effect change in one's life. Although this Coleman finding has been largely ignored for decades, the effects of what may be termed an attitude of hope are most significant in terms of student achievement:

> The responses of pupils to questions in the survey show that minority pupils, except for Orientals, have far less conviction than Whites that they can affect their own environments and futures. When they do, however, their achievement is higher than that of Whites who lack that conviction.
>
> Furthermore, while this characteristic shows little relationship to most school factors, it is related, for Negroes, to the proportion of Whites in the schools. Those Negroes in schools with a higher proportion of Whites have a greater sense of control. This finding suggests that the direction such an attitude takes may be associated with the pupil's school experience as well as the experience in the larger community. (p. 23)

High expectations, then, are embodied within a complex human social system that cannot be boiled down to a set of imposed beliefs, regardless of how noble or harsh or relentless the enforcement of those beliefs become, or how much said beliefs claim the power to alter realities that remain immune, nonetheless, to wishful thinking. While high expectations are absolutely required to raise achievement, they are entirely insufficient to complete the job.

To promote the cynical fallacy that high expectations in schools, alone, hold the key to the problem of low achievement among poor children leads to four possible outcomes, all of them bad: 1) it leads us away from the corrosive socioeconomic realities outside of school, while pushing our attention toward blaming children or blaming schools and their teachers; 2) it requires educators and children to subscribe to an ideology that demands superhuman and/or unhealthy levels of anxiety and stress to attain, even temporarily; 3) it leads to eventual failure to live up to expectations that are more fanciful than reality based, which creates self-loathing or self-blame for failing to achieve the impossible; 4) it leads to totalizing compliance methods in schools that look more penal than pedagogical.

The enormous pressure to remain true to distant, adult goals disconnected from sociological realities requires a blinkered, autonomic acceptance to No Excuses and "by any means required." To substantiate the perverse fallacy that class, income, and race are unrelated to children's achievement scores, there arises a perverse permission to sacrifice both teacher and student autonomy, safety, and health. The imposition of a No Excuses group order leads to displacement of individual autonomy, even though it is autonomy that provides the basis for "pupil attitudes" based on real hope, rather than a manufactured optimism.

We know that the achievement beliefs, or pupil attitudes, are shaped early in life (Heyman, Dweck, & Cain, 1992), and the more often children experience the common failure to live up to KIPP expectations, the harder it is for them to believe in their own worth or in their capacity and potential to succeed. We know, too, from research that "increased surveillance of students . . . and punishment-oriented responses to rule infractions (e.g., pushouts, suspensions and expulsions) do little to create a climate of academic success or teach students prosocial skills" (McEvoy & Welker, 2000, p. 138).

We also know that student confidence is undermined (Roesner, Eccles, & Sameroff, 1998) by organizational practices that are common at KIPP schools, which emphasize competition, public awards, and rewards for "highest grades rather than deep task engagement" (p. 325). Research also tells us that achievement, motivation, and feelings of well-being are enhanced where "authentic learning" or "cooperative learning" (McEvoy & Welker, 2000, p. 138) practices are common, either of which are uncommon in No Excuses schools.

Motivation, achievement, and well-being are enhanced, as well, in schools where students engage in "self-exploration and expression" and where caring teachers have emotionally and academically supportive relationships with students (Roesner, Eccles, & Sameroff, 1998, p. 326). From what former teachers report, teachers at KIPP do not have the opportunity to develop relationships with students, supportive or otherwise, and learning tasks are laser focused on tests and preparing for tests.

A number of former KIPP teachers felt that the laser focus on raising scores kept them from being able to interact with students in effective ways. One teacher felt that the large class size of thirty middle school students (ninety per day) created another barrier to getting to know students: "Not at all was I able to build a relationship with them." The expectations for teacher and student behavior also created barriers to communication with students, as the focus on silent compliance leaves little or no social space for getting to know students. This same teacher found the fixation on testing got in the way of teaching students how to interact with one another, which did not allow students to learn important lessons about social adaptation and empathy.

Some teachers noted that KIPP's absorption with total-compliance demands for procedure and behavior left little time for caring relationships, which created a situation that encouraged a form of detached callousness that both teachers and students reflect in the way they regard themselves and others. An experienced teacher who resigned before the end of his first year at KIPP found school leaders "treating the teachers as though they were tenth-grade children in terms of almost browbeating the teachers" and urging them toward an abrasive militancy aligned with the classroom management expectations of the KIPP Model. More will be said about this in chapter 4.

There is a deep, broad, and long-established empirical basis for believing that Five Pillars may not support KIPP's ideological load and the expectations for disadvantaged students that come with it. Whether we are using fourth-grade standardized tests or college entrance exams, decades of student achievement measures show strong correlations between family income/ wealth and standardized test results (see figure 1.1). In fact, researchers (Orlich & Gifford, 2006; Orlich, 2007; Rampell, 2009) have found from .95 to .97 correlation between family income and SAT and ACT test scores, which means that over 90 percent of the variance in college entrance test scores may be explained by the family income of the test takers (Orlich & Gifford, 2006, p. 1).

Chapter 1

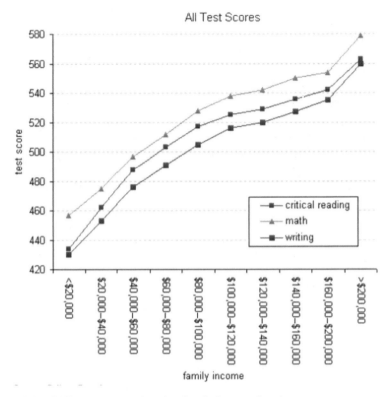

Figure 1.1. SAT scores correlated to family income levels

The same strong correlations between socioeconomic status and test performance can be found, as well, in the standardized tests that public school-children are administered each year. In New Jersey, where District Factor Groups (DFGs) are used to represent school districts' socioeconomic status, six factors are considered to arrive at DFG rankings, A–J, with "A" representing the lowest SES and "J" the highest:

1. percent of adults with no high school diploma
2. percent of adults with some college education
3. occupational status
4. unemployment rate
5. percent of individuals in poverty
6. median family income (New Jersey Department of Education, 2004)

Figure 1.2 shows 2001 to 2002 composite scores for the three state tests administered in public schools: 1) Elementary School Proficiency Test (ESPA), 2) Grade Eight Proficiency Test (ESPA), and 3) High School Proficiency Test (HSPA). In each test case and *without exception*, the average student performance increases as one moves from the poorest (A) to the wealthiest (J) districts.

Do pillars made of high expectations, choice and commitment, more time, power to lead, and focus on results offer KIPP's supporters a legitimate excuse to declare "No Excuses," especially when the expected results are standardized test scores that are more precise measures of house sizes in neighborhoods where tests are administered (Kohn, 2001) than they are any reliable gauge of school quality or teacher/student commitment or expectations? Does a laser focus on the Five Pillars offer us an ethical pass to blot out from our consciousness and conscience any consideration of economic disadvantage as we examine the faces of malnourished, sleep-deprived, or traumatized children getting ready to take the next big math test?

Average Statewide Assessment Score, By 2000 DFG

	ESPA		GEPA			HSPA	
	Lang Arts	Math	Lang Arts	Math	Science	Lang Arts	Math
A	208.9	199.4	201.0	191.3	201.4	209.9	197.4
B	214.1	210.3	213.4	206.4	217.4	221.0	212.3
CD	218.3	219.0	217.2	208.7	224.0	224.7	216.2
DE	221.8	224.8	221.9	214.6	228.6	228.3	220.5
FG	224.1	229.3	224.9	220.5	232.3	230.9	226.2
GH	226.1	233.4	227.8	225.7	235.2	234.6	231.2
I	230.6	240.4	233.4	231.8	240.1	240.1	239.6
J	233.8	247.1	238.5	238.6	244.0	244.1	244.8

Figure 1.2.   Three New Jersey state test results correlated to family income levels

The KIPP Foundation and its political and financial supporters would have us believe that there are, indeed, no excuses, and that its programs prove as much. Are they right, and if they are right, what are the economic and human costs and benefits of such a program, and for whom?

The answers to these questions are teased out in the following pages, but for now one thing is certain: by ignoring or denying the effects of economic disadvantage, segregation, and school resources on student achievement scores, corporate education reformers who support the KIPP mission must push even harder to pressure KIPP personnel to corral and channel the behaviors and attitudes of KIPP children whose lives, from the beginning, have been shaped by the multiple effects of economic deprivation.

To ignore the need to acknowledge and to alter those deprivations places an intense focus and weight upon what happens inside the KIPP classroom to change children so that they become, in effect, impervious to socioeconomic disadvantage. The resulting cultural, character, and behavioral compacting process, then, creates debilitating and unsustainable pressures for teachers and students, alike. In the process of sustaining its ideology and the irrational insistence that the most disadvantaged children will perform at the same levels on standardized tests as the most advantaged, basic human needs of children and teachers become regularly displaced, and many students and teachers, alike, are sacrificed to the grinding KIPP crucible.

Parents of KIPP students, whose own educational experiences are likely to have been shaped, as well, by the many effects of economic disadvantage, often misplace blame on their former teachers for not having forced them to learn more when they were students in school. This rationalization provides, then, a further impetus and permission for KIPP Model schools to use harsh measures to extract total compliance and test scores that serve to burnish the brand.

The children who survive the harsh KIPP gauntlet with high test scores intact serve to perpetuate the myth that teachers and schools, alone, are responsible for differences in student achievement, even as attrition is particularly high among first-year KIPP students who must contend with this insistent claim. Mathematica, Inc., which was commissioned by KIPP (Nichols-Barrer, Gill, Gleason, & Tuttle, 2014) to analyze KIPP's enrollment and performance data, reported in 2014 that KIPP's attrition among fifth-graders was almost one-and-a-half times higher at KIPP (16 percent) than at public feeder schools (11 percent).

In pressing to make the exceptional the perceived commonplace, the KIPP Model stands at the forefront of a national effort to disprove the need for alterations to the long-established institutional and structural inequalities that sustain the vast differences in educational, social, and economic achievement. Preferred by venture philanthropists and corporate foundations are the cheaper and less disruptive educational treatments that have the added benefit of creating new corporate revenue streams and tax savings, all the while tightening the social steering mechanisms within schools to further advantage the business community.

The increasing prominence of standardized testing since NCLB has opened new business opportunities for testing and technology companies, tutoring firms, and professional development consultants. With the migration of high-stakes standardized testing to online formats since 2013, hundreds of billions will have been required to create the infrastructure to administer, transmit, analyze, and store massive amounts of student and teacher data.

At the same time, the prominence of TFA has helped to temporalize the teaching profession, and the expansion of alternative certification schemes has reduced teacher payrolls and weakened collective bargaining. Too, the proliferation of charter schools has shifted control of public education to corporate boards, rather than elected officials.

The belief that economically disadvantaged children will perform on standardized tests at the same levels as privileged students provides a crusader dimension to the KIPP mission and a missionary impulse to both KIPP and TFA. TFA promotional materials used during college recruiting visits (Veltri, 2010) state that inadequate public schools in high-minority and high-poverty areas constitutes "our nation's greatest injustice," which can be "solved" by becoming a TFA corps member.

Feinberg and Levin have used that TFA's missionary zeal to create a schooling environment and methodology to produce test scores, at least for those students who survive the KIPP treatment, that are used to justify the KIPP Model. Large numbers of these children do not survive—60 percent left between fifth and eighth grade in a 2008 study conducted in Bay Area KIPP schools (Woodworth et al., 2008, p. ix). And in a later study (Miron, Urschel, & Saxton, 2011), researchers similarly found that "approximately 15% of the originally enrolled students disappear from the KIPP cohort every year" (p. 12).

Helping, too, to drive up scores for the remaining cohorts is the fact that KIPP leavers are most often not replaced by new students, as they are in public schools that must accept all students who walk through the door. Because they are not replaced, the test scores of students at KIPP schools are inflated and are not truly representative of the original population of students.

The implications of implementing a model of schooling based on KIPP's core values and ideological commitments are many, and they have proven hazardous to the emotional, intellectual, and ethical well-being of many students and teachers, alike, who have been indoctrinated and often discarded by a system that is unforgiving in its ironclad "non-negotiables." During talks with the teachers who volunteered to be interviewed for this book, we came to understand, in part at least, the rupture between KIPP rhetoric and KIPP reality for those who work within the KIPP system.

The level of commitment required of teachers and students assures that large numbers will not survive the KIPP gauntlet. In the brave new world of corporate schooling aimed to build gritty superkids, however, such losses have become entirely unexceptional and forgotten by the survivors who must continue to face the unrelenting demands of a system that assures one's best is almost never good enough. In a system where teaching experience is often not required or even desired, new and inexperienced teachers lack the knowledge or experience to challenge narrow conceptions of learning that are enforced with brute methods.

KIPP's preference for psychological indoctrination to replace children's developmental learning needs and KIPP's insensitivity to sociological and cultural contexts provide a breeding ground for rationalizations and practices to become accepted that, outside the KIPP bubble, would be considered hostile to the well-being of children or tantamount to educational malpractice. There is a treacherous tipping point that separates zealous commitment from cultlike blindness, where moral clarity and educative purpose may become outweighed by relentless fixations on data, chain-gang behavioral regimen, and foggy, futuristic abstractions (Brookfield, 2004, p. 164) that place testing accountability ahead of conscience.

This potential outcome is made more likely when market-based education solutions grounded by amoral capitalism are applied to public institutions that, otherwise, demand deep moral commitments to the public good. The results, too often, are lapses in professional behaviors and in the treatment of children at KIPP that only become discussable after teachers leave KIPP (many examples are shared in the following chapters).

One example worth noting here is referenced in Jay Mathews's chronicle of KIPP founders Feinberg and Levin (Horn, 2009). Even though public reports from visitors to KIPP have documented that rule breakers were labeled (sometimes literally with signs) as "miscreants," Mathews (2009a) never makes note of these labeling practices other than to use the label, himself, to describe a child who received a private tongue-lashing for whispering on the first day of school. The teacher reminds this "miscreant" that

> you are too big for that kind of stuff. From now on, when a teacher is speaking, you are going to track your eyes on the teacher and listen to what he or she is saying. You are in KIPP now. It is time to grow up. I am expecting a lot from you. (p. 67)

Unfortunately for the children of KIPP entering fifth grade who are expected to "grow up," the penalty for even the smallest infraction is clearly demonstrated in various forms of harsh discipline, humiliation, isolation, silencing, and public shaming. Otherwise, pent-up energy is often burned off on a dizzying carousel of chanting, singing, snapping, nodding, waving, and clapping in an exhibition of mechanical unanimity by all "teammates."

When combined with long, silent hours at school and hours more of homework drudgery after school, these practices resemble the same ones commonly used to indoctrinate and maintain control within cults:

> Keeping devotees constantly fatigued, deprived of sensory input and suffering protein deprivation, working extremely long hours . . . in cult-owned businesses, engaging in monotonous chanting and rhythmical singing, may induce psychophysiological changes in the brain. The rhythmical movement of the body can lead to altered states of consciousness, and changes in the pressure or vibration pattern of the brain may affect the temporal lobe. (Cath quoted in Collins, 1982, para. 33)

Without the capacity or intent to change the social, economic, health, safety, and housing conditions that influence KIPP students' levels of achievement and behaviors (or any other student, for that matter), KIPP teachers and those embracing the KIPP Model must focus on changing the children, themselves, in order to alter the educational outcomes as measured by performance character grading and standardized tests.

In short, education reform necessarily merges with thought reform, or coercive persuasion, as defined by the *Encyclopedia of Sociology* as "programs of social influence capable of producing substantial behavior and attitude change through the use of coercive tactics, persuasion, and/or interpersonal and group-based influence manipulations" (Schein, 1961; Lifton, 1961). When the demand for changing student achievement and character traits, or "performance character" (Tough, 2012), routinely ignores sociological realities that shape human beings, then the pressure to control these environmental elements demands ongoing psychological interventions.

More will be said about these interventions in subsequent chapters. Now it is time to turn to the social theory and practices that provide the deeper rationale for schools based on the KIPP Model, where coercion, surveillance, and compliance embody the paternalistic goals inherent in what has come to known as "broken windows theory."

BROKEN WINDOWS THEORY AND THE NEW PATERNALISM

"Broken windows theory" adheres to the belief that social order demands that any rule infraction or unlawful act, whether on city streets, in homeless shelters, or in schools has to be met with strict intervention and corrective measures. Beginning with Rudolph Giuliani's administration in New York City, the restoration and preservation of order on New York streets or public spaces required that any broken window be mended, just as the smallest act of law breaking or defiance to public authority had to be immediately noted and punished.

To bring this philosophy to bear in the delivery of public services to the disenfranchised, Giuliani stepped around legal protections for the poor by contracting services like homeless shelters to privately operated shelters that imposed strict measures that were beyond public oversight. Anyone, for instance, who failed to tuck in his blanket at New York's privatized homeless shelters had to be confronted and corrected; if the homeless individuals didn't like it, then they could choose to return to the underfunded and some-times chaotic environments of the remaining public shelters.

Privately operated facilities would offer the latitude for rules and enforce-ment practices that, otherwise, would not survive the public scrutiny of insti-tutions based on less punitive protocols and legal protections. "Broken win-dows theory" adheres to the notion that any crack in the dam requires an immediate and forceful fixative in order to stem the flood of chaotic rule breaking that threatens social order. At the same time, swift and sure inter-ventions are thought be the best training for the poor and disenfranchised, who are thought to be unable to self-correct and to function as societal assets, rather than liabilities.

Supporters of the "new paternalism" find ideological grounding in the work of political scientist Lawrence Mead, whose writings (1986; 1993; 1997) inspired the get-tough welfare reforms in New York and other U.S. cities during the 1990s. Though often draconian in its applications, Mead's philosophy, nonetheless, represents a less harsh solution than the one advo-cated by people such as Charles Murray, who has argued for severing welfare programs entirely, and consequences be damned (Schram, 1999).

Instead, Mead calls for more effective and efficient management of ser-vices by government bureaucrats, along with accountability measures aimed to wean those receiving public services from the need for them. In fact, the welfare reform legislation, the Personal Responsibility Work and Opportu-nity Reconciliation Act of 1996, reflected the ideas of the new paternalists' call for "holding welfare recipients accountable for making progress toward self-sufficiency" (Schram, 1999, p. 669).

The contributors to Mead's (1997) influential edited volume, *The New Paternalism: Supervisory Approaches to Poverty*, advocate for a system whereby social policy, whether in the area of child support, homelessness, drug treatment, or education, is designed around strategies and tactics for changing the behaviors among the poor and needy who depend upon public services. Those following this line of thinking argue that the poor are inca-pable of changing their attitudes and behaviors on their own without assis-tance. Therefore, it becomes the responsibility of policy elites to create en-forceable expectations that are deemed in the best interests of those whose behaviors are targeted for change.

As a hybrid form of political thought that combines liberal and conservative elements, it advocates, essentially, for using government for conservative ends; that is, to replace government authority with "social authority" as "the key to reducing poverty" (Mead, 2012, para. 6), even if government is required to initiate interventions for achieving that social authority. As Mead summed up his social policy thinking twelve years after publication of *The New Paternalism*, "Welfare recipients must work to get aid, the homeless must obey rules to get shelter, and students must pass tests to be promoted in school" (Mead, 2009).

If government management by force is required to achieve individual conduct that ends the need for government assistance to the poor, then so be it, according to James Q. Wilson, who wrote the concluding essay for Mead's *The New Paternalism*. In 1982 Wilson cocreated (Kelling & Wilson, 1982) "broken windows theory," which is based on the claim that "disorder and crime are usually inextricably linked, in a kind of developmental sequence," and that "if a window in a building is broken and is left unrepaired, all the rest of the windows will soon be broken" (para. 11).

Furthermore, if regulations and legal protections get in the way of enforcement mechanisms and accountability demands, as they did in New York City homeless shelters during the 1990s, then contracting out government services to private firms is seen by paternalists as a viable solution to existing government assistance programs, which represent for paternalists their own forms of governmental "broken windows." As noted already, Giuliani's "choice" vouchers in New York were provided to homeless clients, who could then sign up for private sector shelters that were not bound by government red tape or oversight.

This, in effect, guaranteed compliance by the homeless to strict rules intended to instill character and good habits. Those individuals who refused prescribed behaviors for shelter inhabitants in return for the privilege of having a bed would be forced to return to the remaining public shelters. Included below is a somewhat lengthy quote by Thomas Main (1997), who also had an essay in Mead's *The New Paternalism*. The rationale that Main offers for private sector homeless shelters is the same one that underpins charter schools and the second of KIPP's Five Pillars: "Students, their parents, and the faculty of each KIPP school choose to participate in the program" (KIPP Foundation, 2015b):

> Because clients have no right to a particular shelter, private shelters may require and enforce participation in their program as long as noncompliant clients are free to return to a general shelter. [This] gives clients a degree of choice that is not available in an all-city-run-system. It also makes possible an exercise of authority that is less drastic than the impermissible denial of city shelters. Indeed, the provision of choice and the existence of a usable sanction go hand-in-hand. It is because clients make a voluntary choice to go to a

certain program that the shelters can reasonably expect clients to adhere to
their program. (Main, 1997, p. 174)

Even though education reformists usually base their arguments for the
paternalistic corporate charter schools like KIPP on innovative methods and
an absence of bureaucratic restrictions, the less acknowledged advantages
come into focus when examining KIPP's authoritarian culture, total-compliance demands, and character alteration programs. As schools of "choice,"
KIPP is free to invite anyone who does not wish to abide by a contract
assuring compliance with KIPP expectations to return to the other school
choice that poor communities can usually offer: underresourced public
schools that are ravaged by malignant neglect and generations of battering
from fanciful accountability demands.

Choosing the new paternalist schools is often the only other choice in
town for economically disadvantaged parents. One of the ironies inherent in
the operation of the "Knowledge Is Power Program" is that acquiring the
knowledge and character traits that KIPP advertises to be the solution to
inequality requires a totalizing submissiveness to a domineering and "non-
negotiable" system.

Chester Finn, the doyen of the conservative education reform movement,
has a chapter in *The New Paternalism*, where he lays out his case against any
progressive agenda and for another era of reform centered on the traditional
basics, this time under closer supervision by the new paternalists (Finn,
1997). In 2008, Finn once again offered his full-throated enthusiasm for
paternalism in schools (Finn & Kanstoroom, 2008): "Giving disadvantaged
adolescents a full and fair shot at success in life may require a period of close
supervision and explicit instruction in how to learn and how to live. If this
makes the schools paternalistic, many education reformers will have no ob-
jection to the practice even if they're nervous about the terminology"
(xii–xiii).

As an enthusiastic advocate of the new paternalist agenda, which begins
by fixing any broken window and by "sweating the small stuff," Finn (Finn
& Kanstoroom, 2008) shows no such nervousness about imposing academic,
moral, or cultural values among the children of the poor:

> The [No Excuses] schools are preoccupied with fighting disorder; they fix the
> proverbial broken windows quickly to deter further unruliness. Students are
> shown exactly how they are expected to behave—how to sit in a chair without
> slumping, how to track the teacher with their eyes, how to walk silently down
> the hall, how to greet visitors with a firm handshake, and how to keep track of
> daily assignments. Their behavior is closely monitored at all times and the
> schools mete out real rewards for excellence and real punishments for rule-
> breaking. (p. x)

If nervousness remains at the KIPP Foundation about admitting its paternalist agenda, the words and actions within the KIPP schools leave no doubt as to the conscious efforts to establish adherence among children to values and behaviors that are approved by No Excuses interventionists. With child poverty rates steadily increasing, such alterations have proven over the past twenty years to be no small feat, and extraordinary interventions to change the cultural and psychological realities of KIPP children now indicate a hardened and more systematic commitment to the paternalist program in schools to alter the effects of child poverty by altering children, instead.

REFERENCES

Anderson, J. (1988). *The education of Blacks in the South, 1860–1935.* Chapel Hill, NC: University of North Carolina Press.

Anderson, N. (2011, March 10). Most schools could face "failing" label under No Child Left Behind, Duncan says. *Washington Post.* http://www.washingtonpost.com/wp-dyn/content/article/2011/03/09/AR2011030903089.html.

Banjo, S. (2009, November 11). *Dow Jones—"Getting personal: Gates Foundation invests in charter schools."* http://www.kipp.org/news/dow-jones-getting-personal-gates-foundation-invests-in-charter-schools-1.

Brookfield, S. (2004). *The power of critical theory: Liberating adult learning and teaching.* San Francisco: Jossey-Bass.

Brown, E. (2012, December 11). KIPP DC wins $10 million grant in Race to the Top competition. *Washington Post.* http://www.washingtonpost.com/local/education/kipp-dc-wins-10-million-grant-in-race-to-the-top-competition/2012/12/11/ad6a2802-43c3-11e2-8061-253bccfc7532_story.html.

Cohen, D. K. (1996). Standards-based school reform: Policy, practice, and performance. In *Holding schools accountable.* Edited by H. F. Ladd. Washington, DC: The Brookings Institution.

Coleman, J. S., Campbell, E., Hobson, C., McPartland, J., Mood, A., Weinfeld, F., York, R. (1966). *Equality of educational opportunity.* Washington, DC: U.S. Government Printing Office.

Collins, G. (1982, March 15). The psychology of the cult experience. *New York Times.* http://www.nytimes.com/1982/03/15/style/the-psychology-of-the-cult-experience.html?pagewanted=2&pagewanted=all.

Dillon, S. (2010, August 5). Education Department deals out big awards. *New York Times.* http://www.nytimes.com/2010/08/05/education/05grants.html?_r=0.

Du Bois, W. E. B. (1903). *The souls of black folk.* Chicago: A. C. McClurg & Co.; Bartleby.com, 1999. www.bartleby.com/114/.

Duxbury, S. (2008, July 18). Businesses invest in charter school innovation. *San Francisco Business Times.* http://www.kippbayarea.org/files/2008_07_18_ SF%20Business%20Times.pdf.

Education Week. (2014, January 3). State report cards. *Education Week* 33 (6). http://www.edweek.org/ew/qc/2014/state_report_cards.html .

Ellison, S. (2012). From within the belly of the beast: Rethinking the concept of the "educational marketplace" in the popular discourse of education reform. *Educational Studies* 48 (2), 119–36.

Faulkner, W. (1951). *Requiem for a nun.* New York: Random House.

Finn, C. (1997). Paternalism goes to school. In *The new paternalism: Supervisory approaches to poverty,* 220–47. Edited by L. Mead. Washington, DC: Brookings Institution Press.

Finn, C., & Kanstoroom, M. (1998). Foreword. In D. Whitman, *Sweating the small stuff: Inner-city schools and the new paternalism*, ix–xvii. Washington, DC: Thomas B. Fordham Institute.

Fromm, E. (1955). *The sane society.* New York: Fawcett World Library.

Gabriel, T., & Medina, J. (2010, May 9). Charter schools' new cheerleaders: Financiers. *New York Times.* http://www.nytimes.com/2010/05/10/nyregion/10charter.html?pagewanted=all.

Grant, G. (2009). *Hope and despair in the American city: Why there are no bad schools in Raleigh.* Cambridge, MA: Harvard University Press.

Heyman, G., Dweck, C., & Cain, K. (1992). Young children's vulnerability to self-blame and helplessness: Relationship to beliefs about goodness. *Child Development* 63 (2), 401–15.

Holcombe, R. (2014, August 6). *Vermont's commitment to continuous improvement.* http://education.vermont.gov/documents/EDU-Letter_to_parents_and_caregivers_AOE_8_8_14.pdf.

Horn, J. (2010). Corporatism, KIPP, and cultural eugenics. In *The Bill Gates Foundation and the future of U.S. "public" schools.* Edited by P. Kovacs. New York: Routledge.

Horn, J. (2009, March 5). The KULT of KIPP: An essay review. *Education Review: A Journal of Book Reviews*, 12 (3). http://www.edrev.info/essays/v12n3index.html.

Horn, J., & Libby, K. (2010). The giving business: The New Schools Venture Fund. In *The Bill Gates Foundation and the future of U.S. "public" schools.* Edited by P. Kovacs. New York: Routledge.

Horn, J., & Wilburn, D. (2013). *The mismeasure of education.* Charlotte, NC: Information Age.

Kelling, G., & Wilson, J. (1982, March). Broken windows: The police and neighborhood safety. *The Atlantic.* http://www.theatlantic.com/magazine/archive/1982/03/broken-windows/304465/?single_page=true.

KIPP Foundation. (2015a). *National partners.* http://www.kipp.org/about-kipp/the-kipp-foundation/national-partners.

KIPP Foundation. (2015b). Five pillars. http://www.kipp.org/our-approach/five-pillars.

Kohn, A. (2001, January). Fighting the tests: A practical guide to rescuing our schools. *Phi Delta Kappan* 82 (5). http://www.alfiekohn.org/teaching/ftt.htm.

Kopp, W. (2003). *One day, all children . . . : The unlikely triumph of Teach for America and what I learned along the way.* New York: Public Affairs.

Levenick, C. (2010, Winter). Closing the gap: The philanthropic legacy of Don Fisher. *Philanthropy Magazine.* http://www.philanthropyroundtable.org/topic/excellence_in_philanthropy/closing_the_gap.

Lifton, R. (1961). *Thought reform and the psychology of totalism: A study of "brainwashing" in China.* New York: W. W. Norton.

Main, T. (1997). Homeless men in New York City: Toward paternalism through privatization. In *The new paternalism: Supervisory approaches to poverty*, 161–81. Edited by L. Mead.Washington, DC: Brookings Institution Press.

Mathews, J. (2009a). *Work hard, be nice: How two inspired teachers created the most promising schools in America.* New York: Algonquin Books.

Mathews, J. (2008, Spring). Growing up fast: Will Houston's charter school expansion revolutionize urban education? *Philanthropy Magazine.* http://www.philanthropyroundtable.org/topic/k_12_education/growing_up_fast.

McEvoy, A., & Welker, R. (2000). Antisocial behavior, academic failure, and school climate: A critical review. *Journal of Emotional and Behavioral Disorders* 8 (3), 130–40.

Mead, L. (2012, March 19). James Q. Wilson: Another view. *Public Discourse.* http://www.thepublicdiscourse.com/2012/03/4991/.

Mead, L. (2009, Spring). Econs and humans. [Book review *Nudge: Improving decisions about health, wealth, and happiness*, by R. H. Thaler & C. R. Sunstein]. *Claremont Review of Books*, 18–19. http://www.aei.org/wp-content/uploads/2011/10/Econs and Humans.pdf.

Mead, L. (1997). *The new paternalism: Supervisory approaches to poverty.* Washington, DC: Brookings Institution Press.

Mead, L. (1993). *The new politics of poverty: The nonworking poor in America.* New York: Basic Books.

Mead, L. (1986). Beyond entitlement: The social obligations of citizenship. New York: Free Press.

Miron, G., Urschel, J., & Saxton, N. (2011). *What makes KIPP work: Study of student characteristics, attrition, and school finance.* New York: National Center for the Study of Privatization in Education. http://www.ncspe.org/readrel.php?set=pub&cat=253.

Morris, R. (2011, September 15). KIPP co-founder: "We need to get rid of the government monopoly on education." *Uptown Messenger.* http://uptownmessenger.com/2011/09/founder-of-kipp-schools-speaks-at-tulane-university/ -comment-4836.

New Jersey Department of Education. (2004). *District Factor Groups for school districts.* http://www.state.nj.us/education/finance/rda/dfg.shtml.

New York Times. (1898, November 14). To aid Hampton Institute: Dr. Frissell, the principal, explains the work for colored people and Indians at a church meeting. http://timesmachine.nytimes.com/timesmachine/1898/11/14/102127757.html?pageNumber=2.

Nichols-Barrer, I., Gill, B., Gleason, P, & Tuttle, C. (2014). Does student attrition explain KIPP's success? *Education Next* 14 (4). http://educationnext.org/student-attrition-explain-kipps-success/.

Orlich, D., & Gifford, G. (2006, October 20). *Test scores, poverty, and ethnicity: The new American dilemma.* Phi Delta Kappa Summit on Public Education, Washington, DC. http://macaulay.cuny.edu/eportfolios/liufall2013/files/2013/10/Highstakestesting_poverty_ethnicity.pdf.

Rawls, K. (2013, May 8). Who is profiting from charters? The big bucks behind charter school secrecy, financial scandal and corruption. *Alternet.* http://www.alternet.org/education/who-profiting-charters-big-bucks-behind-charter-school-secrecy-financial-scandal-and.

Roeser, R., Eccles, J., & Sameroff, A. (1998). Academic and emotional functioning in early adolescence: Longitudinal relations, patterns, and prediction by experience in middle school. *Development and Psychopathology* 10, 321–52.

Rumberger, R., & Palardy, G. (2005). Does segregation still matter? The impact of student composition on academic achievement in high school. *Teachers College Record* 107 (9), 1999–2045.

Schein, E. (1961). *Coercive persuasion: A socio-psychological analysis of the "brainwashing" of American civilian prisoners by the Chinese Communists.* New York: W. W. Norton.

Schram, S. (1999). The new paternalism. [Review of the book *The new paternalism: Supervisory approaches to poverty*, by Lawrence M. Mead]. *Journal of Public Administration Research and Theory: P-PART* 9 (4), 667–72.

Tough, P. (2012). *How children succeed: Grit, curiosity, and the hidden power of character.* New York: Houghton Mifflin Harcourt.

Veltri, B. T. (2010). *Learning on other people's kids: Becoming a Teach for America teacher.* New York: Information Age Publishers.

Woodworth, K. R., David, J. L., Guha, R., Wang, H., & Lopez-Torkos, A. (2008). *San Francisco Bay Area KIPP schools: A study of early implementation and achievement. Final report.* Menlo Park, CA: SRI International.

Chapter Two

Broken Windows Theory and the KIPP Teaching Model

The limitation that was put upon outward action by the fixed arrangements of the typical traditional schoolroom, with its fixed rows of desks and its military regimen of pupils who were permitted to move only at certain fixed signals, put a great restriction upon intellectual and moral freedom. Straitjacket and chain-gang procedures had to be done away with if there was to be a chance for growth of individuals in the intellectual springs of freedom without which there is no assurance of genuine and continued normal growth.
—John Dewey (1938/2007)

As we pointed out in chapter 1, underpinning the "new paternalism" of the 1990s was the belief that social order demanded that any rule infraction, whether on city streets, in homeless shelters, or in schools had to be met with strict intervention and corrective measures. Any broken window on New York streets had to be mended, or anyone failing to tuck in his blanket at New York's privatized homeless shelters had to be exorcised. And if the homeless clients didn't like it, then they could choose to return to the under-funded and sometimes chaotic environments of the surviving public shelters.

Privately operated facilities would offer the latitude for rules and the enforcement regimen that, otherwise, would not survive the public scrutiny of institutions with accountable public officials and legal protections for the poor. As noted earlier, any crack in the dam required an immediate and forceful reaction in order to stem the flood of chaotic rule breaking. These same paternalistic underpinnings were cemented into place when Mike Feinberg and David Levin set out to create their KIPP Model for schooling economically disadvantaged children.

Researcher Howard Berlak (Horn, 2010) reported the following from his own visit to a KIPP school in San Francisco:

When I was there, children who followed all the rules were given points that could be exchanged for goodies at the school store. Those who resisted the rules or were slackers wore a large sign pinned to their clothes labeled "miscreant." Miscreants sat apart from the others at all times including lunch, were denied recess and participation in all other school projects and events.

I've spent many years in schools. This one felt like a humane, low security prison or something resembling a locked-down drug rehab program for adolescents run on reward and punishments by well meaning people. Maybe a case can be made for such places, but I cannot imagine anyone (including the *Times* reporter) sending their kids there unless they have no other acceptable options. What is most disturbing is the apparent universal belief by KIPP staff and partisans that standardized tests scores are the singular and most important measure of a truly good education. (p. 95)

One former KIPP teacher told me that she experienced so much anxiety and dread of going to work that she did not sleep the night before returning to her KIPP school after spring break. She realized that in the previous months at KIPP she had become less like a teacher and more like a "referee or a cop," whose principal aim was apprehending offenders of total-compliance expectations.

There was so much pressure to "catch" the kids. Catch them whispering. Catch them doing this. Catch them doing that. It was exhausting. It was all about catching them. One of Doug Lemov's ideas is that if you don't have one hundred percent compliance, one hundred percent authority, then others will think they can question.

Doug Lemov's (2010) book, *Teach Like a Champion*, is sometimes referred to as the No Excuses teaching bible, and it includes forty-nine "techniques" that promise to produce championship teaching. Technique 36 is one referred to above, which states "there's one suitable percentage of students following a direction given in your classroom: *100 Percent*. If you don't achieve this, you make your authority subject to interpretation, situation, and motivation" (p. 168). It would be hard to find a pedagogical dictum that is any more expressive of the new paternalism for schools serving poor and disenfranchised students.

Having spent a good deal of time in Philadelphia's Mastery Charter Schools, a No Excuses corporate chain of fifteen schools, Professor Joan Goodman (Strauss, 2014) used the domino metaphor, rather than broken windows, to explain Mastery's total-compliance school regimen based on the No Excuses model:

These schools believe that behaviors that you might not think are directly related to academic learning can have a domino effect if left unaddressed. Getting up from your chair to go to the bathroom without explicit permission, for example, or not having your hands folded on your desk, or not looking at the teacher every minute, or not having your feet firmly planted on each side of the center of the desk are problematic behaviors. Because if you don't conform to these rules then you are going to precipitate the next domino and the next domino. It's going to have a cascading effect on your behavior and pretty soon you're going to be very disruptive. (para. 9)

In the sections below, former KIPP teachers provide insights and reflections that help us understand the ramifications of the new paternalism for the teachers and students in economically deprived communities. Keep in mind that KIPP Model teachers, often with little classroom management capability, are focused on the enforcement of unbending rules among students, even as they are also subject to punitive enforcement mechanisms to do everything the KIPP way.

Pressure from school leaders to improve test performance and "performance character" takes the form of encouraging teachers to be "militant" and punitive. This regularly produces teacher behaviors that are not like the teacher behaviors in schools we are accustomed to but, rather, more reminiscent of subjects in one of Stanley Milgram's experiments (Milgram, 2009), whereby "teachers" set aside personal conscience to administer increasingly severe shocks in futile efforts to decrease errors by learners.

DISCIPLINE

In the federal report titled *Successful Charter Schools* (U.S. Department of Education, 2004), the KIPP Foundation's flagship, KIPP Academy Houston, was identified as one of nine exemplary charter schools. Even though the KIPP Foundation provides latitude to individual schools in developing disciplinary procedures, the infractions criteria and modes of punishment listed in figure 2.1 from the USDOE report are common in many of the 183 KIPP schools.

The KIPP Model views any infraction as serious enough to bring about any of the punishments listed, from additional assignments to detention to being confined to the "porch," or the "bench," as it is sometimes called. In explaining how the "bench" worked at her school, one former KIPP teacher noted that being benched carries with it a label that no one could miss:

It's meant to tie into the metaphor of this is KIPP as a team and if you don't do something that jibes with the expectations, then you go to the bench, just like you would on a sports team. It was a very overly complex system with—it was just way too complex to be an actual, successfully implemented discipline system. The thrust of it is a student that commits an offense that is really worthy of probation is placed on the bench, and they have to do a certain number of things to work their way off the bench. They go through detention. They carry around a "choices form" throughout the day, which has to be

KIPP: Houston							There are no shortcuts
Level of infraction	1	2	3	4	5	6	Expulsion
	Not following directions	Incomplete assignment	Academic ticket not signed	Negative attitude	Lying	Copying or cheating	Unacceptable items[2] (guns, knives, etc.)
	Not prepared for class	Dress code violation	Unorganized	Porch interaction	Swearing	Inappropriate conduct (harassment)	Gross harassment
	Tardy to class	Missing ticket	Disrespectful	Grossly unorganized	Gross disrespect	Fighting	Other similar offenses at the discretion of the principal
		Insufficient funds to recollect items	Completely missing assignment			Stealing	
		Absent w/o call to school by 8 am					
		Unnecessary items[1]					
		Off task					

[1] An unnecessary item consists of something that should not be brought to school such as electronic toys, game cards, pagers, cell phones, excessive amounts of cash, etc. Such items will be confiscated and held for a parent to recollect.

[2] Unacceptable items are things no child should have in his/her possession at any time such as weapons, drugs, alcohol, etc. In either of these situations, the item(s) will be confiscated and handed over to an administrator to be picked up by a parent, and the proper authorities will be notified.

Strategies to Redirect Disciplinary Violations

KIPP implements some of (but is not limited to) the following techniques to help our students learn from their mistakes and make better choices in the future:

- Additional assignments
- Calling/agenda plans
- Khaki plan (excessive dress code violations)
- Detention (Saturday)

Porch students avoid distractions in the following ways:

- Wearing their shirts/jackets inside out to let others know they are "looking inward", reflecting on their mistakes and should not be disturbed (reversible jackets should not be worn while on porch)
- Not being able to communicate (verbal or otherwise) with their peers without first being granted permission from a teacher

Figure 2.1.   Sample KIPP discipline and punishment chart

signed by each teacher at the end of each period, whether or not they made good choices for that period.

At the end of a period, a teacher will sign off on, yes, he made good choices, or no, he made bad choices today. I think the most striking thing to me about it is that students, while they're on the bench, until they earn their way off by completing these requirements, having multiple days of good choices, having written a reflective essay, having had a meeting with the teacher that put them on the bench originally, that student also each day until they earn their way off the bench, they wear a sticker across their uniform that says *BENCH* on it, in big, bold letters.

The "porch" or the "bench" at KIPP provides a form of psychological solitary confinement, and it functions as a form of public humiliation and ostracism that may last for hours or weeks, depending upon the infraction and how the student behaves while he is on the bench. At one KIPP school, students on the bench had to earn twenty of twenty-nine possible KIPP dollars for three consecutive days in order to get off the "bench." The practice underscores the connection between approved behavior and financial reward.

At other schools, students must write letters of contrition and read them aloud to the class or the entire school. Depending on the school, benched students may be placed in a different part of the room from other students, on a lower chair (porch chair) than the other students, or on the floor. Students on the "porch" must also sit apart from other students during lunch, and they may not communicate with other students away from school.

Students on the "porch" sometimes wear the "miscreant" sign, but more often they are required to turn their KIPP shirts inside out or are forced to wear a different shirt entirely. At some schools, KIPPsters wear blue shirts emblazoned with "Work Hard, Be Nice," unless they have broken a rule and are on the "bench," which may require them to wear a white shirt. Earning the KIPP shirt is a rite of passage, and to lose it is a serious blow to some students.

One former teacher described an incident in which a student was placed in a "porch chair" for making fun of girl who had a gap between her front teeth. The teacher took an example of the perpetrator's writing and posted it on an overhead projector "in front of the entire student body," telling the assembly, "You want to talk about a gap—here's the gap, look at your writing—you're in sixth grade not even capitalizing the letters." Another teacher referred to this kind of public humiliation as "public shaming."

> If a student collects enough demerits, then his shirt is turned inside out, and the kid is "on bench" the way someone, you know, a basketball player would be sitting out. And when a kid's shirt is inside out, you can't talk to him. He's not a member of the class. He might even have to sit on the floor or outside. And the other kids can't talk to him. And if the kids do, then it's, like, wildfire. Then they all have their shirts inside out very quickly.

Another teacher worked at a KIPP school where the "bench" had been replaced by RAA (Reflect, Assess, Act), which was "the equivalent of The Bench, where kids are on detention for a week, and they have lunch separate [and] they don't get to go out to PE, which is—there is no PE, just not going out . . . and playing on the swings and they have to stay after school for an hour."

In reflecting on the use of the "bench" as one of KIPP's devices used to maintain total compliance, one teacher who was still working at KIPP at the time of our interview shared this encounter with a student who had come to see the abnormality of the KIPP regimen:

> I had a kid the other day come up, this just happened this week, but he was like "Ms. _____, . . . the other schools don't have paychecks and they don't have deductions, they don't have detention . . . why can't KIPP be like a normal school?" And I feel like that kind of sums it up. . . . I feel like they aren't given the opportunity to really be kids.

The KIPP Model uses a discipline system that puts tremendous pressure on teachers to maintain straightjacket classroom conditions that are always breaking down under the countervailing influence of students' irrepressible needs to be the children they are. The more teachers put their fingers into the leaks in the dam, the sooner they find that ten fingers are not enough. The anxiety that is created for children and teachers, alike, is counterproductive to efforts to learn and to teach.

One teacher noted that KIPP had made her a worse teacher by forcing her to focus on behavioral compliance, rather than teaching in effective ways that successfully channel the energy of children.

> Retrospectively if I look at it [teaching at KIPP], it has made me a worse teacher because like now I feel I am constantly thinking of these expectations that I am supposed to have in terms of behavior, like having them be silent and all those things, and I feel like it is making me a bad teacher because it is constantly looking at the negative like, "oh they are not doing good". . . . I feel like it has not helped me to focus on the positive things as much.

EQUAL TO CHARACTER AND ACADEMICS

One aspect of the KIPP Model that deserves more public scrutiny is KIPP's "performance character" training, which is inspired by David Levin's association (Tough, 2006) with positive psychology guru Dr. Martin Seligman. Seligman's early research from the 1960s on "learned helplessness" took on an added element of controversy in 2008 and again in 2014, when it was found that Seligman's techniques for achieving total compliance were infamously used by psychologists under contract from the CIA after September 11, 2001 (Mayer, 2008a; Singal, 2014).

Although Seligman has consistently denied knowing anything of plans to use learned helplessness with enemy detainees, he delivered, at the behest of the CIA, a three-hour lecture on learned helplessness in 2002 at the Survival, Evasion, Resistance, and Escape (SERE) school in San Diego. Investigative journalist Jane Mayer (2008b) later wrote that "Professor Seligman says he has no idea why he was called in from his academic position in Pennsylvania, to suddenly appear at this CIA event. He just showed up and talked for three hours about how dogs, when exposed to horrible treatment, give up all hope, and become compliant. Why the CIA wanted to know about this at this point, he says he never asked" (para. 3).

In 2015, the *New York Times* (Risen, 2015) published a report (Soldz, Raymond, Reisner, Allen, Baker, & Keller, 2015) that included new details regarding the involvement of the American Psychological Association in the CIA torture program that occurred during the George W. Bush administration. Included in the report are emails from APA members, CIA officers, and White House officials. Among the emails is one from Kirk Hubbard, the CIA's Chief of the Operational Assessment Division, who obviously viewed Seligman's work on behalf of the CIA as significant. Here Hubbard complains to Susan Brandon (NIH), Dr. Geoffrey Mumford (APA director of Science Policy), and Scott Gerwehr (RAND Corporation contractor) that his bosses at the CIA would not pay for gifts for Dr. Seligman's children. "My office director would not even reimburse me for circa $100 bucks for CIA logo tshirts and ball caps for Marty Seligman's five kids! *He's helped out alot over the past four years* so I thought that was the least I could do. But no, has to come out of my own pocket! And people wonder why I am so cynical!" (p. 41)

It was during the 1960s and early 1970s that Seligman and his colleagues conducted a series of historic experiments that demonstrated dogs receiving "unavoidable electric shocks failed to take action in subsequent situations—even those in which escape or avoidance was in fact possible" (Nolen, 2014). Seligman found that dogs that had once tried to escape their cages never tried to escape after the random series of shocks, even when the doors of their cages were left open. He called the phenomenon "learned helplessness."

The extent of Dr. Seligman's role in developing the KIPP Model surely deserves further study, and central to that inquiry should be this question: How does one tell the difference between a manifestation of learned helplessness and a display of self-control, or self-regulation, particularly when the depressive effects of learned helplessness may be masked by ongoing doses of "learned optimism," which is essential to the happiness training (Hedges, 2010) of positive psychology and the character rehab that KIPP tries to accomplish?

Dr. Seligman's more recent research has been focused on emotional resiliency training to achieve "learned optimism," which Seligman's University of Pennsylvania colleagues put into use among urban adolescent schoolchildren to gauge the effects. Researchers (Gillham et al., 2007) found that the Penn Resiliency Program (PRP) was successful in temporarily reducing depression among late elementary and middle-school children.

Despite the limited success with children and adolescents, and despite the fact that no protocols had been developed for use with adults, Dr. Seligman received a no-bid contract (Benjamin, 2010) in 2010 from the U.S. Army worth $31 million to provide two weeks of training for army drill sergeants, who would then apply their new knowledge with recruits. In doing so, it was hoped that post-traumatic stress disorder among GIs could be averted at some later date.

Subsequently, Seligman's resiliency training program at the University of Pennsylvania's Positive Psychology Center became the centerpiece for a $145 million U.S. Army program to provide ten days of intense training for all of the army's forty thousand drill sergeants. In early 2014, a National Academies Institute of Medicine (Denning, Meisnere, & Warner, 2014) found in an evaluation study that army personnel suffering from PTSD and other reintegration problems had received no benefit from Seligman's programs:

> Resilience, prevention, and reintegration interventions should be based on well- established theoretical frameworks. Assessments of DOD programs conducted by this committee and others show that a majority of DOD resilience, prevention, and reintegration programs are not consistently based on evidence and that programs are evaluated infrequently or inadequately. For example, on the basis of internal research data that show only very small effect sizes, DOD concluded that Comprehensive Soldier Fitness, a broadly implemented program intended to foster resilience, is effective—despite external evaluations that dispute that conclusion. Among the small number of DOD-sponsored reintegration programs that exist, none appears to be based on scientific evidence. (p. 5)

PERFORMANCE CHARACTER

Seligman's influence and that of his protégé, Angela Duckworth, continue to be central in controlling the "noncognitive" behaviors and attitudes that are central to completing the KIPP Model mission. As "KIPP teachers believe their job is to teach 49 percent academics and 51 percent character" (Morris, 2011), "grit" and "self-control" are the two most important character traits that KIPP develops in their students. The other components of character are *zest, optimism, gratitude, social intelligence,* and *curiosity,* although the KIPP Model is principally concerned with developing *grit,* or relentless determination to achieve and to maintain *self-control.*

KIPP further divides *self-control* into two categories, each having four components:

School Work

- came to class prepared
- remembered and followed directions
- got to work right away instead of waiting until the last minute
- paid attention and resisted distractions

Interpersonal

- remained calm even when criticized or otherwise provoked
- allowed others to speak without interrupting
- was polite to adults and peers
- kept temper in check (KIPP Foundation, 2015c)

KIPP refers to its character goals as "performance character," or "achievement character," and KIPP's list of traits represents a distillation of a more expansive list that includes twenty-four characteristics, which was developed by Dr. Seligman and his colleague, Dr. Peterson (Peterson & Seligman, 2004). The narrowing down of the list was the principal work of Duckworth and Levin, who selected those qualities that they believed were crucial for raising the achievement for children who, otherwise, may be distracted by the challenges of living in poverty.

Notably missing are some of the more common elements of moral character that have been traditionally taught in school, such as honesty, integrity, thrift, and humility. According to Paul Tough (2012), Levin contends that moral character is based on moral law that, by necessity, is imposed by some higher authority. In following Seligman and Peterson, Tough claims "moral laws were limiting when it came to character because they reduced virtuous conduct to a simple matter of obedience to a higher authority" (p. 59).

In exchanging goals of moral character for those aimed at developing "performance character," students are likely to grow up with values suited to the needs of the modern workplace, as described by Eric Fromm (1956) in *The Art of Loving*:

> Modern capitalism needs men who co-operate smoothly and in large numbers: who want to consume more and more: and whose tastes are standardized and can be easily influenced and anticipated. It needs men who feel free and independent, not subject to any authority or principle or conscience—yet willing to be commanded, to do what is expected of them, to fit into the social machine without friction; who can be guided without force, led without leaders, prompted without aim—except the one to make good, to be on the move, to function, to go ahead. (p. 85)

David Levin's focus on "grit" and "self-control" suggests a high value attached to a kind of crusty abrasiveness, or personality pumice, that may be used to deal with difficult life situations. According to Tough (2012), Levin believes his approach stands above any charge of indoctrination or cultural colonialism by KIPP because "the character-strength approach is . . . fundamentally devoid of value judgment" (p. 60). We are left to wonder how Levin's preferred values of grit, self-control, gratitude, zest, and the rest are any less of an imposition than, let's say, wisdom, justice, honesty, and temperance.

Levin's proselytizing for positive psychologists' preferred values attempts to cloak any signs of imposition of behaviors among KIPP children, who are routinely taught that grit, self-control, zest, social intelligence, gratitude, optimism, and curiosity are the keys to attracting the best that life has to offer. Those who are unsuccessful at working or wishing hard enough to lure are taught that it is only themselves they have to blame if the best in life remains elusive. Hedges (2010) sums it up this way for those whose positivity efforts fail to attract the best things in life: "For those who run into the hard walls of reality, the ideology has the pernicious effect of forcing the victim to blame him or herself for his or her pain or suffering" (p. 119).

Indeed, students are taught to blame themselves, even if they encounter harsh treatment from others (Horn, 2012). Such mistreatment by an adult in a position of authority is an indicator that they, obviously, are not working hard enough or being good enough to be treated with the respect that comes when one "makes good." The drawing (see figure 2.2) is a copy of a worksheet that Seligman disciple Dr. Angela Duckworth has used in developing performance-character curricula for children in Philadelphia-area schools and for Levin's New York KIPP schools.

In figure 2.2, we see that children are taught that they should "feel okay" about abusive treatment from authority figures, whose verbal assaults and harsh treatment are to be viewed as the earned result for failure to meet expectations, which, in turn, requires more grit and working harder to avoid more justifiable denigration for falling short of expectations. In this new urban character-building regimen and emotional resilience training, children are expected to internalize abusive treatment from authority figures and to blame any such behavior on their own shortcomings.

At the same time, they are expected to maintain emotional resilience and self-control when faced with any of the sociological cancers that are triggered by poverty and that, otherwise, might serve as an excuse for not achieving the expectations from school leaders and teachers who work within the KIPP Model. Too, any anger or resentment among students that may result from punishments becomes suppressed as an improper reaction, rather than as a legitimate expression against KIPP's total control, constant surveillance, and unrealistic demands.

Many of the students who survive at KIPP become docile hard workers, whose submission to the KIPP total-compliance regime embellishes a highly developed sense of self-blame, even as they are effectively dehumanized in the process. If things don't work out for these children in terms of working hard enough or being nice enough to survive in KIPP and, later, to attract the "best things in life" further down life's road, then they will at least have learned along the way that no one will be to blame except themselves. They,

Figure 2.2. Character lesson handout teaching students to "feel okay" about verbal abuse

themselves, will be responsible for the failure that, based on KIPP's definition, the majority of them will experience as a result of not finishing college. No excuses. No shortcuts. Work hard, be nice.

Angela Duckworth's ongoing research projects include working directly with Levin at a KIPP school in New York to develop and fine-tune a report card that can be used to measure and grade what she prefers to call "achievement character" among the disadvantaged KIPPsters in The Bronx. Per the worksheet above, Duckworth is working there and elsewhere to develop curriculum that is intended to inject character and personality traits into children that purports to build immunity against the epidemic of urban poverty and disenfranchisement.

Duckworth, herself, grew up the daughter of privileged Chinese immigrants in the middle-class town of Cherry Hill, New Jersey, and she studied neuroscience as an undergraduate at Harvard (Hartnett, 2012). After a masters at Oxford and then a year at McKinsey and Co., Duckworth became the CEO of the online public school rating company, Great Schools, before she altered course to become a charter school teacher on both the West and East coasts.

After a late-night email exchange with Martin Seligman in 2002 and a face-to-face meeting the next day, Seligman cleared the way for Duckworth to be considered for the doctoral program at the University of Pennsylvania, even after the normal admissions process was closed. Duckworth became Seligman's protégé, and she earned a PhD in psychology in 2006. The next year Duckworth was hired as assistant professor of psychology at UPenn.

Since then, she has earned a reputation as a bold experimenter and unabashed extrovert, who exhibits a particularly salty vocabulary. According to a reporter (Hartnett, 2012) for the *Pennsylvania Gazette*, Duckworth

> uses expletives in a way that might impress even high-powered cursers like Rahm Emanuel. In the course of a 90-minute conversation she called a principal she knew "an asshole," described the opinion of a leading education foundation as "fucking idiotic," and did a spot-on impression of a teenager with attitude when explaining the challenge of conducting experiments with adolescents: "When you pay adults they always work harder but sometimes in schools when I've done experiments with monetary incentives there's this like adolescent 'fuck you' response. They'll be like 'Oh, you really want me to do well on this test? Fuck you, I'm going to do exactly the opposite.'" (p. 61)

With David Levin's promotional prowess, top charter chains such as Aspire, YES Prep, and Uncommon Schools have been significantly influenced by Seligman's techniques (Tough, 2006) that became central to his and Duckworth's research agenda. Seligman's protégé has extended Seligman's resilience methodology known as "learned optimism" to further develop programs for urban schoolchildren to shape their persistence, self-control, adaptability, and patience.

Duckworth's ongoing experiments in the public schools near the University of Pennsylvania attempt to devise ways to measure efforts to inoculate disadvantaged children from poverty's effects and to boost their immunity to the severe measures used in No Excuses schools to instill grit and self-control. Levin and other total-compliance charter operators want to engender a version of Seligman's "learned optimism" that will background the degrading life conditions that, otherwise, remain dispiriting or depressing for children. In doing so, the experimenters hope that KIPP Model students will develop the tenacity to rise above circumstances that would drag down lesser beings. Attitude, Duckworth argues, becomes as important or more important than ability.

In the absence of any program that might modify or eradicate the actual stress, distress, and irrationality of living in poverty, Duckworth and Levin's character performance experiments may be viewed as little more than involuntary behavioral and neurological sterilization techniques that could hinder, in fact, the capacities of children who have to survive daily in environments where internalizing abuse or acquiescing to domination could prove disadvantageous or even deadly. Even so, the unregulated and unchecked experimentation on children without regard for potentially harmful outcomes remains one of the hallmarks of Duckworth and Levin's "ready-fire-aim" approach, which may be very useful for business entrepreneurs (Zwilling, 2012) developing new processes or products, but extremely risky and potentially dangerous when it comes to educating the most vulnerable children.

MAINTAINING CONTROL BY LOSING CONTROL

From talking with former KIPP teachers, it became clear that demands for more grit and self-control and the total-compliance requirements of the KIPP Model result in rules, surveillance procedures, and enforcement strategies that are often discarded when school leaders find that students do not fully comply or that monitoring and enforcement become unmanageable. Failure to achieve total compliance leads to a proliferation of new and, often, more draconian rules that require more time and effort for enforcement by teachers who lack experience, confidence, or skills for establishing realistic classroom management, not to mention the wherewithal to stay above the quicksand of rigid minutiae that characterizes teaching the KIPP way.

Teachers describe KIPP teaching environments as sometimes chaotic and emotionally explosive, and the resulting atmosphere makes the teacher-coach in figure 2.2 above seem a much more plausible and familiar character. One beginning KIPP teacher hired to teach middle school, but with a degree in early childhood education, clearly understood, in retrospect, how his inexperience and unrealistic job expectations worked to his students' disadvantage:

> I didn't have any classroom management at all. They didn't teach me classroom management. I didn't learn as far as setting routines and procedures, so at the beginning of the year I was basically thrown into the deep end and I was trying to swim, but I was constantly drowning. I would come to the administration and constantly tell them that I was drowning because I wasn't able to hold the children up; I couldn't teach because of all the chaos that I was having in the classroom.

Efforts to enforce total compliance, without the requisite skills for basic classroom management, regularly lead to emotional outbursts that could easily jeopardize the health and safety of both teachers and students. This same beginning teacher described his "going crazy," which almost culminated in a violent incident in the classroom, which precipitated this beginning teacher's leaving KIPP before the first year was up.

> I had one child that basically had one of those little skateboards, finger skateboard; I took that away from him and he took my clipboard and that's when I say that I snapped because I have never been disrespected by a child like that.

And then another girl, she just threw her notebook on the ground. For me to try to control, I am thinking, I have to be mean to the children, and so I took the desk and I looked into the corner where I was going to throw the desk. I was aiming for the ceiling. So I didn't do it, but I did move the desk and that scared her and for me doing that, I thought that I was losing myself in the process. I wasn't doing what I felt like I was sent there to do, which was educate children and have them love learning. Those children did not love learning at all and will they ever? I hope so, but from the way it was looking, they are testing constantly, so they will learn how to test. That is what they will learn.

SCREAMING

While students are forced to stay silent for much of the time at a KIPP Model school, teachers are often loud—very loud. At St. Hope in Sacramento, a No Excuses charter school that takes special pride in its adoption of the KIPP Model, one administrator whose title is Dean of Culture regularly encouraged the eighteen or so teachers there to use yelling to maintain control. When the Dean of Culture visited a classroom of one former St. Hope teacher, the dean told her "you're too nice to the kids, you're too soft with them." This teacher said the behavior that the administrators modeled was "very militaristic screaming at the kids—I mean, shouting."

At some KIPP schools, yelling or screaming at students by teachers and school leaders is a sanctioned control technique. Teachers are regularly encouraged to be "forceful" or "militant" in their interactions with rule breakers or those who fall short of expectations. One teacher told me that teachers who do well at KIPP are "forceful and think for the child instead of having them think for themselves." Another young teacher had school leaders who told her that poor, black children expect to be yelled and screamed at, and that any other disciplinary approach will not work. She did not comply, and she resigned after spring break of her first year at KIPP. The following is part of her resignation letter:

The most important issue at [the KIPP school where this teacher worked] is the way students are managed. I imagined that working at KIPP meant a system-atized way of managing behavior (paychecks). However, I came to find out that this is very far from the truth. In fact, [a coworker who was a lead teacher] told me in our first week not to use the paychecks if we could help it. I came to realize that students are managed largely through bullying, screaming and personal insults. At my previous school, teachers did not raise their voice ONCE during the course of the year. At [the KIPP school where this teacher worked], screaming and yelling is ubiquitous.

Unlike at [two other schools], where there are school-sanctioned conse-quences for actions (namely, detention), at [the KIPP school where this teacher worked] students are managed by personal insults. I've witnessed [the coworker lead teacher] calling kids "gay," saying "that's why you have no friends" or other rude comments. And that's on a typical day. I've also seen teachers on my team get in students' faces and scream at them, I've seen teachers slam clipboards on desks until they break, I've seen teachers physically intimidate students. Needless to say, this is not beneficial to the students. In fact, I would never send my student to a school where these actions took place. I can only imagine that it is BECAUSE not many people know that these actions take place that they are allowed to continue. (personal communication)

Another teacher was told something very similar. When she resisted the pressure to be "militant," school leaders countered that because of cultural differences, black students are accustomed to being screamed at: "[Scream-ing] was encouraged because [school leaders] would say, well that's how their parents speak to them. And that's how they listen. . . . That's their justification, yeah, is that it was a cultural difference, and . . . I needed to speak to them in the way that their parents speak to them."

Screaming at students, then, is a common occurrence at KIPP and other schools that emulate the model, even though there are intense public relations efforts to promote the image of zest-filled, optimistic KIPP students engaged in "joyful learning," or the "J-Factor." As with other aspects of KIPP life, academics are key considerations for any manifestation of joy, as in the following examples (Sullivan, 2012) shared on a web page belonging to the venture philanthropy bundler and KIPP supporter the New Schools Venture Fund:

> For [KIPP] middle schoolers, distributing index cards turns into a competition in no time. Fun thrives in the virtual world of education technology as well. Who doesn't want to see a bright orange and red flame to celebrate a hot streak of test prep questions answered correctly on Grockit? [a computerized plat-form for test preparation] And chances are great that the whimsical characters of Class Dojo [a computerized class management tool] are much more effec-tive at catalyzing positive classroom behavior than listing students' initials under "Leading Scholars" ever was on my whiteboard. (para. 2)

While celebrating a "hot streak of test prep questions answered correctly" may fail to evoke the elusive "J-Factor" in many classrooms, the conse-quences of off-task behavior at KIPP are certain to produce the opposite of joy. Teachers under the constant stress of test performance expectations and KIPP's strict character catechism aimed to instill grit and self-control offers little patience for wandering student attention or any lapse in acceptable behavioral responses. One of the teachers who found it impossible to "follow their model" had this to say about the KIPP Model's regimen, which she said reminded her of "a concentration camp."

> There's nothing wrong with thinking outside of the KIPP values but you weren't allowed to. . . . There's one leader, there's a group of people who are just in it following a day to day routine that's exactly the same. . . . And you either hang in there or you drop out. The ones that are hanging in are barely hanging in. No one is just bright and cheery and coming to work happy. It's like they're coming to work and from the minute they walk in, they are screaming and yelling. . . . One thing the school leader worked on was—you have to smile. If you're not smiling, something's wrong. . . . No one was smiling.

At the same time, then, that KIPP teachers are told to smile and to focus on learned optimism and the "J-Factor," school leaders insist, either explicitly or implicitly, that teachers should be more "militant." This same teacher elaborated, when I asked her who was screaming and yelling:

> I . . . was free to move from classroom to classroom because I was over the _____ program. Almost every type classroom I went into, some worse than others, I couldn't stand the screaming. The teachers were at their end. They were screaming . . . to get attention from children, and you know your last step is just screaming. . . . There's a lot of yelling and screaming from the teacher trying to get control of the classroom. There's a lot of discipline problems in a KIPP school, which are not usually discussed at all. I would say that is usually the number one reason teachers leave—lack of classroom management skills.

Not every KIPP school is as chaotic as this one. In many of the 183 KIPP schools and the thousands of other schools that emulate the KIPP Model, however, a consistent absence of classroom management preparation contributes to KIPP teachers and leaders resorting to the authoritarian power play of screaming and yelling to control student behavior and to establish a total-compliance environment. Another teacher reported:

> Teachers yelled at students . . . [but] I'm not that person. . . . And you know, some of the teachers that were most effective were the loudest, and they came down on the kids. So I think that was more of the discipline that they were looking for.

This teacher, however, noted that the school leader, who was a "screamer," too, sometimes reminded teachers that "we really need to tone it down—we need to watch the way we're speaking to our students." As a result, this teacher was caught in a double bind that resulted from personal conscience and school leader reminders coming in conflict with practices that were encouraged and that brought the results that school leaders were looking for. This same teacher noted that some of the teachers with the best test scores were "screamers," and she remained uncertain during her time at KIPP as to whether she was to yell more to establish her "militancy."

Three KIPP teachers interviewed had direct knowledge of abusive practices by teachers at KIPP that went beyond yelling and screaming. The first teacher talked of a "foul-mouthed teacher," in particular, that she eventually reported for his yelling obscenities at children. Even though he "said the four-letter S word and the four-letter F word in class" on a regular basis, he was still teaching at KIPP when our interview took place, which was months after her leaving. A second teacher referred to a neighboring teacher as a "screamer, swearer, humiliator": "I had never seen anybody who would go to the lows that he did to really just knock a kid down, you know way down, but there was a lot of yelling and that was something that really bothered me."

A third teacher had similar experiences with a "hostile environment" next door. Hearing her neighbor's tirades caused her to feel "shaky" and have "that feeling of knots in my stomach."

> He would literally be yelling "what's wrong with you, are you an idiot?" He was the only one that I saw doing this. . . . He was, perhaps, an anomaly—I think he was, but "Jesus Christ" and "Goddamn it," and he would really work through humiliation. So when students would take a quiz, when the quiz was over they would correct it, and then he would call on each student and they would have to say their score out loud. Then he would start harassing the ones that got low scores—it was a bloody battlefield. That is what his classroom looked like.

When she reported the abusive teacher, the administrative reaction registered no alarm. There are many things that can trigger a teacher being fired at KIPP, but screaming and abusive language do not seem to be on that list.

> I couldn't take it anymore for the kid's part and for my own health. It was really a hostile environment. So I finally talked to the second principal and said "this is what is going on, I don't know if you know and I want to remain anonymous" and she said "okay thank you for telling us—he has had trouble in the past, we've talked to him in the past, and we will do more visits to his room."
>
> Great, I thought, wonderful. I can tell you even without being able to see his classroom door, I would know when somebody came into his room—it was like a switch went on, it was scary. So that went on and they knew about it and I said something again . . . and I got the same thing. "Oh yes he has been talked to, we will work on that." But it never changed.

One teacher attributed the screaming and verbal abuse at KIPP to a student management system "that doesn't reward kids for doing well" nearly as often as it "penalizes them for doing poorly." He added, "I saw teachers literally screaming at kids, and I'd never seen that before. I saw teachers, you know, slamming books and clipboards down on the desk, and I had never seen that before. . . . things like that. And so, you know, that whole process is demoralizing."

Screaming at KIPP may erupt for major or minor offenses. One teacher witnessed screaming for "back talking, dishonesty, talking in the middle of class, not staying in line." Having since found a teaching job in a public school, this teacher remembered the yelling as an element of the humiliation that students at KIPP endured:

> In terms of the humiliation, I know that I've seen it, I've slipped over, I've crossed that line, that's part of why I don't yell anymore. I've watched other teachers do it. . . . There's a bit of a mob mentality when you work for KIPP, and it's different at different schools. . . . But when it crosses that line to [where] you're just angry and a kid has gotten on your last nerve, I've seen teachers just yell at a kid in their face—full blown yell—the kind of thing that I would not want done to my daughter. I think KIPP long term will have to deal with that issue of short-term discipline that works with 5th and 6th graders for longer term.

When asked about specific books or classroom management techniques, another teacher responded, "Yelling. . . . It [discipline] was just kind of paying attention to the culture of the school, which was very in-your-face yelling, 'everything is everything' sort of model. Instead of deescalate, escalate. But it's not an approach that's effective, like spanking."

One former KIPP teacher first encountered teachers yelling even before she was hired. During her interview day at a KIPP school, she was taken to the cafeteria, where she saw "children sitting at the lunch tables, and they were just being yelled at and berated by a number of different teachers in the room who were taking turns. . . . The kids had nothing in their hands, no books, nothing. . . . I think that the reason that they were getting yelled at, as I remember, was that they had had very low homework completion that week."

Other teachers reported they, too, had encountered yelling and berating students at KIPP, which was sometimes accompanied by confrontations: "There was a lot of yelling, a lot of berating students, a lot of physically confronting students." One teacher saw the berating begin on the "first day students were on campus." During his time at KIPP, there was never a day, he said, that he "did not hear an adult raise their voice to a student, and not just in the stern command issuing tone kind of way, but just loudly berating students." When this teacher was asked to be more specific, he said, "The content was never anything like cursing, name-calling, anything like that."

During an assembly on the first day students were present, "there was one student that was, I think, fidgeting or talking to his neighbor, something like that. A staff member just came out of nowhere and interrupted the principal in the middle of her presentation, interrupted the whole thing and started shouting at the student. I expected the principal to appear taken aback or disoriented, but the principal jumped right on board."

As with some other teachers who talked about official sanctioning for screaming, this teacher, too, felt "pressure from the administration, in my observation, to yell more":

> I felt like that was the subtext to a lot of the feedback I got in terms of, "you need to be more strict, you need to be more heavy handed." I felt the subtext was "raise your voice, scream more," that kind of thing. It was a school with an open door policy, but we always said if we saw a closed door that meant that the teacher was screaming. And that was something that was part of the culture. Teachers would go, they'd close the door to their classroom and they would just erupt.

He noted, too, that "screaming," as it was referred to, was the "number one reflection that most kids had when asked 'if you could change one thing about your school,' what would it be."

When I asked one teacher how his new teaching position since leaving KIPP differed from his KIPP experience, it was the yelling that was most figural to him.

> The first thing would be there wasn't the sense of dread hanging over the place at all times, of someone's going to yell at any minute. It could be at any time. I could be in the middle of a lesson; someone could come in and start yelling. Kids could be walking from class to class; someone could start yelling. There was this sense of an iron curtain over everything [at KIPP] at all times.

Not surprisingly, the teachers who talked about participating in yelling felt badly about it, and engaging in tantrums or screaming fits provided the impetus for a number of these teachers to decide to leave KIPP. The following teacher decided just that, when she found that her yelling became a barrier to communication with her students:

> I just felt like I was constantly yelling at them all the time and I felt like that was a barrier between me and my students and because I was always yelling at them for talking or for not being in a straight line, that I could never really get to know who they were and that for me was so unnatural. That was something that was never brought up in my interview [for a teaching position at KIPP], and I had no idea what I was getting into, and once I realized what it was, I was like I got to get out. This is not for me.

While some of the KIPP teachers had uncomfortable memories of their own screaming, others could recall screaming by their colleagues at KIPP. One teacher, however, could recall screaming in her own classroom by another teacher from down the hall, a teacher she described as "downright mean."

> The teacher down the hall, the same one with the _____ chant, came
> over. The kids—getting them to settle down wasn't working despite all the
> things that I had in my toolbox from ten years of teaching. And the guy from
> across the hall would just come in and just scream at the kids. And they would
> instantly be silent because they were terrified of him. It wasn't out of respect
> for him. Some of the other teachers, they had their respect. But this guy, they
> just feared him. And they would instantly be quiet.

Near the end of every interview, former KIPP teachers were asked if they had anything they would like to discuss that they had not been asked about. One teacher who was subsequently hired by a public school came back to the subject of yelling as a mode of character remediation and control, and this time she suggested what many critics of KIPP have pointed out: If KIPP schools were not poor, black, or brown, our society would not allow KIPP's disciplinary methods to be used:

> There are things I really liked about my time at KIPP; there are things that I
> wish I had changed. I think KIPP—I'm Caucasian . . . KIPP _____ is
> mostly Hispanic, KIPP in _____ was mostly African American. I think
> there's a broader question when you look at the heavy discipline of KIPP.
> Would we let this happen if the students were white middle class? Would we
> be okay with the yelling? . . . I think that's a pretty valid question: is part of the
> reason that KIPP is allowed to get away with things that couldn't be done in a
> traditional school. I mean the things I did at KIPP would get me fired at my
> school now. The yelling—I've watched a teacher slam a door and the glass
> broke—I think that's a question worth analyzing, how much is race. . . . I don't
> know if I'm saying that right.

Another teacher with previous experience in public schools expressed his dismay at the encouragement from school leaders to be more punitive: "Definitely the school culture at KIPP was, I mean, militant and I was expected to be much more punitive as a teacher than I was at my previous position. . . . KIPP took over my life in a way that the previous experience did not. I at least had a few hours to myself working in the public school system to relax or to reflect." When asked to be more specific, he said, "Much more of a disciplinarian—more actively engaged in delivering the consequences that we had as part of the discipline plan. And that was a very strict code of conduct."

Later in the interview, this same high school teacher pointed to the "militant" culture of his No Excuses KIPP school as the thing he would change first about KIPP if he could. He also noted the bitter irony he found in

KIPP's desire to change student behavior, while remaining entirely silent about changing the conditions of the students' impoverished community:

> I would change the culture of the school. It's way too militant. I think the whole no excuses thing kind of drives this idea of every individual being accountable for his or her own circumstances in life. . . . I guess I wish that poverty was addressed and that the KIPP organization took up more genuine concern with the current state of education and inequality, because they always talk about closing the achievement gap. But it's just like, again, there's no mention of doing things in the community or improving circumstances for people in _____. Nothing about some of the reasons things are so bad in the first place for people. There's no real engagement of those topics, and so the students just sometimes feel, I think, like they're carrying a huge burden because they're told that there's this certain strict set of behaviors, that if you don't meet expectation, it's all your fault—it's up to you sort of thing.

The milder form of teacher "militancy" takes the form of what KIPP calls "preaching." One teacher from a New York KIPP school described a "preach" that came about after a visit from the executive director, who had begun screaming at a student when he saw a pushing incident during his walk-through. This embarrassing breach in the rules (no one was embarrassed by the screaming) during the director's visit led later to a "preach" by the school leader that had students "taken down," quite literally, as desks were pushed to the back of the room before students were brought in silently and lined up in their assigned seating arrangement, but on the floor.

The floor treatment was part of being "taken down." His description offers this look inside KIPP Model culture:

> There was this issue around pushing, and the reason it came to a head is because this Executive Director was in our school, kind of doing a walk through, and he saw this boy push this other boy, and they were best friends, and he got really mad at them, screamed at them.
>
> They both got suspended, and then we had to have a whole class meeting where the principal came to preach, and that meant that the kids—my classroom was taken down, like the desks and chairs were all moved to the back; the kids would come in and sit down in their rows, and they have their independent reading book with them, so they had to be silent, read their independent reading book until it was time for the principal to preach. Then they put the books down, everything out of their hands, hands in their lap.
>
> And then the principal did this kind of like—created a narrative, and it was usually around a single theme. She would say something like, "Okay, I want you to think of the number seven; keep the number seven in your mind," and then the whole speech would be around this concept, and for her the concept . . . was the seven spots—that there were seven openings in our incoming fifth-grade class left, and that there were 350 families or something that wanted those spots—she was telling them that there are 350 people trying to get seven spots. Well, what does that tell you about our school—how many

people want to be here, and how fortunate you are to have your spot here, and when you do things like push in line you're really jeopardizing—you're not playing your part in the KIPP community.

She didn't threaten them like they were going to get kicked out. It wasn't like that, but it was reminding them of how privileged and special they were to be there, and that this kind of behavior isn't what KIPP is about. So, it was like a lecture. . . . And different teachers did it differently. I mean, I saw other teachers do more of a class conversation. But the way we were instructed during professional development was to just preach at the kids, and lecture them about character. Yeah, the preaching was always about character.

KIPP-NOSIS

They have to be KIPPnotized early on . . .
—Mike Feinberg (Smith, 2005b)

The initial phase of KIPP performance character building and enculturation is known as "KIPP-notizing" (Brancaccio, 2007), and it is a central socialization component of the program that has received much less attention from the media than the test scores of KIPPsters who survive at KIPP long enough to take the state tests. The first dose of KIPP-notizing occurs during three-week summer sessions leading up to initial enrollment.

In 2005, the *Washington Post* published these details of the initial KIPP-nosis for new fifth-graders:

Mornings at the summer program at one of the District's newest public charter schools typically began with the principal, Khala Johnson, striding down the aisles between tables in the cafeteria/auditorium/gym commanding the students to get funky. "Give me a beat!" she shouted, her shoulder-length dreadlocks shaking.

The 80 or so fifth-graders obliged, stomping their feet and pounding on the tables. On the fourth beat, the chanting began: "You got to read, baby, read! You got to read, baby, read! 'Cause reading is knowledge and knowledge is power, the power for college and I want it!"

It's called "KIPPnotizing"—what officials at KIPP DC: AIM Academy say is their way of indoctrinating students into a culture of high expectations. (Haynes, 2005, para. 1–3)

New students must learn the SLANT rules, which mean to "sit up straight, look and listen, ask and answer questions, nod to show understanding, [and] track the speaker" (Browne 2009, p. 58). Students learn that any rule infraction will bring an instant corrective response, and they learn that the smallest misdeed will be no more tolerated than the most egregious offense. They learn that teachers or principals might, without warning, begin "preaching," which means to loudly castigate rule breakers and to provide long-winded explanations for why rules are as they are.

New KIPP enrollees practice walking in a silent, straight line, getting off the bus the KIPP way, sitting silently in the cafeteria, flawlessly following directions, and going to the bathroom only at times that are appointed for that. Learning to be silent starts early during KIPP-notizing. New fifth-graders are gathered together to comprehend "important aspects of KIPP" and how KIPP is different from the schools they have known in the past.

Students learn "how to walk silently in line, to never shout out and distract the speaker, use hand signals for asking to go to the bathroom or asking to get a drink of water or asking to sharpen a pencil without having to interrupt the class." At one KIPP school, a teacher said, "There were lines painted on the concrete walkways and they would line up when it was time to switch for their next class, and they would walk in a single file line to their next class, not talking."

"SCOWLING TEACHERS AND SILENT KIDS"

New KIPP students learn that silence is the rule of the realm for students. While screaming, yelling, preaching, and ranting are common practices for teachers and school leaders at KIPP schools, much of it springs from the inability to keep children entirely silent for most of the school day. Those students who comply with the expectations for silence and submission are rewarded with dollars added to paychecks that travel with them from room to room.

This system allows teachers to see how students behave in other classes, without using academic time to ask what kind of day the students might be having. Those students who don't submit to the enforced silence are punished with isolation, labeling, public humiliation, repetitious writing chores, written apologies, subtracted paycheck dollars, or a scream event. One teacher told me that at his school, which used the "bench" to isolate troublemakers, "the ones that were on bench for a long time, they weren't meeting the expectation of being silent."

As for teachers, those who have difficulty maintaining the enforced silence find themselves under the supervisory microscope much of the time. The emphasis on silence certainly provides an unadvertised counterweight to the emphasis that KIPP puts on the "joy factor." Specific protocols for maintaining silence vary from school to school, but all former KIPP teachers recounted experiences where enforced silence provided a school climate that one teacher called the "iron curtain."

The KIPP Model requires silence for most of the school day, and for some schools, silence is required even on the bus to and from school. One former

KIPP teacher said, "There were very little opportunities for any kind of social interaction at school that I recognized from my own experience in school as healthy social school interactions between students." Breakfasts, which begin around 7:10 a.m., are expected be silent work time.

One teacher's first memory of KIPP was the beginning of her interview day, when just after 7 a.m. "I went in to the cafeteria where all teachers were and the kids were all eating a silent breakfast." Homerooms, or "advisory," are expected to be entirely silent, with teachers poring over homework assignments to make sure they are complete while students do "morning work," which could be a crossword puzzle or a worksheet or some other task to distract them from the desire to interact.

If work is missing or sloppy, a note must be made for each child, which will have explicit consequences. Silence is maintained at all times, except during chanting or singing, or when students raise their hands to answer or ask a question. Lunches at some KIPP schools offer a few moments to interact with others, but the privilege can easily be lost by talking too loudly. Transitions between classes are silent, too, with students walking in straight lines near the wall.

One teacher saw the long hours of sitting in silence as contributing to hostility and tension within the classroom: "If you never saw [the] outside until 5:00, I think anybody would be hostile, and we saw constantly those four walls and those children . . . it was prison for them—the desks were their prison. They would sit at those desks all day, at that same desk all day, so they were definitely hostile."

The student privilege of talking at lunch has to be earned by remaining silent during lunch for the first two weeks of school. When students demonstrated they were unworthy of this privilege, silent lunches were demanded: "So for the first two weeks, everybody is silent in lunch. And following that, if your grade level earns the right, you can earn the right to talk at lunch, or lose it again." Another teacher noted, "Lunches were often silent, depending on the mood of the administrator looking over lunch that day."

One teacher who had worked at two different KIPP schools found lunch very different at the two schools. At one school, students who weren't on the "bench" having a segregated lunch were allowed to go into the courtyard during lunch. At the other school, however, lunch had much more in common with descriptions from other teachers:

> All of the kids would file into the cafeteria silently, take their seats, take out a book and start reading, and eat their lunch silently. After all of the kids were seated and reading, then they would be allowed to talk at a level-two volume to the people that were in their vicinity, but they weren't allowed to get up and leave the tables, to go to the bathroom unless they had permission from a teacher. They weren't allowed to get up and throw something away or to get napkins unless they had permission from a teacher.

One of the teachers who "was eating with the kids . . . to keep them quiet" offered what she understood to be the rationale for silent lunches: "Rather than having them be loud and rowdy and then trying to go to class next period, you know, they were silent and they were focused. And on one hand I can kind of get where she is coming from . . . but on the other hand you have to remember that you are dealing with middle schoolers, and they need to get that energy out."

Except for the two teachers from states with duty-free lunch mandated by law, the KIPP teachers were with their students during lunch. During lunch, they were "expected to sort of regulate the students. . . . You don't have any time to eat during lunch, which is a 30-minute time period. You are responsible for your children. You have to be inside the lunchroom. If you were to eat lunch, you would have to walk around and eat a sandwich real quick that you made at home in the morning or the night before."

Some KIPP schools have what is termed "academic lunch," where students who come to school with unfinished homework must complete their work as they eat. Sometimes it is held in the lunchroom, and at other schools, students on "academic lunch" must eat at their desks. Others have "lunch detention," whereby students are assigned to a teacher who maintains silence among offenders during that time.

KIPP lunch is commonly a half-hour, but because students must line up silently and walk silently to the cafeteria in single file, both teachers and students usually have fifteen to twenty minutes to eat. When students were allowed to talk during lunch, one teacher noted that "many lunches were turned into silent lunches simply because the volume got too loud in the cafeteria."

It is not uncommon for KIPP schools to locate in office buildings without kitchens, cafeterias, libraries, art rooms, or other physical elements we normally associate with school. One such teacher I talked with taught in a 20 x 20 basement room with no windows, where she was in charge of thirty children. Lunches were delivered, and it was her job, as well as her colleagues', to assemble the lunches, pass them out, maintain 100 percent silence, and keep children from eating until all children received every part of the meal:

> So one thing that the teachers had to do, every teacher, was to assemble lunches for the 30-something kids in your class. So I'm here with my 30 kids in this 20 by 20 room, and I'm assembling their lunches. And they sit down. And again, this is just telling. They sit down and they're not allowed to talk during lunch. And they're not allowed to eat until everyone has received every part of the meal.

The pressure cooker created by enforced silence is compounded at some KIPP schools on interim assessments (IA) days, which are monthly tests to determine if the school is on course to pass the next state test. On IA days, one teacher told me that children are not even allowed any interaction the entire day: "The days that they take these tests, the entire day they are not allowed to talk at all, or they automatically get detention even if they whisper."

The enforced silence takes a toll on normal child development, and it also curtails KIPP teachers' ability to get to know and, therefore, understand their students. One teacher said, "Keeping the kids silent during most of the day was just something I found extremely hard, especially in the morning when I want to greet a child or say hello or catch up on the weekend. We weren't allowed to do that."

Another teacher said that it was the "silent lunches and the silent lines" that he remembered most as a low point at KIPP: "For me that just sucks the life out of it [teaching], and I think I had really amazing kids there who I never got to know until right towards the end." Just before leaving KIPP, this teacher, in defiance of the administration, asked students to write personal narratives, which he then discussed with them. This last assignment turned out to be his high point at KIPP.

Although most of the teachers who shared their stories were middle school teachers, silence reigns, it seems, in the high school and elementary level as well. One high school teacher who left in midyear to take a job with a big pay cut said, "Most lunches were supposed to be silent. And we were supposed to walk around and make sure the kids were being absolutely quiet, as though we were in a prison."

All teachers had lunch duty at this high school, and most of the teachers were very young. This teacher who left midyear was not: "They [administrators and teachers] were so worried about keeping kids quiet during the lunchroom, which, to be honest, never made any sense to me. It makes sense to a 23-year-old. But it's not prison. A 15- or 16 year-old isn't just a student. They're still a kid. And they want to talk to their friends."

As noted already, minimizing distraction from academic purposes appears to be a primary purpose of maintaining silence, and no one would argue against the need for classrooms to be orderly for learning to be optimized. The fixation on a totalizing silence, however, disallows the kinds of interactions that can optimize learning levels that require understanding, analysis, synthesis, and application. Since these are surely academic skills that are highly valued by society and that are placed at the top of most learning taxonomies, we have to accept that there are other reasons that KIPP classrooms are kept silent, except for the group chanting and singing.

New KIPP students must learn that rules apply inside and outside of school. "Miscreants" must learn, for instance, that isolation and ostracism from the KIPP "team and family" is total as long as administered punishments last, and children who talk to "miscreants" at or away from school risk the same punishment if apprehended. In fact, it becomes the duty of other students to report offenders who are associating in any way with "miscreants" who become temporary untouchables. If they do not, they, too, risk the same punishment. New recruits, then, learn compliance through both coercion and constant surveillance.

LEARNING COMPLIANCE TO EARN A DESK

An element of KIPP-notizing that the mainstream media has largely ignored is the common practice of requiring new or returning students to sit on the floor until they earn their desks and classrooms. Evidence of children forced to sit on the floor as a form of punishment first surfaced in 2009, when the *Atlanta Journal-Constitution* (Vogell, 2009) published a story about angry parents who had removed their children from the school as a result of excessive punishment:

> The parents said a group of children were mistreated by teachers who separated them from their peers in class and at lunch. The students, parents said, reported sitting on the floor and said one girl urinated on herself after not being allowed to use the restroom immediately.
>
> School administrators said they erred in not calling parents as soon as their children got in trouble. First-year principal Jondré Pryor said he also should have done more to warn parents about the high expectations for conduct, as well as academics.
>
> "I'm really saddened that the kids are gone," Pryor said.
>
> David Jernigan, executive director of KIPP Metro Atlanta, said the group has no plans to remove the administrators or teachers involved, adding, "We sincerely have learned from this mistake." (para. 3–6)

One Atlanta student was removed after he told his parent, India Wood, "I can't take them yelling at me 10 hours today" (para. 13). Parent Cordelia Johnson said, "I just feel like these kids have been mistreated. They shouldn't have to sacrifice the emotional for the academic" (para. 14).

Two years later, another *Journal-Constitution* reporter (Dodd, 2011) found that, at the same KIPP school in Fulton County, eighth-graders obtain "classrooms and desks when they demonstrate they have earned them by meeting their student goals." This quote is from the photo caption (Dodd, 2011), which shows eighth-grade KIPP students sitting on the floor in neat rows doing their schoolwork.

This reality was confirmed by one of the former middle school teachers interviewed for this book, who reported that during KIPP-notizing, students "wouldn't have desks at first, so they would sit on the floor and that's how they would have class at first and then they were teaching how to SLANT, how to track the teacher and making sure that they keep their eyes on the teacher. . . . they had to earn their desks and they had to earn that chair."

Another KIPP middle school teacher recounted a most harrowing part of her KIPP-notizing experiences, when I asked her near the end of our interview if she had anything else she would like share about KIPP. This teacher witnessed one hundred fifth-graders, in a room designed for thirty children, who were forced to sit on the floor during the first week of KIPP-notizing (Horn, 2013). She seemed relieved to finally have the opportunity to share her story:

TEACHER: One thing I did want to tell you was, we started school the middle of July. And they did something totally illegal. And I knew then that I didn't want to work there anymore. For the fifth-graders coming into the school for the first time, they sat 100 fifth-graders on the floor of one class in rows for a week, 100 fifth-graders in one classroom for a week until they could follow directions. And at that point, I said, why am I here?

INTERVIEWER: This was during the, what is sometimes referred to as the KIPP-notizing?

TEACHER: Yes.

INTERVIEWER: And what do these children do all day if they were sitting on the floor?

TEACHER: They would sit there and do homework on the floor. They would fill in forms and pass them. And they had to all do it correctly, otherwise, they'd do it again and again and again. And so what we would do, by Thursday, all the teachers would vote . . . should we let them go into desks? In front of them, we had to vote. You know? And I voted yes, put them in desks. You know? It's like treating like animals. They weren't animals. They were children. And so by Friday, I think they figured, well, a week is long enough. You know? And so we all voted, yeah, let them go in the desks. And that's how they decided to go in the desks.

INTERVIEWER: Did all the teachers have to vote yes before they were given desks?

TEACHER: Yeah. Yeah. But we were encouraged to vote yes. Is that a KIPP thing to do? I don't know. But you wouldn't do that ever in a public school.

INTERVIEWER: I'm sure you wouldn't. I've heard of children sitting on the floor, but I haven't heard of 100 in a single room.

TEACHER: It was 100. It was all the fifth-graders in a classroom.

INTERVIEWER: And this is like a classroom designed for 30 desks?

TEACHER: Yes. They were stuffed in. They were stuffed in.

INTERVIEWER: How many teachers were in this room during this time?

TEACHER: Five. I think five teachers were there. And the principal would walk in every once in a while.

INTERVIEWER: So when all these children were sitting there, they were sitting there at all times unless they were going to recess or going to lunch?

TEACHER: Right. And those were only, I think those were only minimum days also. So it wasn't like eight hours. It was, like, four hours.

INTERVIEWER: OK. So they were there for half day.

TEACHER: Yeah, they were there for half day. You know? I don't think they had PE, but they did have lunch and they did have recess.

INTERVIEWER: OK. So they were just on the floor for four hours. So when the children got their desks, were they sent into different classrooms?

TEACHER: Yes, they were, three different classrooms, yes.

INTERVIEWER: And what was the reaction among students and among teachers?

TEACHER: Once they went to classroom?

INTERVIEWER: Yeah, once they got their desks.

TEACHER: They were a lot happier, because they had their own place to put their backpack. They had their own places to put books. They had their own place to put stuff. You know? They had their own space. And they needed that. They needed their own space. They needed to feel comfortable being an individual, not just being a classmate. (Horn, 2013)

While some KIPP schools require children to earn a desk, it is not uncommon for children to lose their desks for rule infractions. One teacher offered a sampling of offenses that could lead to losing desk privileges for minutes, hours, or days.

> If they were to talk to somebody when they were in line, if they didn't have their homework done, if their homework was messy, if their shirt wasn't tucked in, you know those are the minor ones all the way to if they were being disrespectful or bullying to a fellow student, they could get on it for rolling their eyes at a teacher, for talking back to a teacher, for talking during lunch, for talking during breakfast.

At the completion of weeks of intense KIPP-notizing, students become KIPPsters with the ritual of receiving the KIPP shirt (Browne, 2009, p. 58). This symbolic reward and acknowledgement of new students becoming part of the KIPP "team and family" marks the conclusion of the initial indoctrination phase. Some uniform shirts will carry the message "Work Hard, Be Nice"; others will read "No Shortcuts, No Excuses." Shirts are subject to being taken away for failure to comply with expectations, or sometimes students are forced to wear them inside out as a form of punishment.

KIPP was the creator and remains the exemplar of standardized No Excuses schooling. Its extreme form of educational paternalism serves as a model for others focused, above all else, on improving achievement test scores and raising levels of "performance character." KIPP preaches the gospel of working hard and being nice as the ticket to someday escaping the ravages of social and economic deprivation, which remain off the radar screens and beyond the actionable concerns of KIPP's elite supporters, whether venture philanthropists, bond investors, hedge funds, or corporate foundations that invest heavily in KIPP as the solution to the "poverty problem."

For the children, as well as teachers, who have been indoctrinated to believe that they are captains of their own educational fates, they must wonder what character deficiencies prevent them from persisting and succeeding, as the majority of them will fall short of KIPP's expectations. To avoid the attrition epidemic, themselves, the well-intentioned teachers, many of whom are neophytes from the best colleges, often attach themselves with unerring loyalty to the KIPP Model and the "attentive malevolence" that it engenders (Foucault, 1977, p. 137).

In doing so, these teachers come to insist that they and their students make any sacrifice, pay any price, to overcome the social and economic obstacles that politicians and philanthropists find too risky to try to change. In bearing the inhumane expectation of changing themselves in order to change their sociological realities, children are forced to give up being children. They are forced to put KIPP's demands above all else, as they are pried away from their community and family connections and forced to undergo a form of cultural neutering aimed to produce a ghettoized version of the white, middle-class child.

Something similar happens to teachers at KIPP, as their family and friends move to the background and KIPP takes over the foreground. Personal health needs become sacrificed to the grinding acceptance that "anything less than total exhaustion indicates a falling short of the mark of complete professionalism" (Brookfield, 2004, p. 101). As we know, many students and teachers fall by the wayside as a result. This book offers some of the stories of former teachers who could no longer accept or enforce the KIPP Model's form of educational "enslavement with pride" (p. 101).

The insistence on "complete professionalism" masks a paternalistic No Excuses rationale that results in an authoritarian organizational model that easily breeds a "dark moral nihilism" (Hedges, 2009). This nihilism infects teachers and school leaders and suffuses the KIPP school climate with an irrational hardness, where vulnerable and high-needs children are subjected to control measures and psychological interventions that are carried out without public oversight.

The consideration of any shortcoming as another excuse for not performing as expected encourages a hardness and single-minded focus by school leaders and teachers that is often abusive and unsympathetic to reality. The result is a psychological machismo celebrated among KIPP school leaders, which mimics the heedless "let the stallions run" mentality (Mathews, 2009a) that began when David Levin and Mike Feinberg were Teach for America recruits.

The KIPP Model embodies a predominating expectation of exceptionalism and even superhuman feats from inexperienced and vulnerable teachers, most of whom lack the teaching background or training to understand that what is expected of them is imbued with a sadistic quality. Chris Hedges (2009) describes this phenomenon and quotes from Theodore Adorno:

> He [Adorno] knew that radical evil was possible only with the collaboration of a timid, cowed and confused population. . . . He feared a culture that banished the anxieties and complexities of moral choice and embraced a childish hypermasculinity. . . . [Hedges quoting Adorno:] "This educational ideal of hardness, in which many may believe without reflecting about it, is utterly wrong. . . .The idea that virility consists in the maximum degree of endurance long ago became a screen-image for masochism that, as psychology has demonstrated, aligns itself all too easily with sadism." (pp. 91–92)

One teacher that I interviewed recounted an incident of unhealthy "masochism" at her school, which had become a subject of lore and that carried with it a moral: no sacrifice for KIPP is too much.

> This one teacher I am talking about had been in the hospital for a major operation of some kind. He was in for awhile. And he had gotten out in a wheelchair with an IV drip—and he came back to his classroom. I think it was before a test. And they joked about it, like, ha, remember when that happened? And it was just, like, no, that's terrible. You know, people coming in sick, them [school leaders] telling us, "we don't care if you're sick. You come in anyway—we can't be absent for the kids."

Another teacher I talked with found it necessary to take off for a year following her KIPP experience, which left her with "a PTSD thing." She said that year was spent on the Web trying to find others who could help her understand the trauma she felt.

> I do go on the Internet and try to find stuff about KIPP. What's going on, what are people saying, what are people writing. . . . Because it is healing in a way to be able to know, yeah that's right, it wasn't just me, even though I know that I am still looking for outside validation because it was such a horrendous time. As I am talking to you about this, my hands are sweaty, my feet are clammy, so I mean it brings up a lot. It was a really hard time.

It is not uncommon for KIPP teachers to feel pressure to push themselves to the breaking point. One said, "There's just this assumption that you're on [duty] all the time, and any hour that you're awake is one that you're doing things for the kids. And if you don't, you don't care about them. And that's pretty much it. It's like you give your life." This same teacher, too, noted a kind of contagious masochism that ensued among teachers who competed with one another to take on even more duties than required, such as covering the classes for teachers who had to be absent from school.

To understand how the intense and, sometimes, disturbing accounts by former KIPP teachers fit the broader social and political contexts for education policy and No Excuses schooling practices, we must first understand the background from which current economic motives, corporate steering aims, test-based accountability practices, and productivity measures for K–12 education have emerged and gained ascendancy. How other education purposes and aims generally associated with humanistic and communitarian ends have been supplanted by corporate education reforms is the subject taken up next by Scott Ellison.

REFERENCES

Benjamin, M. (2010, October 14). "War on terror" psychologist gets giant no-bid contract. *Salon.* http://www.salon.com/2010/10/14/army_contract_seligman/ .

Brancaccio, D. (2007, June 22). *The report card and lending a hand.* NOW with David Brancaccio. http://www.pbs.org/now/transcript/325.html .

Brookfield, S. (2004). *The power of critical theory: Liberating adult learning and teaching.* San Francisco: Jossey-Bass.

Browne, L. W. (2009). *A character education approach to founding a KIPP college preparatory charter school.* (Doctoral dissertation). Retrieved from Dissertation and Theses database. (UMI No. 3344513).

Denning, L., Meisnere, M., & Warner, K. (Eds.). (2014). *Preventing psychological disorders in service members and their families: An assessment of programs.* Washington, DC: National Academies Press.

Dewey, J. (1938/2007). *Experience and education.* New York: Simon & Schuster.

Dodd, D. (2011, August 15.) KIPP schools' get-tough rules, lessons get results. *Atlanta Journal-Constitution.* http://www.ajc.com/news/news/local/kipp-schools-get-tough-rules-lessons-get-results/nQKYw/ .

Foucault, M. (1977). *Discipline and punish: The birth of the prison.* New York: Vintage Books.

Fromm, E. (1956). *The art of loving.* New York: Harper & Row.

Gillham, J., et al. (2007). School-based prevention of depressive symptoms: A randomized controlled study of the effectiveness and specificity of the Penn Resiliency Program. *Journal of Consulting and Clinical Psychology* 75 (1), 9–19.

Hartnett, K. (2012, May/June). Character's content. *The Pennsylvania Gazette*, 58–64. http://www.upenn.edu/gazette/0512/PennGaz0512_feature4.pdf.

Haynes, V. (2005, August 25). Charter schools expand in several new directions. *Washington Post.* http://www.washingtonpost.com/wp-dyn/content/article/2005/08/24/AR2005082400731.html.

Hedges, C. (2010). *Empire of illusions: The end of literacy and the triumph of spectacle.* New York: Nation Books.

Hedges, C. (2009). America is in need of a moral bailout. *Truthdig: Drilling beneath the headlines.* http://www.truthdig.com/report/print/20090323_america_is_in_need_of_a_moral_bailout/ .

Horn, J. (2013, December 17). KIPP forces 5th graders to "earn" desks by sitting on the floor for a week. *Alternet.org.* http://www.alternet.org/education/kipp-forces-5th-graders-earn-desks-sitting-floor-week.

Horn, J. (2012, September 12). A former KIPP teacher shares her story. [Blog post]. http://www.schoolsmatter.info/2012/09/a-former-kipp-teacher-shares-her-story.html

Horn, J. (2010). Corporatism, KIPP, and cultural eugenics. In *The Bill Gates Foundation and the future of U.S. "public" schools*. Edited by P. Kovacs. New York: Routledge.

KIPP Foundation. (2015c). *Character strengths and corresponding behaviors.* http://www.kipp.org/our-approach/strengths-and-behaviors.

Lemov, D. (2010). *Teach like a champion: 49 techniques that put students on the path to college (K–12).* San Francisco: Jossey-Bass.

Mathews, J. (2009a). *Work hard, be nice: How two inspired teachers created the most promising schools in America.* New York: Algonquin Books.

Mayer, J. (2008a). *The dark side: The inside story of how the war on terror turned into a war on American ideals.* New York: Doubleday.

Mayer, J. (2008b, July 17). Mayer on Seligman. *The Atlantic.* http://www.theatlantic.com/daily-dish/archive/2008/07/mayer-on-seligman/214016/.

Milgram, S. (2009). *Obedience to authority: An experimental view.* New York: Harper Perennial Modern Classics. (Original work published 1974.)

Morris, R. (2011, September 15). KIPP co-founder: "We need to get rid of the government monopoly on education." *Uptown Messenger.* http://uptownmessenger.com/2011/09/founder-of-kipp-schools-speaks-at-tulane-university/ -comment-4836.

Nolen, J. (2014). Learned helplessness. *Encyclopedia Britannica.* http://www.britannica.com/EBchecked/topic/1380861/learned-helplessness.

Peterson, C., & Seligman, M. (2004). *Character strengths and virtues: A handbook and classification.* New York: APA/Oxford University Press.

Risen, J. (2015, April 30). American Psychological Association bolstered CIA torture program, report says. *New York Times.* http://www.nytimes.com/2015/05/01/us/report-says-american-psychological-association-collaborated-on-torture-justification.html?ref=topics&_r=0.

Singal, J. (2014, December 9). Meet the psychologists who helped the CIA torture. *New York Times Magazine.* http://nymag.com/scienceofus/2014/12/meet-the-shrinks-who-helped-the-cia-torture.html.

Smith, H. (2005b). *School-by-school reform: Interview with Mike Feinberg.* Headrick Smith Productions. http://www.pbs.org/makingschoolswork/sbs/kipp/feinberg.html.

Soldz, S., Raymond, N., Reisner, S., Allen, S., Baker, I., & Keller, A. (2015). *All the president's psychologists: The American Psychological Association's secret complicity with the White House and US intelligence community in support to the CIA's "enhanced" interrogation program.* http://www.nytimes.com/interactive/2015/05/01/us/document-report.html.

Strauss, V. (2014, September 19). *Why "no excuses" charter schools mold "very submissive" students—starting in kindergarten.* [Blog post]. http://www.washingtonpost.com/blogs/answer-sheet/wp/2014/09/19/why-no-excuses-charter-schools-mold-very-submissive-students-starting-in-kindergarten/.

Sullivan, C. (2012, July 11). *The J-factor.* [Blog post]. http://www.newschools.org/blog/the-j-factor.

Tough, P. (2012). *How children succeed: Grit, curiosity, and the hidden power of character.* New York: Houghton Mifflin Harcourt.

Tough, P. (2006, November 26). What it takes to make a student. *New York Times Magazine.* http://www.nytimes.com/2006/11/26/magazine/26tough.html?pagewanted=all.

U.S. Department of Education. (2004). Successful charter schools. http://www.p12.nysed.gov/psc/documents/USDOESuccessfulCharterSchoolsreport.pdf.

Vogell, H. (2009, March 22). Charter school faces withdrawals over punishment. *Atlanta Journal-Constitution.* http://charterschoolscandals.blogspot.com/2010/05/kipp-south-fulton-academy.html.

Zwilling, M. (2012, November 17). 6 right times to be a ready-fire-aim entrepreneur. *Forbes.* http://www.forbes.com/sites/martinzwilling/2012/11/17/6-right-times-to-be-a-ready-fire-aim-entrepreneur/.

Chapter Three

Neoliberalism Goes to School

Scott Ellison

> Just as modern mass production methods require the standardization of commodities, so the social process requires standardization of man, and this standardization is called "equality."
> —Eric Fromm (Brookfield, 2004, p. 161)

In popular debates over education policy, it has now become quite common to see terms such as *neoliberalism* and *neoliberal education reform* bandied about in political debates in order to describe this current era of education reform. The neoliberal descriptor is indeed apt, but there is a problem with its common usage. Unfortunately, it is all too often the case that this terminology is used as a substitute for analysis, a pejorative shorthand used alongside terms such as *corporate reform* and *privatization*.

This unfortunate use of terminology obscures the reality that neoliberalism represents a dynamic political ideology, with a specific intellectual and political history, that has come to dominate not only debates over education policy but also the political discourse and major institutions of American society. This chapter will attempt to flesh out what is known as neoliberal education reform by tracing three overlapping, mutually reinforcing societal trends that have fundamentally restructured the landscape of education policy over the past thirty to forty years.

The first section will trace the development of a political convergence around a set of education policy reforms in the United States informed by neoclassical economic theory and globalization practices that have radically shifted education policy talk and implementation to the political Right. The second section will examine the power dynamics behind this political convergence by examining the emergence of an increasingly assertive business and philanthropic community that has constructed a private superstructure around public education policy in order to transform America's schools. The third section will look at how economic globalization and orthodox neoclassical economic theory entered into popular discourse and how these ideas came to define both the "why" and "how" of public education.

It is, of course, not possible to give an exhaustive account of the broad transformations taking place in the politics of education policy over the past thirty-five years in the space provided here. However, what will be made evident in the chapter that follows is that the No Excuses school model can be viewed as the paradigmatic institution of an education reform movement shaped by neoliberal ideology.

Or, to be more precise, the KIPP charter school model is one very prominent manifestation of an ongoing political project to remake American society in the image of an imagined marketplace of rationality and human liberty. Unpacking this political project will amplify the analysis in the chapters that follow to provide new perspectives on the KIPP Model.

POLITICAL CONVERGENCE

The purpose of public schooling is often treated as being self-evident or commonsensical: to transmit to the young the skills and knowledge they will need as adults. This may seem rather straightforward, but it papers over the complexity of the question. The kinds of knowledge and skills we believe young people will need to enter into adult life are predicated on a specific set of assumptions about the nature of social reality, in terms of "what is" and "what should be," and the nature of the individuals who inhabit it.

This is not a trivial point to consider. As John Dewey (1944) went to great pains to point out, the ends and means of public education are reciprocally determined, each informing the other. That observation is nowhere more true than current debates over public schools and reform.

In the second decade of the twenty-first century, the intended outcomes of public schooling are conceptualized from an economic perspective. Leaders and public intellectuals may offer hollow platitudes to citizenship and human development, but it is increasingly the case that the ultimate goal of public schooling is to produce good workers for a social reality defined by economic globalization.

The commonsense answer to the question of why we educate is so that young people can prepare for the workplace. In the modern parlance of education policy, the task of schools is to prepare children to be "college and career ready" competitors in the global economy. The politics of the shifting discourse in and around public education takes us back to the Reagan era and to what David Berliner and Bruce Biddle (Berliner & Biddle, 1995) referred to as the manufactured crisis emanating from *A Nation at Risk (ANAR)* (1983).

The Manufactured Crisis and *A Nation at Risk*

Published in the format of an open letter to the American public, *ANAR* painted a dire picture of American education, and it identified a litany of ills threatening the nation, including 1) low academic achievement of American students in comparison to their international peers, 2) low student achievement on standardized assessments (particularly among minority populations), 3) a lack of "higher order" skills among high school graduates, 4) falling achievement of college graduates, 5) the large number of functionally illiterate adults, and 6) a workforce lacking the skills for a high-tech economy.

The picture that emerged from *ANAR* was an education system in crisis, and this tragic situation was attributed to several causes. First, *ANAR* singled out high school curricula as being "homogenized, diluted, and diffused to the point that they no longer have a central purpose . . . a cafeteria-style curriculum in which the appetizers and desserts can easily be mistaken for the main courses" (NCEE, 1983, p. 18).

ANAR painted a picture of a high school curriculum that is a mile wide and an inch deep, allowing students to earn a high school diploma without having mastered even the basics of learning. *ANAR* pointed toward the low number of students taking challenging math or foreign language courses and the corresponding ease of general track studies, in which credits are earned for "physical and health education, work experience outside the school, remedial English and mathematics, and personal service and development courses," as evidence of a general decline in academic standards (p. 19).

Second, alongside this watering down of high school curricula, *ANAR* argued that American high schools could be characterized as having shockingly low expectations of its students. The amount of homework expected of high school seniors had plummeted while overall grades were rising, despite declining overall achievement. Further troubles were located in easy high school graduation requirements, "minimum competency" examinations that were too easy, low entry requirements for four-year colleges and universities, and inadequate textbooks (pp. 20–21).

Third, *ANAR* argued that American students spent much less time in school than their peers in other industrialized nations, and much of the time they spent in school was wasted due to inefficiency and superfluous activities, such as driver's education and home economics (pp. 21–22). Finally, while arguing against scapegoating any one particular group, *ANAR* did single out teachers as being one of the big problems in education.

ANAR characterized teachers as being poorly paid professionals drawn from the lowest achievers in college, who have taken large numbers of courses "in 'educational methods' at the expense of courses in subjects to be taught," such as mathematics and science (p. 22). To anyone following current debates in education policy, the problems identified in *ANAR* are all too familiar. The concepts of standards, excellence, assessment, and accountability continue to dominate public debates over education and schooling, and each of these concepts can be traced directly back to *ANAR*.

The publication of *ANAR* spawned a flurry of reports, research, and opinion that were both supportive and critical of the report (Holton, 1984; Tomlinson, 1987; Bennett, 1998; NCEE, 2007). Then and now, critics charged that *ANAR* used misleading and imagined statistics to paint a dire picture of American schooling that looked nothing like reality and that offered nothing new beyond the "more math and more science" mantra of the post-*Sputnik* era. As Gerald Bracey (2003) noted:

> [T]he report's recommendations were, as [William F.] Buckley and others observed, banal. They call for nothing new, only more of the same: more science, more mathematics, more computer science, more foreign language, more homework, more rigorous courses, more time-on-task, more hours in the school day, more days in the school year, more training for teachers, more money for teachers. Hardly the stuff of revolution. And even those mundane recommendations were based on a set of allegations of national risk that Peter Appleborne of the *New York Times* later called "brilliant propaganda." Indeed, the report was a veritable treasure of slanted, spun, and distorted statistics." (p. 617)

Nevertheless, despite its numerous flaws and somewhat clichéd recommendations, it is clear that, as a historical document, *ANAR* constitutes a clear turning point in the history of American education in that it sparked a three-decade march toward reform (Hunt & Staton, 1996) by the way the report framed educational failure and defined the resulting "risk" facing the nation.

The success of *ANAR* can be attributed to the way in which it constructed linkages between the economic malaise and deindustrialization of the 1970s with the purported decline in public schooling. *ANAR* made the explicit argument that the economic troubles facing the nation were in large measure educational problems. This frequently quoted passage from *ANAR* gives the reader a taste of the overall economic framing of the document:

> The world is indeed one global village. We live among determined, well-educated, and strongly motivated competitors. We compete with them for international standing and markets, not only with products but also with the ideas of our laboratories and neighborhood workshops. America's position in the world may once have been reasonably secure with only a few exceptionally well-trained men and women. It is no longer. The risk is not only that the Japanese make automobiles more efficiently than Americans and have govern-

ment subsidies for development and export. It is not just that the South Koreans recently built the world's most efficient steel mill, or that American machine tools, once the pride of the world, are being displaced by German products. It is also that these developments signify a redistribution of trained capability throughout the globe. Knowledge, learning, information, and skilled intelligence are the new raw materials of international commerce and are today spreading throughout the world as vigorously as miracle drugs, synthetic fertilizers, and blue jeans did earlier. If only to keep and improve on the slim competitive edge we still retain in world markets, we must dedicate ourselves to the reform of our educational system for the benefit of all—old and young alike, affluent and poor, majority and minority. Learning is the indispensable investment required for success in the "information age" we are entering. (NCEE 1983, pp. 6–7)

ANAR was able to successfully tap into Americans' anxiety over economic turmoil at home and increasing economic competition from abroad, particularly from Japan and the other so-called Asian Tigers, in order to make a case for large-scale education reform. *ANAR* successfully established linkages between the economic malaise of the time with educational failure and, in so doing, gave rise to the looming specter of an existential crisis in the not-so-distant future. More importantly, the global economic framing of *ANAR* changed the way we, as a society, talk about public education by introducing new concepts that are now dominant in the field, such as the "knowledge economy," "life-long learning," and the "information age." In the post-*ANAR* era, the name of the game in education policy and reform is globalization.

Shifting Politics of Education Policy

The political rhetoric of the late 1970s was still largely defined by the post–World War II divide between the progressive liberalism of the Democratic Party and the neoclassical liberalism of the Republican Party. Dominated by the legacies of Roosevelt's New Deal and Johnson's Great Society, the progressive liberalism of the Democratic Party understood public schooling as a functional mechanism to alleviate societal ills and resolve social conflict.

Liberals envisioned a positive federal government role in providing adequately resourced public schooling as a means for ensuring equality of opportunity and, as a result, the smooth functioning of a liberal democracy. The neoclassical liberalism of the Republican Party was defined by a strong commitment to an absence of federal obstacles to public schooling, which was viewed as a state and local issue. Conservatives opposed federal initiatives in public education, and (at the state level) they argued for a "traditional" education to produce good citizens and workers.

On the surface, the rhetoric of education politics offered Americans two very different visions for public schooling, although the reality of educational politics was always more dynamic and complicated. However, shifts taking place within the Republican Party and the conservative movement would ultimately shift American politics further to the political Right and, with it, the political landscape of education policy (Mehta, 2013).

Berliner and Biddle (1995) identified three overlapping, and somewhat contradictory, groups within the conservative movement that gained ascendancy over education policy after the election of Ronald Reagan in 1980. The Far Right was the libertarian-leaning wing of the Party that rejected all federal involvement in education: "At a minimum, this mean[t] abolishing the Department of Education, closing down federal support for educational research, eliminating funds for categorical grants in education that support minorities, and reducing the influence of federal courts" (p. 134).

The Religious Right, the second group, was represented by national religious figures, such as Pat Robertson and Jerry Falwell. From this perspective, many of the social ills that had befallen society were the product of public schooling and its commitment to humanist principles and cultural relativism: "In general, the Religious Right argue[d] that federal controls have been used to deny students the 'right' to pray in schools; to restrict unfairly the teaching of 'scientific creationism'; to encourage the appearance of 'dirty,' 'anti-family,' 'pro-homosexual,' and 'anti-American' books in school curricula; and to enforce 'cultural relativity' in courses on values and sex education" (p. 136).

Railing against "secular humanism," the Religious Right carved out a rather contradictory space in the conservative movement that, on the one hand, argued against further federal intrusion into public schools while, on the other hand, argued for federal and state government to mandate policies, funding, and curricula that reflected its values, including school choice and voucher programs that would allow parents to send their children to parochial schools at the taxpayers' expense.

The third group, the neoconservatives, was the new up-and-comers in the Party. They rejected any perceived attempt at social engineering in federal policy, asserting that it inevitably led to a lowering of standards and achievement. That said, the neoconservatives envisioned a strong role for the federal government in public schooling to ensure that they were reaching the following goals:

> [S]chools should recommit themselves to academic excellence and require a larger number of basic-skills courses; higher academic standards should be encouraged through tougher grading procedures and national tests of student achievement; schools should maintain discipline and reassert their rights to discharge students who cannot meet reasonable standards for behavior; stress should be given to competitiveness and other values thought to be "traditional" in America; and greater effort on the part of teachers should be encouraged through merit pay, competency testing, and stronger requirements for teacher certification. (p. 137)

The neoconservatives were, by far, the most comfortable with the idea of a strong federal role in public education, seeing it as a mechanism for accountability and ensuring that schools are fulfilling their institutional mission. It is important to note that the neoconservatives were heavily influenced by an increasingly assertive business community concerned about workforce skills, and it is clear that the neoconservatives saw human capital development as integral to the mission of public education.

The Reagan Revolution of 1980 brought to the Department of Education this unwieldy and rather paradoxical coalition of groups that advocated for strict federalism (Far Right); groups that argued for rolling back federal involvement in public schooling while also arguing for using federal leverage to encourage "traditional" curricula and school choice policies (Religious Right); and groups that envisioned a strong federal role in public education in order to ensure system accountability and human capital development (neoconservatives).

In an impressive feat of political maneuvering, Terrell Bell was able to successfully negotiate the Reagan White House and use the publication of *A Nation at Risk* to unify the three divisions of the Right that made up the Republican coalition of the early 1980s (Bell 1988/1993). Bell was able to unify the party in openly criticizing public schools and teachers, articulating a relatively unified vision for education reform, and advocating for using the leverage of the federal government to push these reforms at the state level. Bell was able to carve out a federal role in education policy by, in effect, becoming its biggest critic.

Policy changes during the Reagan years, however, remained modest at best. Resistance from the more libertarian-leaning members of the Republican coalition and outright opposition from liberal Democrats in Congress quickly cooled the jets of education reform. However, the political legacy of the Reagan Revolution for education policy wasn't so much one of radical change as it was the emergence of a new vision of federal education reform centered on the ideas of internationally "competitive" standards, assessment and accountability, and school choice. It was a vision that would come to influence the presidential administrations that followed, both Republican and Democratic.

President George H. W. Bush campaigned as the "education president" in 1988 and, upon winning the election, set about establishing a governor's conference to chart a course for education reform during his administration (McGuinn, 2006, p. 216). The Charlottesville Education Summit of governors was held in September of 1989, and the six principles that emerged from that conference formed the backbone of Bush's America 2000 education initiative:

1. annually increasing the number of children served by preschool programs with the goal of serving all "at-risk" four-year-olds by 1995
2. raising the basic-skills achievement of all students to at least their grade level, and reducing the gap between the test scores of minority and white children by 1993
3. improving the high school graduation rate every year and reducing the number of illiterate Americans
4. improving the performance of American students in mathematics, science, and foreign languages until it exceeds that of students from "other industrialized nations"
5. increasing college participation, particularly by minorities, and specifically by reducing the current "imbalance" between grants and loans
6. recruiting more new teachers, particularly minority teachers, to ease "the impending teacher shortage," and taking other steps to upgrade the status of the profession. (Vinovskis, 1999, p. 37)

The America 2000 initiative scored few legislative victories. However, the Charlottesville Summit was successful in further nationalizing the issue of standards-based education reform, and the Bush administration was able to successfully launch federally funded programs to assist states in developing national standards (DeBray 2006, pp. 27–28). States across the union began reform efforts to raise academic standards, develop assessments, and experiment with new teacher evaluation methods. The push for standards-based education reform and test-based accountability was on, and the administration of President Bill Clinton took up the cause with zeal in 1992.

As the embodiment of "third way" education policy enactment and the rightward shift of the Democratic Party, President Clinton scored a legislative victory in 1994 with the passage of his Goals 2000 legislation and major revisions to the Elementary and Secondary Education Act (ESEA), which had been a bedrock of Lyndon Johnson's Great Society initiatives. Goals 2000 sought to use federal funding (specifically Title I) to push states toward developing higher academic standards, rigorous assessments, and accountability policies for schools and teachers.

Unfortunately for Clinton, resistance from Congress was successful in loosening the requirements of Goals 2000, and the entire project appeared to be threatened by the dramatic Republican takeover of both the House and Senate in the 1994 midterm elections. Led by firebrand Newt Gingrich, Congressional Republicans pushed for, among many other legislative goals, the abolition of the Department of Education and the rollback of the standards-based reforms implemented by Clinton.

However, after two years of legislative clashes with the White House and the defeat of Bob Dole in the 1996 presidential election, polling data showed that education was an important issue for strategic voting groups, such as suburban women. This, in turn, led to a strategic shift in American politics. Congressional Republicans "accommodated themselves to the continued existence of federal education programs but set out to reform them in line with conservative principles" (DeBray-Pelot & McGuinn, 2009, p. 24) that focused on school choice initiatives and test-based accountability.

This shift opened up a space in American politics for the emergence of a new, and somewhat unlikely, coalition of interest groups to push for standards-based and business-friendly education reform and for using federal Title I funding as leverage to initiate reform and "innovation," the new buzzword of the education reform movement at the state level. Despite the increasing rancor in Washington, D.C., the two parties had found one arena in which compromise had become possible. Federal education reform increasingly became a bipartisan initiative that defined a "third way" previously uncharted.

By the turn of the century, the political landscape of education policy had been fundamentally transformed. As DeBray-Pelot & McGuinn (2009) note, the new bipartisan consensus over education policy was possible due to an unlikely convergence of political interests. The business lobby had played an important role in publicizing *A Nation at Risk* and contributed to standards-based reform initiatives at the state level during the Reagan and G. W. H. Bush administrations.

However, by the late 1990s, the Business Roundtable of the U.S. Chamber of Commerce had lost faith in the efficacy of state-level reforms and began to advocate for federal intervention to push for tougher standards, market-based education solutions, and a greater focus on "twenty-first-century job skills" in Science, Technology, Engineering and Mathematics (STEM). At the same time, civil rights leaders were growing increasingly frustrated by the lack of progress in resolving long-standing educational achievement issues in urban school districts.

Liberals in Congress worried that the lack of movement on addressing these issues might strengthen arguments for voucher programs (long popular in the conservative movement), and the growing interest in a new urban school model that promised local control and latitude for pedagogical innovation, the charter school concept, created a new space for political compromise among progressive, civil rights, and business elites. The stronger appetite for reform among the liberal wing of the Democratic Party led by Ted Kennedy strengthened the position of the more "centrist" Third Way wing to push for stronger enforcement of Goals 2000 and the revisions to ESEA that called for more testing accountability. The stage was set for dramatic change in 2000.

Touting his success as governor of Texas, George W. Bush came to Washington with education reform at the top of his agenda. The signature legislation of the Bush administration, the No Child Left Behind Act of 2001 (NCLB), was a political compromise that built on an ideological shift in Washington politics toward using Title I funding to pressure states into creating internationally "competitive" standards and accountability policies for teachers and schools.

Specifically, NCLB mandated the development of "challenging state standards," "annual testing of all students in grades 3–8," and for states to develop "annual statewide progress objectives ensuring that all [racial and ethnic] groups of students reach proficiency within 12 years" (p. 1). Schools and school districts identified as not making Adequate Yearly Progress (AYP) became subject to an increasing array of penalties for each successive year of "failure."

These "corrective actions" are the following: 1) restructuring (where entire school staffs are replaced), 2) state or mayoral takeover (where entire school districts are put under state or mayoral control), and 3) school closures (where traditional public schools are closed and students are shifted into charter schools or rezoned to another traditional public school). The Bush administration was able to forge this political compromise by bringing on board the more libertarian-leaning and religious wings of the Republican Party by pushing for expanding school choice in the forms of charter schools and voucher programs for students in schools identified as failing.

At the same time, the liberals of the Democratic coalition were able to continue their push for raising standards for all and addressing funding inequities, both important issues in the civil rights community. The symbolism of a conservative president and former governor of Texas working with the so-called liberal lion of the Senate, Ted Kennedy, to usher through one of the most sweeping pieces of federal education policy since the 1960s is a powerful testament to the convergence of interests among competing groups in American politics, and the repercussions of NCLB would define the education politics of the 2000s.

The wave of reform and changes in public education set off by NCLB was unprecedented in the history of American schooling. Heated debates broke out in state houses and school board meetings across the nation as urban schools tried desperately to stay ahead of steadily escalating annual testing targets. School leadership and teachers became increasingly focused on test scores as a means of survival, and nontested subjects and social missions long associated with public schools were largely sacrificed to the NCLB demands for Adequate Yearly Progress. Waves of school closures in "failing" school districts were accompanied by the exponential growth of both nonprofit and for-profit charter schools, and politicians of all stripes voiced strong commitments for the disruptive innovation introduced by the charter school sector.

While the post-NCLB era has been a time of dramatic change for teachers and families in urban communities, it has proven to be profitable for the new education industry that has emerged and grown up around it. International publishing companies such as Pearson, CTB/McGraw-Hill, Riverside, and Harcourt have carved out important lucrative niches in the education market, producing standardized assessments, scripted curricula, professional development materials, and test scoring services.

The growth of charter schools in urban school districts has produced an ever-expanding constellation of charter school networks and standalones that have, in turn, fed into a growing sector of property management, real estate, and supplementary education service, or tutoring, companies. Not surprisingly, the exponential growth taking place in the education market and the increasing demand for data collection, analysis, storage, and sharing have drawn the attention of technology companies and investors on Wall Street.

As Jonathan Kozol (2007) noted, the Wall Street investing class has come to see the K–12 market as being the "Big Enchilada" for extracting profit from public tax dollars, while hardware, software, and technology infrastructure companies see huge potential for growth in online testing, virtual learning, and new forms of content delivery that are advertised to increase learning while lowering costs. However, these dramatic changes have also contributed to a growing chorus of criticism that NCLB was just another unfunded or underfunded federal mandate that produced a good deal of change in the structural makeup and steerage of public schooling without producing substantive gains in academic achievement or reducing achievement gaps among different student groups.

NCLB's fanciful expectations of 100 percent proficiency for all students by 2014, regardless of the circumstances, and the increasingly hostile rhetoric aimed at public schools, teachers, and local school boards (an institution that commentator Jonathan Alter [2010] pejoratively labeled "The Blob") has led many public school advocates and education researchers to see NCLB as a mechanism to produce the failure it was supposedly designed to address—a Trojan horse to create the perception of educational crisis and, thereby, accelerate reform.

In the run-up to the 2008 presidential election, then-candidate Barack Obama frequently characterized NCLB as being "flawed," leading many public school advocates to project onto him their hopes that his presidency would reverse the tide of education reform sweeping the nation. After all, education scholar and Stanford University researcher Linda Darling-Hammond had advised Obama on the campaign trail and served in his transition team. These hopes were dashed, however, when Darling-Hammond was swept aside, and President Obama named as his Secretary of Education Chicago Public Schools chief Arne Duncan, a champion of high-stakes testing accountability, school closures, alternative certification programs, test performance pay, and charter schools.

Duncan was given a chance to make his mark on American public schools early on in his tenure, when the American Recovery and Investment Act of 2009 set aside $4.3 billion in discretionary funding for school improvement. The money was used to fund the Obama administration's Race to the Top initiative that built on and expanded the mandates of the supposedly "flawed" NCLB. States suffering from budget crises brought on by the Great Recession of 2008 were incentivized to compete for badly needed funding from the federal government.

In order to be eligible, states had to sign on to the development and implementation of a set of national standards; the development of high-stakes assessments attached to those standards; the introduction of accountability policies that would tie teacher evaluations to student test scores on those assessments; improved data collection and storage systems; and to the lifting of caps on the number of charter schools. More than anything else, the indistinguishable overlay of Barack Obama's education policies with those of his Republican predecessor testifies to the dramatic transformation in education policy since the Reagan administration and the publication of *A Nation at Risk*.

The new politics of education is defined by bipartisan consensus and seemingly paradoxical relationships, and the nationwide tour to promote charter schools featuring Reverend Al Sharpton, former Speaker of the House Newt Gingrich, and New York's mayor Mike Bloomberg provide a good example (Johnson, 2009). While the two parties go to great rhetorical lengths to distinguish themselves on education, the reality of public school policy is one in which the two parties draw from the same lexicon of business language to justify virtually identical education policies built on standards, assessment, accountability, and choice. This convergence is made possible in the post-NCLB era by prominent advocacy and funding from an increasingly assertive business community, along with the growing number of venture philanthropies and corporate foundations.

ADVOCACY RESEARCH AND PHILANTHROPIC ENTREPRENEURSHIP

In order to understand shifts in the educational politics over the past forty years, it is important to consider the broader transformations taking place in American society. The crises of the 1970s marked the closing of the post–World War II era of industrial capitalism and broadly shared wealth and the opening of a new era of economic globalization, deindustrialization, and the reemergence of an increasingly speculative financial sector that has produced levels of economic polarization not seen since the stock market crash of 1929.

As more and more of the productivity gains have accumulated at the top of the economic pyramid, the United States has witnessed the rise of a newly assertive business community that has sought to shape political policy and debate through an ever-expanding sector of think tanks, policy institutes, and philanthropic organizations. Today, the driving force behind the national conversation over public schooling and education reform is a new elite that is using its economic and political muscle to achieve political goals that will open up new revenue streams for American business in the name of addressing educational inequality and preparing workers for the new global economy.

The history of the think tank in the United States goes back to the Progressive era and its faith in the use of newly emerging social sciences to manage societal issues through policy. The idea behind the think tank was to be a bridge between the academy and government that produced relevant scholarship tailored to the particular needs of policymakers. Funded by large endowments from the philanthropic organizations of industrialists and populated by PhDs, these new institutions, such as the Bureau of Municipal Research, carved out an important niche in the American political system.

Their ability to gain access to policymakers and continued sources of funding hinged on the credibility and neutrality of the research they produced (Rich, 2005, pp. 34–40). To be sure, the relationship between think tanks and the power elite in Washington, D.C., was always troubled, the strong ties between the American military and the RAND Corporation being a good example. However, in comparison to the politically polarized think tank sector of the early twenty-first century, the think tank model of the first half of the twentieth century is now widely regarded as somewhat of a golden age in which the research was measured and ideologically tempered.

It was in the 1970s that conservative activists in politics and business began what they understood to be a War of Ideas against the perceived liberal and leftist ideologies dominating academia, media, and popular culture. Drawing upon the ideas of luminaries such as Friedrich Hayek and Walter Lippmann, a new cadre of conservative public intellectuals set out to reverse the tide of populism and legislation that defined the civil rights, antiwar, and environmental movements of the 1960s.

These efforts resulted in new institutions to promote what these "thought leaders" saw as the spirit of free market capitalism. Feeling threatened by "collectivist" ideologies and the growing regulatory framework of the post–New Deal era, they were joined by the business community and the economic elite, who were interested in building a countermovement to the sweeping social changes of the 1960s.

Gabbard and Atkinson (2007) point toward a memo written in 1971 for the U.S. Chamber of Commerce by future Supreme Court justice and former tobacco industry lawyer Louis F. Powell Jr. as marking the starting point of this countermovement. Decrying an all-out attack on the free enterprise system from the media, universities, religious institutions, and intellectual journals, the memo calls for the U.S. Chamber of Commerce to become more politically active.

Powell urged individual companies to set up well-funded public relations divisions to counter attacks on free enterprise and for individual companies to take united action in funding new research and policy institutions to "monitor schools and universities, the media, the courts, and politics for anti-business ideas, and aggressively target them for the distribution of pro-business/neoliberal ideas" (p. 99). Powell called on the business community to create its own institutions of knowledge production, policy development, and media outreach to champion free market ideology in order to play a significant role in public debate and policy development. In retrospect, it is clear that Powell's advice was taken to heart by a broad swath of the economic elite.

The period from the early 1970s until the present has been one of phenomenal growth in the number of think tanks, policy institutes, and advocacy research centers funded by corporate money. Changes to the tax code in 1969 that limited a traditional source of foundation funding for established think tanks, along with the appearance of a newly assertive business community, led to a dramatic transformation in the think tank model of the early twentieth century and to the emergence of a new crop of think tanks and policy institutes characterized by distinct ideological orientations and sophisticated media outreach operations (Rich, 2005).

Powell had placed a good deal of faith in the growing field of public relations as being the key component of the countermovement, and that faith appears to have been well-placed. The significant advances in the field of marketing over the past four decades have informed the development of the modern think tank. The same tools used to market consumer goods are being employed to sell ideas and to shape public debate. Think tanks are, in many ways, well-funded media operations producing advocacy research aligned to the interests of their funders.

The modern think tank carries out a wide range of activities: producing issue-specific research that is marketed to major news organizations; hosting conferences and seminars to disseminate ideas, generate media coverage, and inform policymakers; and publishing books, magazines, web pages, and news blogs to shape public debate. Whether concerned with a broad range of issues or more narrowly focused on one or two policy areas, think tanks rely on individual and corporate funding aimed to shape public debate, gain access to policymakers, and have an impact on policy development.

In the field of education policy, the number of think tanks carrying out research and disseminating policy proposals has grown significantly, and they have been quite successful at shifting the tenor of public debate over schooling toward the neoconservative ideas that emerged from *A Nation at Risk* (Kovacs & Boyles, 2005). Even an incomplete listing that focuses on the major players in the field offers the reader a good idea of how large this sector has become:

American Enterprise Institute
American Legislative Exchange Council
Brookings Institution
Cato Institute
Center for American Progress
Center on Education Policy
Center on Reinventing Public Education
Education Trust
Fordham Institute
Foundation for Excellence in Education
Friedman Foundation for Educational Choice
Heartland Institute
Heritage Foundation
Hoover Institution
Lexington Institute
Mackinac Center for Public Policy
Manhattan Institute for Policy Research
Mathematica Policy Research
National Council on Teacher Quality
New Teacher Project
Progressive Policy Institute
RAND Corporation
StudentsFirst
Third Way

Beyond the big national players, there are many more narrowly focused regional and local think tanks and advocacy groups working in the field. Together, they form an expansive network of knowledge and opinion production, policy development, and political marketing that dominate education policy at the federal and state levels. Think tanks are closely associated with party politics, and their scholars and fellows enjoy extensive access to policymakers.

However, their most significant avenue for promoting the interests of their funders is through their access to media outlets. Think tank fellows maintain a significant presence in popular news media. Cloaked in the patina of academic legitimacy, think tank fellows are presented in popular news media as being unbiased experts in the field of education (Haas, 2007), and they increasingly offer a unified discourse of policy reform, regardless of their self-identified political affiliations (McDonald 2013).

At the beginning of the contemporary education reform movement in the 1980s, many of the policies that have come to dominate the discourse of education reform were ideas closely associated with conservative think tanks that had strong ties to the business community, such as the American Enterprise Institute and the Heritage Foundation. However, with the rise of third-way politics in the 1990s, corporate money began to flow toward both traditional and new think tanks associated with the Democratic Party to advocate for more corporate-friendly policies, the Brookings Institution's Hamilton Project being a good example.

New sources of wealth emerging in the 1990s from a postindustrial economy based on financial innovation from Wall Street and technological innovation in Silicon Valley helped to produce a new elite far less interested in social issues associated with the culture wars than their industrialist predecessors. The willingness of this new corporate elite to fund think tanks and advocacy groups associated with the Democratic Party coincided with the political convergence over education policy between the two parties.

Not surprisingly, the culmination of this political convergence, NCLB, produced an explosion of new education policy organizations and advocacy groups linked in an increasingly complex web of money and social networking that has helped to solidify a new paradigm for education policy based on standards, testing accountability, and choice. During the early years of the twenty-first century, three names came to dominate American education reform: Gates, Walton, and Broad.

The Bill & Melinda Gates Foundation, the Walton Family Foundation, and the Broad Foundation have achieved a dominant presence in political debates over education reform and, as a result, wield a great deal of sway over policy formation at the federal, state, and local levels. They represent a new form of philanthropy that uses funding as investments to leverage fundamental societal change, an important difference that distinguishes this model from the traditional philanthropic model of the Industrial Era.

In its most simple form, it can be understood as a shift from providing funds for the public good, such as arts and cultural projects, to the strategic use of grants and structural supports to bring about "disruptive" change to society that favor corporate constituents. Janelle Scott (2009) notes that, while this new form of philanthropy has certainly generated a lot of attention (not to mention a good deal of criticism), the break between these two institutional models of philanthropy isn't nearly as clear-cut as it would appear.

In many ways, this model was pioneered by conservative institutions in the 1950s and 1960s, such as the Olin and Bradley foundations, which played a pivotal role in funding the development of conservative think tanks like the

American Enterprise Institute and the Manhattan Institute. Nevertheless, it is clear that a new form of philanthropic organization has emerged with a specific interest in education policy and reform. This new model of philanthropy takes its ethos from the venture capitalist model of Silicon Valley and Wall Street, where the majority of the funds that these organizations use originate.

> Like venture capitalists, venture philanthropies expect aggressive returns on their investments. They measure such returns not necessarily by profit generated but by growth in student achievement, expansion of particular educational sectors, such as education [management organizations] or charter schools, and the growth of constituencies who will place political support on public officials to support particular educational reforms. (Scott, 2009, p. 116)

A new crop of billionaires emerging from the tech boom in Silicon Valley and the financial "innovation" of Wall Street have created a new institutional model for philanthropic organizations working in the education field, and this new model is increasingly being adopted by more traditional, well-established foundations.

Several characteristics distinguish venture philanthropies from their more traditional cousins of the first half of the twentieth century. First and foremost, these new players in the politics of education reform have a clear preference for building new private sector institutions to challenge the public sector. Venture philanthropies fund charter school management organizations as well as individual charter schools in order to build a hybrid form of schooling and school management outside of the public sector.

Charter management organizations or CMOs (such as Achievement First, KIPP, and Green Dot) are nonprofit entities that manage multiple charter schools, and education management organizations or EMOs (such as UNO Charter School Network) are for-profit entities that manage a much smaller number of U.S. charter schools. According to the National Alliance for Public Charter Schools, management organizations "provide back office functions for charter schools to take advantage of economies of scale, but some also provide a wider range of services—including hiring, professional development, data analysis, public relations and advocacy" (Warne 2013).

To staff these nonprofit and for-profit charter schools, venture philanthropies also provide substantial funding for alternative teacher licensure programs (such as Teach for America) as well as alternative leadership training programs (such as the Broad Residency and the Broad Academy). Second, venture philanthropies are enamored with the concept of innovation. They demonstrate a clear preference for funding new approaches to schooling and student learning that generate new efficiencies through computer and information technology. "Blended" schools, virtual academies, and computer-based credit recovery and "competency-based" programs receive substantial funding.

Finally, venture philanthropies have worked to establish a new model for educational research that works outside of the traditional peer-review process of academia. Venture philanthropies provide targeted funding to national think tanks (such as the Center for American Progress and Center on Inventing Public Education) and even university-based programs (such as the School Choice Demonstration Project at the University of Arkansas) to conduct educational research and publish reports on the initiatives pursued by the philanthropies. The importance of this practice cannot be overstated.

Working through think tanks, corporate foundations, and policy institutes with clear ideological agendas, venture philanthropies are an important source of funding for the production and marketing of educational research to build the appearance of a consensus among the research community, often where none exists (Lubienski et al., 2009). In order to build national support, these foundations aggressively market to news organizations think tank studies that demonstrate the efficacy of the reform initiatives. Of course, studies that fail to demonstrate the efficacy of those initiatives are not aggressively marketed to media outlets and subsequently disappear down our collective memory hole.

According to the Foundation Center (2014), philanthropic organizations spent a total of $2.4 billion in 2011. The "big three" of the Gates, Walton, and Broad foundations spent $448 million, $159 million, and $42 million, respectively. While this might appear to be a significant amount of funding to drive educational change, it is important to note that total educational spending in the United States is approximately $600 billion annually. This raises the question of how large an impact these philanthropies really have if the amount of funding they are providing constitutes a drop in the bucket of total spending. The answer is that they have significant impacts.

Sara Reckhow (2013) points out that these new venture philanthropies use their funds strategically to drive national change. Venture philanthropies target their funding efforts toward large urban school districts that are geographically representative of the nation as a whole in order to create new institutional and organizational models that can be "scaled-up" nationally. They demonstrate a clear preference for urban districts under mayoral control with a robust network of partnering organizations and environments that are supportive of their reform initiatives.

The top five urban areas targeted by venture philanthropies are New York City, Los Angeles, Oakland, Boston, and Chicago (pp. 35–51). Other notable test sites include New Orleans, Houston, Memphis, and Washington, D.C. By focusing their resources on specific sites, venture philanthropies use these districts as models of reform that can be researched, managed, and marketed to policymakers in order to foster change at the national level. The importance of these new philanthropic organizations isn't necessarily the dollar amounts they spend, although they do spend a substantial amount of money. What makes venture philanthropies important is their ability to leverage their funding to promote national change.

Beyond funding advocacy research in think tanks that principally target policymakers and news media organizations, the venture philanthropists have several ways to promote their initiatives in popular culture so as to build political support for education reform. The "big three" of the Gates, Walton, and Broad foundations figured significantly in the production and promotion of the major motion picture *Waiting for Superman*, a film that was clearly designed to demonize traditional public schools, teachers, and teachers' unions as being self-interested proponents of the status quo who remain resistant to educational reform and equity.

At the same time, charter schools and a new crop of educational leaders (such as Michelle Rhee and Geoffrey Canada) are portrayed as saviors of struggling urban student populations. Promoters of the film were able to obtain prominent feature stories in magazines (including the *New Yorker* and *Time*) national newspapers (*New York Times*), exclusive interviews with the film director Davis Guggenheim on the *Oprah Winfrey Show*, and a nationwide speaking tour to promote the film put on by Bill Gates, who appears in the film as an educational expert (Goldstein, 2010).

Similar strategies were used in the production and promotion of the major motion picture *Won't Back Down*, a fictional story of a working-class mom and burned-out teacher who win the battle to "pull the trigger" on a failing public school and transform it into a privately run charter school. The film was a production of Walden Media, which is owned by Philip Anshutz, a longtime activist known for funding conservative causes such as school choice. The film was distributed by 20th Century Fox, a unit of NewsCorp that also owns the school technology company Amplify, which is headed by former New York City Department of Education chancellor Joel Klein.

In 2013, Amplify won contracts to develop assessment software and learning tools for the federal Common Core Initiative (Cavanaugh, 2013). These media companies partnered with CBS and the Walton family's Wal-Mart to broadcast the television special *Teachers Rock* to promote the release of *Won't Back Down*. Featuring performances by famous music stars, the television special was part of a well-executed media strategy to use the guise of celebrating teachers in order to promote the film and the education reform movement.

Other notable successful marketing strategies funded by venture philanthropies in recent years include MSNBC's (and more recently sponsored by NBC) annual *Education Nation* series and nationwide tour that aggressively markets advocacy research, standards-based education reform, and charter schools. Then there is the Center for Public Broadcasting's ongoing feature

American Graduate: Let's Make It Happen, which put on the PBS special *Ted Talks: Education*, which was heavily funded by the Gates Foundation and featured Bill Gates as an educational expert.

In short, venture philanthropies are one of the driving forces behind the contemporary education reform movement. They pursue disruptive innovation in public education by targeting urban school districts as laboratories for reforms, using their significant funding as leverage to introduce and expand charter schools and virtual schools. Venture philanthropies then market their initiatives in these laboratories of reform by funding and publicizing sponsored advocacy research by think tanks, which are, themselves, sleekly styled marketing machines.

NEOLIBERALISM AND EDUCATION

Hailed by Edward Lazear (2000) as the triumph of economics imperialism, the dominant ideas informing education policy in this modern era of reform come from neoclassical economic theory (Allais, 2012). Both the why and the how of public education are now defined by an economic logic of global competition for human capital, whose worth is weighed by knowledge acquisition. In the words of Barack Obama, it is now "an undeniable fact that countries who out-educate us today are going to out-compete us tomorrow" (Obama, 2011).

In this new global reality, the goal of public schooling is to produce human capital in the form of college-ready graduates well versed in STEM curricula and eager to pursue careers in science, engineering, and computer technology. As these ideas have risen to ascendancy in recent years, a political convergence on education policy emerged that is largely informed by human capital theory and neoclassical economic theory. This convergence involved a coalescence around three broad policy reforms: raise academic standards and create challenging assessments to test student mastery; hold teachers and schools accountable for student scores on these assessments, often by using value-added measures borrowed from econometrics; and introduce market competition into public education in order to produce innovation and to close persistent achievement gaps between student populations.

These three broad policy reforms are seen as being not only the key to producing human capital but also for achieving equitable outcomes. The rhetoric of equity has been adopted by a new breed of venture philanthropists and business leaders whose neoliberal assumptions are shaped by neoclassical economic theory, and whose money played a prominent role in bringing about a political convergence over education policy. Over a period of time when real incomes stagnated in the United States, a new economic elite has set about remaking society in its own perceived interests.

In this New Gilded Age, the corporate philanthropic community has set about constructing an elaborate architecture of think tanks and policy institutes to shift education policy talk and implementation to the political right through advocacy research and marketing. Venture philanthropies have chosen struggling urban school districts as laboratories of education reform; have funded sympathetic think tank research on the reforms being pursued; and have aggressively marketed education reform and sponsored research results across a spectrum of media.

Michael Peters (2011) traces the origins of neoliberalism to a meeting of prominent philosophers, political theorists, and economists organized by the French philosopher Louis Rougier in 1938. *La Colloque Walter Lippmann* was a meeting of intellectuals held to discuss Walter Lippmann's 1937 book *The Good Society*. Lippmann argued for the revitalization of liberalism as a middle ground between laissez-faire capitalism and European socialism.

The term *neoliberalism* was coined at *La Colloque Walter Lippmann* by the future father of the West German state, Alexander Rustow, who sought to differentiate a new form of liberalism marked by a free economy *and* a strong state from the small, laissez-faire state of classical liberalism. Indeed, despite the more libertarian rhetoric often bandied about in discussions on neoliberalism, the combination of a "free" market economy and a strong activist state is a defining characteristic of neoliberalism. The proponents of neoliberalism will frequently argue that their goal is to liberate individuals from the burdensome regulations of an overbearing nanny state, but the liberty they envision is a peculiar one.

The nature of this peculiar form of liberty can be located in the ideas of Frederick Hayek, a prominent thinker who was an attendee at *La Colloque Walter Lippmann* and whose work would come to have a profound influence on the American Right. His *Road to Serfdom* (1944) argued that all forms of "collectivism" posed the risk of a creeping authoritarianism that inevitably sacrificed the natural rights of individuals at the altar of bureaucratic logic. For Hayek, the threat from collectivism was everywhere, from the corporatism of fascism to the communism of the Soviet Union to the Keynesianism of the welfare state. Each represented a threat to the individual.

In opposition to the creeping authoritarianism of collectivism, Hayek held up the spontaneous order of the marketplace as the ideal model for organizing human society so as to maximize individual liberty. For Hayek, markets are information processors, or signaling machines, in which market actors continuously "signal" the price/value of commodities to one another through the buying and selling of goods and services. Left to its own devices, Hayek argued, the marketplace would spontaneously achieve an equilibrium in which intersecting supply-and-demand curves ensure the efficient and rational allocation of resources.

More importantly, individuals would achieve authentic liberty through the pursuit of their own self-interested goals in a competitive marketplace. Hayek's ideal was a spontaneous order of rationality achieved through the (mostly) rational activity of self-interested individuals, a market democracy in which the state was largely absent. Nevertheless, there was a role for the state in Hayek's work (Hoppe, 1994). According to Hayek, the role of the state was to provide the legal and judicial infrastructure to ensure the smooth functioning of markets and to provide the services that, for whatever reason, cannot be taken care of by the market.

At the time, the attendees of *La Colloque Walter Lippmann* appeared to be fighting an uphill battle. It was an era in which Karl Polanyi's "Great Transformation" was very much in ascendancy and the formation of the post–World War II welfare state was well underway. However, what ultimately emerged from the colloquium was a political ideology that would later influence a new crop of neoconservative thinkers and business leaders in the United States and beyond. In the era of post-Fordism and the erosion of the welfare state, the ideology of neoliberalism has risen to dominate the two-party system of American politics, the world of economics and finance, and the world of high technology and social entrepreneurship.

Neoliberalism can be understood as an ideology that adheres to a logic that divides social reality into two mutually exclusive spheres: the public sphere vs. private sphere. This public-private distinction separates out the functions of the state from the private individual and the state from the marketplace, the sphere of self-interested individuals. Neoliberalism asserts the primacy of the private individual over the state. Through the pursuit of their own self-interests, individuals achieve authentic liberty in the marketplace, and the outcome of this, shall we say, collective activity is a spontaneous order that ensures efficient, rational outcomes. This rationalizing function of markets is the foundation for neoliberal social policy.

In order to rationalize society and maximize individual liberty, neoliberalism advocates that the state should decentralize the majority of the services it provides to the private sphere, where possible, and to introduce quasi-market processes into the institutions of the state where privatization, for whatever reason, is not possible:

> Under neo-liberalism, the role of the government shifts from regulating markets to enabling them, and replacing public services with private enterprise, in the process, weakening the nation-state and public political participation. The state becomes a handmaiden to the creation and defense of markets and the monetary system on which they are based. (Sleeter, 2008, p. 1947)

Neoliberalism assumes that opening state institutions to market competition will bring about the spontaneous rationality of the marketplace, all the while maximizing individual liberty. However, these newly decentralized and quasi-marketplaces look dramatically different from the popular notions of the marketplace still colored by the legacy of classical liberalism.

> The private sphere to which neo-liberalism seeks to shift the responsibilities of the state apparatus is one that is actively created by the state. Neo-liberalism tasks the state with creating the markets that will deliver social services by determining which organizations are allowed to compete in newly constituted marketplaces and by establishing the roles and responsibilities of individual economic/political actors, both as an individual consumer-citizen and corporation, in those markets. Behind the populist rhetoric of ensuring individual freedom from the heavy hand of governance, there is a perhaps smaller but intrusive government envisioned by neo-liberalism that differentiates it from its classical predecessor. (Ellison, 2012a, p. 131)

In contrast to the image of the unrestrained individual pursuing her/his own self-interest, the fetishized markets of neoliberalism are circumscribed places of observation, measurement, and accountability. The privatization of state services envisioned by neoliberalism requires that the state create, manage, and participate in politicized markets that situate individuals in circumscribed spaces designed to "rationalize" their behavior. John Clarke (2004) explains:

> Of course, this "privatisation" is not merely a process of transfer to an unchanged private space. The private is re-worked in the process—subject to processes of responsibilisation and regulation; and opened to new forms of surveillance and scrutiny. Both corporate and state processes aim to "liberate" the private—but expect the liberated subjects to behave responsibly [as consumers, as parents, as citizen-consumers]. (p. 33)

The goal of neoliberalism isn't to free the individual to participate in market exchange as a consumer; the goal is to produce consumers of state services whose behavior is structured by the rules of market exchange.

Clarke (2004) notes that neoliberalism is not so much a description of social reality as much as it is a political strategy: "Put crudely, neo-liberalism tells stories about the world, the future and how they will develop—and tries to make them come true" (p. 30). Neoliberalism can be accurately considered an ideology or a discourse. Both conceptualizations provide rich avenues for further inquiry. However, from the time of *La Colloque Walter Lippmann* to the present, it is important to remember this: neoliberalism is and always has been a visionary political project to restructure society in the imagined image of an unfettered marketplace for others to emulate, even if the visionaries' own success in the marketplaces look dramatically different from those of their imagined model.

The neoliberals' task is to remake the world in their own imagined image. However, it would not be entirely accurate to characterize neoliberalism as the ideology of the elite. Neoliberalism has proven to be a seductive ideology that speaks to the daily experiences of the managerial class where competition, monitoring, surveillance, quantifiable outcomes, and accountability measurements are common practices. Neoliberalism speaks to technocratic assumptions as to how to organize institutions, and the oft-repeated political bromide that we should "run government like a business" resonates with many who view reality through the corporate lens.

At its core, neoliberalism is a political project that works to subsume human societies beneath a distinctly corporate logic that entails setting measurable performance goals for individuals, evaluating individual performance using statistical analyses, and instituting carrot-and-stick incentive structures to "rationalize" human behavior. It is a project that focuses on individual performance within circumscribed spaces. Neoliberalism is not a social-psychological theory that explains individual human behavior; neoliberalism is a political project to produce "rational" human beings who adhere to the "laws" of an imaginary marketplace.

CONCLUSION

This chapter has traced the political and ideological development of the modern education reform movement. In many ways, the charter school model represents the actualization of the dominant ideological and strategic structures at work in the realization of the neoliberal values applied to federal and state politics; it is, perhaps, the paradigmatic institution of neoliberal education reform. The KIPP Model, specifically, provides an excellent example of Foucault's idea of productive power that works not to control or restrict but to produce students/teachers with the specific aptitudes or habitus for the imagined marketplace of a neoliberal social order.

This new order is defined by hierarchy and domination and informed by the uniquely neoliberal science of positive psychology (Ellison, 2012b). When considering how KIPP fits into the framework presented in this chapter, the No Excuses charter school model should not be considered as an isolated unit of analysis to be abstracted from the larger social reality presented here. Rather, it should be understood as the most tangible example of a "singularity born out of multiple determining elements of which it is not the product, but rather the effect" (Foucault & Lotringer, 2007, p. 64).

In closely examining the grueling experiences of former KIPP teachers and the brutalizing experiences of students that these teachers recall, it will be helpful to keep in mind that both teachers and students in these total-compliance schools are subject to an institutionalized exercise of power aimed to coercively salvage the maximum amount of human capital from human beings that are, otherwise, disposable:

> The human body was entering a machinery of power that explores it, breaks it down and rearranges it. A "political anatomy," which was also a "mechanics of power," was being born; it defined how one may have a hold over others' bodies, not only so that they may do what one wishes, but also so that they may operate as one wishes, with the techniques, the speed and the efficiency that one determines. Thus discipline produces subjected and practised bodies, "docile" bodies. Discipline increases the forces of the body (in economic terms of utility) and diminishes these same forces (in political terms of obedience). In short, it dissociates power from the body; on the one hand, it reverses the course of the energy, the power that might result from it, and turns it into a relation of strict subjection. If economic exploitation separates the force and the product of labour, let us say that disciplinary coercion establishes in the body the constricting link between an increased aptitude and an increased domination. (Foucault, 1977, p. 138)

REFERENCES

Allais, S. (2012). "Economics imperialism," education policy and educational theory. *Journal of Education Policy* 27 (2), 253–74.

Alter, J. (2010, September 20). Obama's class project. *Newsweek* 156 (12), 58.

Becker, G. (1993). *Human capital: A theoretical and empirical analysis, with special reference to education* (3rd ed.). Chicago: University of Chicago Press.

Bell, T. (1993). Reflections one decade after "A Nation at Risk." *The Phi Delta Kappan* 72 (8), 592–97.

Bell, T. (1988). *The thirteenth man: A Reagan cabinet memoir*. New York: Free Press.

Bennett, W. (1998). A nation still at risk. *Policy Review* 90, 23–29.

Berliner, D., & Biddle, B. (1995). *The manufactured crisis: Myths, fraud, and the attack on America's public schools*. Reading, MA: Addison-Wesley.

Bracey, G. (2003). April foolishness: The 20th anniversary of "A Nation at Risk." *Phi Delta Kappan* 84 (8), 616–21.

Brookfield, S. (2004). *The power of critical theory: Liberating adult learning and teaching.* San Francisco: Jossey-Bass.

Cavanaugh, S. (2013). Amplify Insight wins contract from common-core testing consortium. http://blogs.edweek.org/edweek/marketplacek12/2013/03/amplify_insight_wins_contract_from_common_core_testing_consortium.html?cmp=ENL-EU-NEWS2.

Clarke, J. (2004). Dissolving the public realm? The logics and limits of neo-liberalism. *Journal of Social Policy* 33 (1), 27–48.

DeBray-Pelot, E., & McGuinn, P. (2009). The new politics of education: Analyzing the federal education policy landscape in the post-NCLB era. *Educational Policy* 23 (1), 15–42.

DeBray-Pelot, E. (2006). *Politics, ideology, & education: Federal policy during the Clinton and Bush administrations*. New York: Teachers College Press.

Dewey, J. (1944). *Democracy and education*. Champaign, IL: Project Gutenberg.

Ellison, S. (2012a). From within the belly of the beast: Rethinking the concept of the "educational marketplace" in the popular discourse of education reform. *Educational Studies* 48 (2), 119–36.

Ellison, S. (2012b). It's in the name: A synthetic inquiry of the Knowledge Is Power Program [KIPP]. *Educational Studies* 48 (6), 550–75.

Foucault, M., & Lotringer, S. (2007). What is critique? In *The politics of truth*, 41–82. Los Angeles, CA: Semiotext(e).

Foucault, M. (1977). *Discipline and punish: The birth of the prison.* New York: Random House.

Foundation Center. (2014). Aggregate fiscal data for top 50 FC 1000 foundations awarding grants for education, 2011. http://data.foundationcenter.org/ -/fc1000/subject:education/all/ top:foundations/list/2011 .

Foundation Center. (2008). Top 25 foundations awarding US focused grants for education. http://foundationcenter.org/focus/gdf/F_Educ_Dom_2007.pdf.

Gabbard, D., & Atkinson, T. (2007). Stossel in America: A case study of the neoliberal/ neoconservative assault on public schools and teachers. *Teacher Education Quarterly* 34 (2), 85–109.

Gilead, T. (2009). Human capital, education and the promotion of social cooperation: A philosophical critique. *Studies in Philosophy and Education* 28 (6), 555–67.

Goldstein, D. (2010, September 1). Grading "Waiting for Superman." *The Nation.* http://www.thenation.com/article/154986/grading-waiting-superman.

Haas, E. (2007). False equivalency: Think tank references on education in the news media. *Peabody Journal of Education* 82 (1), 63–102.

Hanushek, E., & Kimko, D. (2000). Schooling, labor-force quality, and the growth of nations. *American Economic Review* 9 (5), 1184–1208.

Hayek, F. (1944). *The road to serfdom.* Chicago, IL: University of Chicago Press.

Holton, G. (1984). A nation at risk revisited. *Daedalus* 113 (4), 1–27.

Hoppe, H. (1994). F. A. Hayek on government and social evolution: A critique. *Review of Austrian Economics* 7 (1), 67–93.

Hunt, S., & Staton, A. (1996). The communication of educational reform. *Communication Education* 45 (4), 271–92.

Johnson, J. (2009, January 1). Gingrich, Sharpton, Duncan launch education tour in Philadelphia. http://www.ed.gov/blog/2009/10/al-sharpton-newt-gingrich-and-secretary-duncan-begin-education-tour-to-expose-challenges-and-highlight-reforms-in-philadelphia/.

Kovacs, P., & Boyles, D. (2005). Institutes, foundations and think tanks: Neoconservative influences on U.S. public schools. *Public Resistance* 1 (1), 1–18.

Kozol, J. (2007). The big enchilada. *Harpers Magazine.* http://harpers.org/archive/2007/08/the-big-enchilada/.

Lazear, E. (2000). Economic imperialism. *Quarterly Journal of Economics* 115 (1), 99–146.

Lubienski, C., Weitzel, P., & Lubienski, S. (2009). Is there a "consensus" on school choice and achievement?: Advocacy research and the emerging political economy of knowledge production. *Educational Policy* 23 (1), 161–93.

Madison, J. (1900/1822). *The writings of James Madison.* Edited by Gaillard Hunt. New York: G. P. Putnam's Sons.

Mathematica Policy Research. (2012). Charter-school management organizations: Diverse strategies and diverse student impacts. http://www.mathematica-mpr.com/publications/ PDFs/Education/CMO_Final_updated.pdf.

McDonald, L. (2013). Think tanks and the media: How the conservative movement gained entry into the education policy arena. *Educational Policy* 28 (6), 845–80.

McGuinn, P. (2006). Swing issues and policy regimes: Federal education policy and the politics of policy change. *Journal of Policy History* 18 (2), 205–40.

Mehta, J. (2013). How paradigms create politics: The transformation of American educational policy, 1980–2001. *American Educational Research Journal* 50 (2), 285–324.

National Center on Education and the Economy. (2007). *Tough choices or tough times: The report of the New Commission on the Skills of the American Workforce.* San Francisco: Jossey-Bass.

National Commission on Excellence in Education. (1983, April). *A nation at risk: The imperative for educational reform.* Washington, DC: U.S. Federal Department of Education.

Obama, B. (2011, January 1). Remarks by the president on No Child Left Behind flexibility. http://www.whitehouse.gov/the-press-office/2012/02/09/remarks-president-no-child-left-behind-flexibility.

Peters, M. (2011). *Neoliberalism and after?: Education, social policy, and the crisis of Western capitalism.* New York: Peter Lang.

Reckhow, S. (2013). *Follow the money: How foundation dollars change public school politics.* New York: Oxford University Press.

Rich, A. (2004). *Think Tanks, public policy, and the politics of expertise.* Cambridge, UK: Cambridge University Press.

Scott, J. (2009). The politics of venture philanthropy in charter school policy and advocacy. *Educational Policy* 23 (1), 106–36.

Scott, J., Lubienski, C., & DeBray-Pelot, E. (2009). The politics of advocacy in education. *Educational Policy* 23 (1), 3–14.

Sleeter, C. (2008). Equity, democracy, and neoliberal assaults on teacher education. *Teaching and Teacher Education* 24 (8), 1947–57.

Tomlinson, T. (1987). A nation at risk: Towards excellence for all. *Annals of the New York Academy of Sciences* 517 (1), 7–27.

Warne, L. (2013, July 18). Business behind charter schools. http://educationblog.ncpa.org/business-behind-charter-schools/.

Chapter Four

Whence No Excuses?

What avail is it to win prescribed amounts of information about geography and history, to win ability to read and write, if in the process the individual loses his own soul: loses his appreciation of things worth while, of the values to which these things are relative.
—John Dewey (1938/2007)

In a 1993 commentary that attacked Jonathan Kozol and Gerald Bracey for questioning the veracity of the dramatic warnings of *A Nation at Risk* ten years after its publication, conservative education policymaker Denis Doyle (1993) was one of the first policymakers to use the term *No Excuses*, in an educational context:

If they [public schools] begin to benchmark seriously, they will compare themselves to the best of the best, not just in public elementary and secondary schools, but also in high-performance organizations. The power of benchmarking is that it does internally what competition is supposed to do externally: it holds organizations to high standards of performance, measurement, and reporting. It accepts no excuses. It is continuous. There is no finish line. (p. 631)

The term *No Excuses*, was used two years later by policymaker Anne Lewis (1995), who admonished folks like Denis Doyle for a narrow focus on accountability outcomes at the expense of adequate resource allocation. Lewis offered a reminder to budget cutters and efficiency seekers that there was no escape from the ultimate responsibility to educate all children, without excuse or failure. Specifically, Lewis took to task the newly empowered conservative budget hawks in Washington for their efforts to slash federal funding for welfare and education programs. She warned in pointed terms that as "the culpable may get off the hook temporarily, the responsibility of education to prepare young people for the legitimate economy cannot be

93

passed off. No matter what panaceas are offered by the budget cutters, the bottom line for kids is the classroom. And the work they do there must be demanding, with no failures and no excuses" (p. 660).

Over the next five years, however, the conservative targets of Lewis's castigation successfully turned the phrase *No Excuses* back to Doyle's original intent, so that it came to represent a cudgel used against those victimized by the kinds of budget cutting that Lewis had railed against. By 2000, neoliberals and neoconservatives had launched a "No Excuses Campaign" (Carter, 2000) sponsored by the Heritage and Bradley Foundations, which placed the blame for low academic achievement on schools, educators, and children.

The No Excuses Campaign was launched with the publication of Samuel Carter's *No Excuses: Lessons from 21 High-Performing, High-Poverty Schools*, which includes the following declaration of intent before readers get to the table of contents page:

> The No Excuses campaign is a national effort organized by The Heritage Foundation to mobilize public pressure on behalf of better education for the poor. The No Excuses campaign brings together liberals, centrists, and conservatives who are committed to high academic achievement among children of all races, ethnic groups, and family incomes.
>
> Participants in the No Excuses campaign may hold differing views about vouchers, the federal role in education, and other policy issues. But we agree that there is no excuse for the academic failure of most public schools serving poor children. All children can learn. Hundreds of public, private, and religious schools serving low-income children have proved it. Help us to shine a spotlight on their success and join us in demanding that failing schools meet their standard. (p. iv)

In 2003, the No Excuses campaign got a turbo boost with the publication by Simon and Schuster of *No Excuses: Closing the Racial Gap in Learning*, authored by policy elites Abigail and Stephan Thernstrom (2003). Although Stephan Thernstrom's previous academic research at Harvard had documented the immovable roadblocks for the working classes in America to achieve upward social mobility during prior centuries, the Thernstroms presented a case in their *No Excuses* to the contrary. They claimed that "the breakdown of racial barriers in America had opened up limitless horizons for African Americans in the 21st Century to achieve what the white working classes had been unable to do previously" (p. 112).

And while the Thernstrom's *No Excuses* shared Carter's belief that educators' laziness, indifference, and low expectations played significantly in maintaining low academic achievement among African Americans, the Thernstroms placed the majority of blame for their plight on "cultural patterns" of African Americans, themselves. The Thernstroms claimed that

"African-American children appear quicker to take offense and more prone to conflict" (p. 137).

The Thernstroms (2003) argued that academic achievement and success in life depend upon deliverance from the bad habits and traits derived from flawed cultural patterns among non-Asian minorities, for which society has too long offered excuses. The Thernstroms announced that these excuses, which range from racial inequality to socioeconomic disadvantage, would not be acceptable any longer to the tough-love advocates of the No Excuses campaign. The solemn and difficult crusade to educate black urban children, specifically, is laid out plainly by the Thernstroms:

> The process of connecting black students to the world of academic achievement isn't easy in the best of educational settings—and such settings are today few and far between. But that only means that in order to "counter and transform" African-American "cultural patterns," . . . fundamental change in American education will be necessary—change much more radical than that contemplated by the most visionary of today's public school officials. Recognizing the problem is the first step down that long and difficult road. (p. 147)

Cultural characteristics, according to the new No Excuses creed, are racial characteristics, and they can be separated out from economic or class characteristics that shape behaviors. The Thernstroms (2003) argued that race is defined by culture, which, by some unexplained formula, exerts twice the influence on academic achievement than do family income, accumulated wealth, and skin color. The Thernstroms announced that two-thirds of the achievement gap between black and white children is attributable to culture, whereas one-third may be determined by poverty, parental education, and the environment (p. 147).

Richard Rothstein (2004) has challenged the No Excuses argument by pointing out that social class, rather than flawed culture, functions as the primary contributor to school achievement differences. According to Rothstein, family income, accumulated wealth, skin color, and culture define social class. In his critique of the Thernstroms' framing of the achievement discussion by separating out influences into percentages, Rothstein claimed "the debate about whether the low achievement of black students is rooted in culture or economics is largely fruitless because socioeconomic status and culture cannot be separated" (p. 51).

Rothstein argued that the neat separation of influences that the Thernstroms (2003) devised, with culture constituting the weightier chunk on the achievement scale, missed the larger point that cultures cannot escape the systemic influence of poverty or economic privilege in the formation and activity of culture. Aside from the dubious moral stance of altering other cultures to suit the values of those who are providing the cultural improvement plans, any attempt, Rothstein claimed, to alter cultural values without taking into account family income, wealth/poverty, and ethnicity will always remain blind to the essential elements of culture.

The interventions that the Thernstroms label "cultural" may yield results if enough control, force, and leverage are exerted at the most vulnerable points. This requires the imposition of unwavering demands, unalterable routines, and the use of punitive pedagogies aimed at altering, over time, children's neurological pathways and, thus, their culture and character.

SKEPTICS OF NO EXCUSES LABELED AS BIGOTS WITH LOW EXPECTATIONS

The Thernstroms' book came at a time when skepticism and resistance to the No Excuses ideology triggered harsh rhetoric from the highest levels of government. George W. Bush (2000) declared his candidacy for president on June 12, 1999, and in his announcement, he reminded the Cedar Rapids, Iowa, audience of his belief that disorder in school, drug abuse, and out-of-wedlock children represented an ominous cultural drift that required society to redraw moral lines of engagement for combatting cultural mutations:

> Some people think it's inappropriate to draw a moral line. Not me. For our children to have the lives we want for them, they must learn to say yes to responsibility, yes to family, yes to honesty and work. I have seen our culture change once in my lifetime, so I know it can change again.
>
> We can write laws to give schools and principals more authority to discipline children and protect the peace of classrooms. We must encourage states to reform their juvenile justice laws. We must say to our children, "We love you, but discipline and love go hand in hand, and there will be bad consequences for bad behavior."

In September 1999, Bush spoke to the Latin Business Association in Texas and offered this preview of the direction that his presidency would take, when elected. It was the first of many opportunities for labeling any belief regarding socioeconomic status and achievement as an excuse that bordered on racism, or at least the "bigotry of low expectations":

> In coming weeks, I plan to talk about safety in our schools, the character of our children, education standards we should set and the accountability we should expect. But I want to start where educational failure has had its highest price. I want to begin with disadvantaged children in struggling schools, and the Federal role in helping them. . . . No child in America should be segregated by low expectations, imprisoned by illiteracy, abandoned to frustration and darkness of self-doubt. . . . Now some say it is unfair to hold disadvantaged children to rigorous standards. I say it is discrimination to require anything less—the soft bigotry of low expectations. (*New York Times*, 1999, para. 2–4)

Bush's first "bigotry of low expectations" speech and his subsequent policies represented a clear shift in education policy talk and implementation. Despite the escalating reseparation of whites and minority children in schools, a trend that had begun afresh in 1988 (Orfield & Yun, 1999; Orfield, 2001), Bush signaled that segregation or resegregation had, in effect, become a literacy issue.

According to the Bush administration, adults with low expectation who make excuses for children and their parents were responsible for children "imprisoned by illiteracy," rather than segregation. Under Bush and No Child Left Behind, the crusade for ending segregation of children based on race or class as a condition for achieving equal educational opportunity would take a backseat to the goal of equalizing test expectations.

As a result, calling attention to segregated schools and economic disadvantage became just another excuse for not closing the literacy gaps among black, brown, and white children in reading and math. Challenging inequality among test scores, then, was advertised and accepted by many as the next civil rights crusade. Unfortunately, it was a goal made impossible to reach by the act of disregarding the importance of socioeconomic influences.

With Bush's election and the quick passage of the No Child Left Behind Act following the national disaster on September 11, 2001, the struggle for educational equality that began with *Brown* in the 1950s fell victim once more to a new generation of testing accountability expectations. As a result, the demand for equality in measurable test results replaced older urgencies aimed at achieving social and racial equality, school desegregation, and equitable resource allocation.

It did not take long for education policy elites to accept the No Excuses mission as the centerpiece for a new educational crusade that would become the purported civil rights issue of a generation. Educational equality for the poor became concretized in a stringent, total-compliance pedagogy that looked very different from the types of schooling enjoyed by middle-class children not labeled as culturally deficient.

No one seemed concerned that the unearned disadvantages of race and culture suddenly required interventions that would appear more penal than educational within the urban pockets of poverty where they came to be applied with strict corporate efficiency. Those committed to this new middle-class version of imposed civil rights found no irony in the fact that the new equality would be achieved through oppressive educational interventions that brought huge financial benefit to corporate reform school operators.

Not only would these new No Excuses schools be untethered from public oversight and protections of children and workers, but new tax structures would incentivize lavish financial support for the creation and spread of intensely segregated and publicly funded charter schools. The new charter schools would be staffed by teachers recruited and trained to believe that increasing test results and altering child behavior and character provided the raisons d'être for their new vocation, temporary though it be.

The No Excuses campaign, then, became a central interlocking element in the emerging educational ideology that included 1) a culture alteration program to instill middle-class "free market" values, 2) testing accountability based on fanciful expectations, 3) paternalistic and authoritarian educational interventions demanding total compliance and unending sacrifice, and 4) market-based educational solutions funded by public monies and venture philanthropists.

The new ideology represented a modern-day Children's Crusade, whereby hard work, delayed gratification, behavioral docility, and soldierly commitment to KIPP Model goals would lead to the human liberation that 150 years of civil rights struggle could not. For policy elites long unwilling to risk political disfavor for suggesting disruptive structural alterations to social arrangements that favored the resegregation of schools, Bush's recasting of segregation as a literacy issue that resulted from low expectations offered an affordable and even lucrative moral uplift.

Additionally, Bush policies provided an opportunity to impose psychological and character remediation to those whose academic and cultural shortcomings would, otherwise, exclude them from economic opportunity. For those embracing the Bush reform agenda and the No Excuses mantra, the imposition of the most stringent behavior-and-character-altering interventions became equated with cultural and character improvement to enhance equal educational opportunity for the poor.

Schools that promised to close the test score gaps between rich and poor without the need for disruptive sociological interventions or economic restructuring came to be viewed as the proper vehicle to carry forward the civil rights struggle. The equalizing of high achievement expectations during the Bush era made possible, at least rhetorically, what hard facts had otherwise disallowed. For in declaring that no children would be left behind, issues of segregation and economic inequality were simply added to the list of unacceptable excuses that could be berated like trouble-making students.

In doing so, civil rights and social justice advocates that could be intimidated were silenced, and any remaining argument against the official Washington delusion of 100 percent proficiency in math and reading was labeled as an expression of bigotry. Closing the test score gaps suddenly became the civil rights issue of another accountability era, even though the continuing blindness to economic inequality and segregation made it as likely to fail as former efforts focused only on what could be changed within the school walls.

The power and appeal of the new ideology for those with the least to lose and the most to gain was made clear by President Barack Obama's continued animated embrace of No Excuses in his keynote speech (Sweet, 2009) at the 100th NAACP Convention in 2009:

We've got to say to our children, yes, if you're African American, the odds of growing up amid crime and gangs are higher. Yes, if you live in a poor neighborhood, you will face challenges that somebody in a wealthy suburb does not have to face. But that's not a reason to get bad grades—(applause)—that's not a reason to cut class—(applause)—that's not a reason to give up on your education and drop out of school. (Applause.) No one has written your destiny for you. Your destiny is in your hands—you cannot forget that. That's what we have to teach all of our children. No excuses. (Applause.) No excuses. (para. 40)

President Obama's new Secretary of Education, Arne Duncan (Change.gov, 2008), formally declared in 2008 the shared conviction that education "is the civil rights issue of our generation." The depth of policy elites' rhetorical linkage of civil rights with No Excuses schooling was most apparent, perhaps, in Duncan's reaction to the Hollywood documentary *Waiting for Superman*, which had been financed by venture philanthropists and fashioned to inspire public support for No Excuses charter schools as the urban education solution (*PR Newswire*, 2010). Following the gala opening of the film in Washington, D.C., Duncan described the film as "a Rosa Parks moment" (Fernandez, 2010). That statement, alone, made it clear that corporate education reform had moved to the front of the bus.

HIGHER EXPECTATIONS AND DOWNWARD MOBILITY

KIPP and the other No Excuses charter schools argue that if teachers and children work hard enough, and if parents are supportive of those efforts, then the KIPP Model can clearly demonstrate that economic disadvantage, race, or geography present no barriers to academic achievement as measured by standardized tests. In 2010, President Obama's Secretary of Education, Arne Duncan, declared that "poverty is not destiny," and if policymakers "get the students the support they need, get them the best principals, get them the great teachers, I promise you those students would do extraordinarily well. I have seen it all my life" (*PBS News Hour*, 2010).

Across the Atlantic in 2012, Britain's education secretary, Michael Gove, shared the same conclusion that "deprivation is [not] destiny," and that with "the right teachers and the right values," the economically deprived can outperform public expectations (GOV.UK, 2012). Even if doing "extraordinarily well" or outperforming public expectations is limited to mean higher performance on standardized tests, that conclusion must come with qualifiers, caveats, or skepticism, as we will show later in this book.

If "to do extraordinarily well" is to mean upward social mobility or economic sustainability, then empirical research shows us that the most rigorous, rigid, or behaviorally "militant" schools offer little help or hope for the disadvantaged and economically segregated to get ahead economically or "do extraordinarily well." In a series of reports by the Brookings Institution and Pew Charitable Trust (Isaacs, 2007a; Isaacs, 2007b; Isaacs & Sawhill, 2008; Pew, 2012; Pew, 2013a, 2013b), the simplistic nature of education policymakers' claims regarding student achievement scores and socioeconomic mobility become ever clearer.

Using four decades of data from black and white families in the Panel Study of Income Dynamics (PSID), Pew and Brookings researchers (Isaacs, 2007b; Isaacs & Sawhill, 2008) found disturbing trends when examining questions related to 1) how children fare economically when compared to their parents, and 2) how race, class, and gender affect mobility. As summed up in the *Washington Post*,

> Nearly half of African Americans born to middle-income parents in the late 1960s plunged into poverty or near-poverty as adults, according to a new study—a perplexing finding that analysts say highlights the fragile nature of middle-class life for many African Americans.
>
> Overall, family incomes have risen for both blacks and whites over the past three decades. But in a society where the privileges of class and income most often perpetuate themselves from generation to generation, black Americans have had more difficulty than whites in transmitting those benefits to their children.
>
> Forty-five percent of black children whose parents were solidly middle class in 1968—a stratum with a median income of $55,600 in inflation-adjusted dollars—grew up to be among the lowest fifth of the nation's earners, with a median family income of $23,100. Only 16 percent of whites experienced similar downward mobility. At the same time, 48 percent of black children whose parents were in an economic bracket with a median family income of $41,700 sank into the lowest income group. (Fletcher, 2007)

In an analysis of research that included the data from the Isaacs (2007b) report above, researchers (Sawhill & Morton, 2007) examined the implications of these findings for the American dream of upward mobility based on the long-held belief in hard work, skill, and knowledge. The researchers found the American Dream remains a viable concept in terms of "absolute mobility," which is measured by how economic growth, or the overall standard of living, changes from one generation to the next.

The current generation, as of 2007, remained above the last in terms of living standard. However, the American meritocracy becomes more mythical and less reality based when viewed through the lens of "relative mobility," as defined by how individuals or groups change "relative to others, moving up or down in the ranks as one would expect in a true meritocracy" (p. 8).

Despite their high expectations, Secretary Duncan or Secretary Gove might have been surprised to learn that Great Britain and the United States, respectively, have the lowest upward mobility among other Western nations that include France, Germany, Sweden, Canada, Finland, Norway, and Denmark. According to OECD figures (DeSilver, 2013), the United States ranked second highest among Western nations in after-taxes income inequality. Interestingly, none of these other countries have put so much pressure on schools to provide solutions to inequality and lack of economic opportunity.

The belief, however, that hard work, ambition, and access to education are the primary determinants in a person's economic well-being is widely shared among the American public, and it is one that underpins many of the assumptions guiding the No Excuses KIPP Model. In 2013, Pew researchers (Sharkey & Graham, 2013) found, for instance, that 80 percent of Americans viewed

> factors such as hard work, ambition, and access to education as key drivers of upward mobility, while less than half viewed growing up in a good neighborhood as an important factor. On the contrary, respondents strongly agreed that a young person with drive, ambition, and creativity growing up in a poor neighborhood is more likely to get ahead economically than someone growing up in a more affluent neighborhood who lacks those attributes. (p. 1)

Pew research (Sharkey, 2009; Pew, 2013b) shows, too, that zip code is a central element in shaping social and economic outcomes of residents, with neighborhood poverty increasing the likelihood of moving down the income ladder. The following data clearly suggest that poverty-reduction efforts, neighborhood investment projects, fair housing policies, and ending segregation may prove to be more effective education reform strategies to raise test scores and to breed attitudes of hope than devising total-compliance schools with psychological treatment regimen and character remediation programs:

- For children whose family income is in the top three quintiles, spending childhood in a high-poverty neighborhood versus a low-poverty neighborhood (say, experiencing a poverty rate of 25 percent compared to a rate of 5 percent) raises the chances of downward mobility by 52 percent.
- Over the course of childhood, two out of three black children (66 percent) born from 1985 through 2000 were raised in neighborhoods with at least a 20 percent poverty rate, compared to just 6 percent of white children.
- Four in five black children who started in the top three quintiles experienced downward mobility, compared with just two in five white children. Three in five white children who started in the bottom two quintiles experienced upward mobility, versus just one in four black children.
- Neighborhood poverty alone accounts for a greater portion of the black-white downward mobility gap than the effects of parental education, occu-

pation, labor force participation, and a range of other family characteristics combined.

• Black children who lived in neighborhoods that saw a decline in poverty of 10 percentage points in the 1980s had annual adult incomes almost $7,000 greater than those who grew up in neighborhoods where the poverty rate was stable. (Sharkey, 2009, pp. 2–3)

In 2012, another Pew study (Pew Charitable Trusts, 2012) added more evidence of low *relative mobility* among those born at the top and bottom of the income ladder: "Sixty-six percent of those raised in the bottom of the wealth ladder remain on the bottom two rungs, and 66 percent of the those raised in the top of the wealth ladder remain on the top two rungs" (p. 2). Even more troubling, for poor and middle-class black families, upward *relative mobility* is even less likely:

> Half of blacks (50 percent) raised in the bottom of the family wealth ladder remain stuck in the bottom as adults, compared with only a third (33 percent) of whites. More than two-thirds of blacks (68 percent) raised in the middle fall to the bottom two rungs of the ladder as adults compared with just under a third of whites (30 percent). (p. 3)

More recent Pew research (2013b) focused on the linkage between economic segregation in U.S. cities and economic mobility. Almost fifty years after James Coleman (1966) found that school segregation has a negative impact on school achievement, Pew researchers found that economic achievement is similarly affected by segregation. In more integrated urban communities, the descendants of poor families living in highly segregated communities can expect to take four generations to reach the area's mean income, while poor families in more integrated communities can expect to take three generations to reach median income levels (p. 12).

> The most economically segregated U.S. metro areas—those where the very rich and the very poor live far from each other—are also the least economically mobile, and vice versa. Moreover, neighborhood economic segregation has risen across U.S. metro areas for more than 30 years, suggesting that climbing the economic ladder is more challenging in some places than in others. (p. 12)

With this kind of data available to policymakers and to corporate foundations that remain fixated on funding for total-compliance charter schools, it is difficult to calmly accept philanthrocapitalists' stubborn insistence that even the poorest children can become prosperous adults by becoming more disciplined and dedicated test takers in school. Given the slim odds that school interventions alone, even good ones, can accomplish such formidable results, the "no excuses" ideology takes on an aspect of dangerous fantasy when set alongside the empirical evidence: "Only 4 percent of those raised in the bottom quintile make it all the way to the top as adults, confirming that the 'rags-to-riches' story is more often found in Hollywood than in reality. Similarly, just 8 percent of those raised in the top quintile fall all the way to the bottom" (Pew Charitable Trusts, 2013a, p. 12).

Admitting reality would be a first step toward social, economic, and educational changes that are consistent with our human rights and constitutional guarantees. By depending upon more flawed educational fixes for deeply rooted social and economic problems, not only does a grittier Horatio Alger myth become further perpetuated by those who have never known lack of privilege, but the more expensive and politically risky structural changes such as fair housing enforcement, job creation, and economic livability standards get shoved to the bottom of the policy priority list (Rose, 2014) for another generation.

Is it worth asking, then: Can entrepreneurial imagination and organizationally disruptive practices be used to address entrenched and systemic problems in urban communities, rather than as a mad method to replace public community schools with corporate reform schools that claim the ability to scrub the effects of poverty from children's behavior and psyches? Will venture philanthropists find reasons to invest in ending the entrenched and inequitable systems of urban housing, economic deprivation, child neglect, food deserts, and crumbling public services that continue to feed the poverty monster now consuming large swaths of our population? Or will philanthrocapitalists continue to promote an unending parade of miseducative, though lucrative, acts that represent a minstrel version of educational justice?

REFERENCES

Bush, G. W. (2000). *Bush for President announcement.* George W. Bush for President Website. http://www.4president.org/speeches/bush2000announcement.htm.

Carter, S. (2000). *No excuses: Lessons from 21 high-performing, high-poverty schools.* Washington, DC: Heritage Foundation.

Change.gov. (2008, December 16). *President-elect Obama nominates Arne Duncan as Secretary of Education.* http://change.gov/newsroom/entry/president_elect_obama_nominates_arne_duncan_as_secretary_of_education/.

Coleman, J. S., Campbell, E., Hobson, C., McPartland, J., Mood, A., Weinfeld, F., et al. (1966). *Equality of educational opportunity.* Washington, DC: U.S. Government Printing Office.

DeSilver, D. (2013, December 19). *Global inequality: How the U.S. compares.* Pew Research Center. http://www.Pewresearch.org/fact-tank/2013/12/19/global-inequality-how-the-u-s-compares/.

Doyle, D. (1993, April). American schools: Good, bad, or indifferent? *Phi Delta Kappan* 74 (8), 626–31.

Fernandez, J. (2010, September 16). How did 'Superman' fly with D.C. elite? *The Hollywood Reporter.* http://www.hollywoodreporter.com/news/how-did-superman-fly-dc-27963.

Fletcher, M. (2007, November 13). Middle class dream eludes African American families. *Washington Post.* http://www.washingtonpost.com/wp-dyn/content/article/2007/11/12/AR2007111201711_pf.html.

GOV.UK. (2012, May 10). *Education secretary Michael Gove's speech to Brighton College.* https://www.gov.uk/government/speeches/education-secretary-michael-goves-speech-to-brighton-college.

Isaacs, J. B. (2007a). *Economic mobility of black and white families.* Washington, DC: Brookings Institution. http://www.brookings.edu/~/media/research/files/papers/2007/11/blackwhite isaacs/11_blackwhite_isaacs.pdf.

Isaacs, J. B. (2007b). *Economic mobility of families across generations.* Washington, DC: Brookings Institution. http://www.brookings.edu/research/papers/2007/11/generations-isaacs.

Isaacs, J. B., & Sawhill, I. (2008). *Reaching for the prize: The limits on economic mobility.* Washington, DC: The Brookings Institution.

Lewis, A. (1995, May). Schools and preparation for work. *Phi Delta Kappan* 76 (9), 660–61.

New York Times. (1999, September 3). Excerpts from Bush's speech on improving education. http://www.nytimes.com/1999/09/03/us/excerpts-from-bush-s-speech-on-improving-education.html.

Orfield, G. (2001). *Schools more separate: Consequences of a decade of resegregation.* Cambridge, MA: Harvard University Civil Rights Project. http://la.utexas.edu/users/hcleaver/330T/330TPEEOrfieldSchoolsMoreSeparate.pdf.

Orfield, G., & Yun, J. (1999). *Resegregation in American schools.* Cambridge, MA: Harvard University Civil Rights Project. http://escholarship.org/uc/item/6d01084 .

PBS News Hour. (2010, December 7). *Secretary Duncan: Schools must become centers of communities.* [Transcript]. http://www.pbs.org/newshour/bb/education-july-dec10-duncan_12-07/.

Pew Charitable Trusts. (2013a, November). *Moving on up: Why do some Americans leave the bottom of the economic ladder, but not others?* Washington, DC: The Pew Charitable Trusts.

Pew Charitable Trusts. (2013b, December). *Mobility and the metropolis: How communities factor into economic mobility.* Washington, DC: The Pew Charitable Trusts.

Pew Charitable Trusts. (2012, July). *Pursuing the American dream: Economic mobility across generations.* Washington, DC: The Pew Charitable Trusts. http://www.Pewtrusts.org/~/media/legacy/uploadedfiles/pcs_assets/2012/PursuingAmericanDreampdf.pdf.

PR Newswire. (2010). *Paramount Vantage acquires worldwide rights to a new film by Oscar winning documentarian Davis Guggenheim and Participant Media.* http://www.prnewswire.com/news-releases/paramount-vantage-acquires-worldwide-rights-to-the-new-film-by-oscarr-winning-documentarian-davis-guggenheim-and-participant-media-82294712.html.

Rose, M. (2014, October 22). *Character education: A cautionary note.* Washington, DC: The Brookings Institution. http://www.brookings.edu/research/papers/2014/10/22-character-education-cautionary-note-rose.

Rothstein, R. (2004). *Class and schools: Using social, economic, and educational reform to close the black-white achievement gap.* Washington, DC: Economic Policy Institute.

Sawhill, I., & Morton, J. (2007, May). *Economic mobility: Is the American dream alive and well?* Washington, DC: Brookings Institution.

Sharkey, P. (2009). *Neighborhoods and the black-white mobility gap.* The Economic Mobility Project. Washington, DC: Economic Mobility Project of the Pew Charitable Trusts.

Sharkey, P., & Graham, B. (2013). *Mobility and the metropolis: How communities factor into economic mobility.* Washington, DC: Economic Mobility Project of the Pew Charitable Trusts.

Sweet, L. (2009, July 16). Obama's NAACP speech, New York, July 16, 2009. [Transcript]. *Chicago Sun-Times.* http://blogs.suntimes.com/sweet/2009/07/obamas_naacp_speech.html.

Thernstrom, S., & Thernstrom, A. (2003). *No excuses: Closing the racial gap in learning.* New York: Simon and Schuster.

Chapter Five

KIPP and the Teaching Profession

> Our teachers have normal lives, and many have families and children.
> —Richard Barth, KIPP CEO (*Philanthropy News Digest*, 2009)

The KIPP Foundation has no requirements for professional preparation, and the state charter school statutes where each of the 183 KIPP schools is located govern certification requirements. While a few KIPP advertisements state a preference for teaching credentials, no ads could be located that required anything more than what the state charter laws stipulate. The KIPP Foundation website (2015d) states,

> The primary requirement for teaching at a KIPP school is a belief in a very simple concept: that we will do whatever it takes to help each and every student develop the character and academic skills necessary for them to lead self-sufficient, successful and happy lives.

The Foundation leaves it to each school to determine the qualifications required for new teachers. While many KIPP schools list two years of experience as a requirement in their ads, the necessity of replacing teachers who quit or who are fired make these requirements less applicable in real life. The KIPP website (KIPP Foundation, 2015d) points out that some schools have special programs for teachers with no prior experience.

In 2008, David Levin joined another charter school operator, Norman Atkins, and hedge fund mogul Larry "L-Train" Robbins to found a nonprofit corporation, the Relay Graduate School of Education, which focuses on preparing prospective teachers for the No Excuses charter school environment. Begun as Teacher U in 2006 by KIPP, Achievement First, and Uncommon Schools, Relay requires evidence that degree candidates can raise test scores before receiving their Master of Arts in Teaching (MAT) degree.

In one of the first cohorts, "seven out of 110 teachers did not receive Master's degrees because they could not show that their students had made at least a year's worth of academic progress" (Green, 2011). The "pedagogical content" curriculum at Relay is based largely on Doug Lemov's (2010; 2015) text, *Teach Like a Champion*. Lemov holds an MBA from Harvard and is founder and Board member of Uncommon Schools, a charter chain that largely emulates the KIPP organizational model.

Showing steady growth, Relay has campuses in New York, Newark, New Orleans, Houston, and Chicago, with plans in 2015 to open a location in Memphis. Prominent among Relay's philanthropic investors are the Gates Foundation, Credit Suisse, the Walton Family Foundation, the New Schools Venture Fund, and the Doris and Donald Fisher Fund. These same organizations and many others with them channel millions of dollars of tax-exempted donations through their corporate foundations to supplement the hundreds of millions of dollars in public education funds that go to KIPP each year.

When Bill Gates delivered a TED talk in 2009 on two of the world's most pressing problems, malaria and bad teachers, he provided a copy of *Work Hard, Be Nice* to all attendees, and in 2014 Gates told an interviewer from the American Enterprise Institute that he had concluded "the greatest cause of inequity" in America comes from "the failures of the education system" (American Enterprise Institute, 2014, p. 3). Gates's preferred solution, for poor urban children at least, is the KIPP Model.

KIPP has an attrition rate among teachers that would be unsustainable if it were not for the large numbers of recruits from Teach for America that replace the 30 to 40 percent of KIPP teachers who leave KIPP each year. When David Levin and Mike Feinberg founded KIPP in 1994, it is likely that they envisioned TFA, with its two-year service contract for inexperienced teacher candidates who are heavily recruited from top-tier colleges and universities, as a prime source of new teachers to sustain, perhaps, the heroic demands and test performance standards that the KIPP Model imposes (Horn, 2010).

While former TFA Corps Members make up between 30 and 40 percent of KIPP teachers nationally, some schools have a much higher concentration. At the KIPP Endeavor Academy in Kansas City, for instance, 80 percent of KIPP teachers were TFA Corps Members in 2014. Even though TFA has always attracted more applicants than it has teaching slots, the organization regularly spends more money for advertising and recruitment (Teach for America, 2007, p. 29) than it spends on preservice training, which lasts for just over four weeks.

One would-be recruit from a few years back (Chernicoff, 2006) wrote this assessment in the *Yale Daily News*:

> In just a few years, TFA has established itself as one of the smart-people-who-just-graduated-with-liberal-arts-degrees-and-now-have-no-idea-what-they-want-to-do-with-their-lives-but-are-pretty-sure-it-isn't-remain-in-the-spin-cy-cle-of-academia-or-move-on-to-the-next-preset-hierarchy-in-the-finance-world demographic. Used to be those poor souls could only go to law school or move to New York and "go into, like, publishing or something." But TFA positioned itself in such a way that it gets the lost souls who have an impulse to do something to help the world immediately upon graduating. (para. 12–13)

New TFA recruits who are not assigned directly to KIPP are commonly harvested after two years into KIPP teaching and leadership positions. As KIPP school leaders, they are given CEO power in the principal's office to make policy and rules that were once the responsibility of public school boards.

KIPP's teacher turnover rate became a public fact in 2008, with the publication of the SRI evaluation report *San Francisco Bay Area KIPP Schools* (Woodworth, David, Guha, Wang, & Lopez-Torkos, 2008). SRI researchers found KIPP's teacher annual attrition rate ranged from 18 to 49 percent at the five Bay Area KIPP schools that researchers studied.

> Since 2003–04, the five Bay Area KIPP school leaders have hired a total of 121 teachers. Of these, 43 remained in the classroom at the start of the 2007–08 school year. Among teachers who left the classroom, at four of the schools they spent a median of 1 year in the classroom before leaving; at one school, the typical teacher spent 2 years in the classroom before leaving. (p. 32)

While SRI found KIPP teachers committed, they also found them clearly doubtful of their capacity to continue under the stress of sixty to eighty hours of school-related work per week (which includes two hours per night for telephone homework duty). As one KIPP teacher told SRI researchers, "The consequence is I can't do this job very much longer. It is too much. I don't see any solution with our structure and our nonnegotiables. No one has really presented any way to solve that problem" (p. 35).

Browne (2009) found the average KIPP teacher leaves after three years of service (p. 174). KIPP researchers (KIPP Foundation, 2013) reported in 2013 that 33 percent of teachers left their teaching positions in 2012 (p. 26). Teacher attrition in KIPP's largest district, Houston, was 36 percent across twenty-four schools in 2014. Two other No Excuses chains that are based on the KIPP Model, YES Prep and Achievement First, report the average length of service for teachers is between 2 and 2.5 years (Rich, 2013).

In an analysis by the National Center on School Choice at Vanderbilt University, Stuit and Smith (2009) found the teacher attrition problem severe across all types of charter schools. Using NCES data from 2003 to 2004, the authors "found the odds of a charter school teacher leaving the profession versus staying in the same school are 132% greater than those of a traditional public school teacher. The odds of a charter school teacher moving schools are 76% greater" (Abstract).

THE KIPP SUMMIT: PROFESSIONAL DEVELOPMENT REVIVALISM

An important element of "teacher KIPP-notizing" comes each year when the KIPP Foundation hosts an annual summit that brings together all KIPP teachers just before the new school year begins. Part celebration, sales meeting, revival, and professional development opportunity, the KIPP Summit serves to indoctrinate new staff into the KIPP culture, which is referred to by the KIPP founders as "Team and Family." One former teacher enthused about the KIPP Summit for the "interesting atmosphere" and opportunity to "learn new things" and the chance to hear teachers and school leaders "talk about successes that they had with kids going to college." Interestingly, she found the Summit "fun . . . [and] real, even though it was like a good educational Nuremberg Rally, but a good educational Nuremberg Rally—they really got you pumped up." When I asked her to elaborate, she said,

> It's kind of rah-rah-rah, really this is what our mission is, and I . . . everybody is marching in the same direction. In this case it's a good direction. We want the kids there to get to college, but in a way it is kind of the same direction, and kind of a lot of hype, and . . . there's banners, and each school had their banner, and that's probably the worst reference to make, but there is a certain correlation between the two [KIPP Summit and Nuremberg Rally] in terms of—it's an enthusiasm that a whole crowd is getting, and kids would come up, and they would talk about their achievements, and everybody would clap and cheer, and it was really, everyone moving in that same direction.
>
> And I think it was a good direction, but I'm a history teacher so part of me was kind of outside my body going, "This is interesting. I'm glad this is for a good reason, it's really kind of whipping people up to go this direction." So I'm glad it's a good direction, but I can see where, if you were in another place in time, it could be whipped up into that way.

Summits are often held in popular tourist destinations such as Orlando, Miami, or Las Vegas. In 2011, for example, the KIPP Foundation's 990 nonprofit federal tax return showed that $1,008,633 was paid to Opryland Hotel in Nashville for hotel and hospitality during one Summit, while almost $4 million was spent on travel that year. Most Summit expenses are paid by the KIPP Foundation, but then KIPP recoups some of that money from each KIPP franchise, which must pay up to $30,000 each year to use the KIPP brand name. In 2011, KIPP, Inc., collected a total of $2,050,256 from individual schools in these licensing fees.

One former KIPP teacher who had witnessed the extravagances of the 2014 Summit wondered why KIPP would claim there is no money for hiring substitute teachers, all the while renting huge arenas for general sessions and lavish hotel ballrooms for after parties that featured an array of desserts and snacks, an open bar, and DJs. "To me it seemed like if we have the money for a summit and we don't have the money for substitute teachers, then we should kill the summit and find the money for substitute teachers."

Several of the teachers I interviewed talked about their experiences at the annual summits that always come just before school starts, thus leaving new teachers, in particular, feeling unprepared to meet students. As teachers worry about a lack of lesson planning, the Summit vendors sell books and kits that are advertised to fill those needs and assuage those fears. One teacher said, "They were pushing products and they were pushing new ideas from business perspectives."

One first-year teacher attended a KIPP Summit in Las Vegas, which she described as a "whole big feel-good session." She saw students receive awards, and she heard "inspirational stories with how KIPP changes lives." She said some of her colleagues "who had been in teaching for awhile thought it was a waste of time," but she said, "I enjoyed it because I'm completely new, and I know nothing. . . . It was fun. I enjoyed myself. I got to go to Vegas for free so that was pretty nice. Then we get back and immediately, I mean I started work July 19 and did not physically stop working until Christmas."

When another teacher mentioned the KIPP Summit as she described the beginning of school, I asked what she thought of the Summit. She replied:

> Honestly, I was just kind of like what the hell did I get myself into. It was just really weird. . . . I don't mean everybody, but it was like they were just so beyond enthusiastic, and I am kind of like, this is a little off putting because, I don't know—it felt cheesy in a lot of ways. . . . I mean I am definitely a passionate educator and I think education is so important, and I definitely get enthusiastic about my content area, but it was just a little over the top, and I just felt like I didn't fit in because I wasn't that way, and KIPP is really big on little songs and chants and things like that, and that is just like not me at all. I mean there were a couple of points where I kind of got into it, and it was kind of goofy.

Besides feeling out of place at the Summit, this teacher thought the professional development had much in common with other professional development she has experienced during her six years in charter schools, where young teachers are teaching other young teachers who know only slightly less than they.

> It was kind of like the blind leading the blind. It is kind of hard to remember all the details, but I just remember thinking okay I feel like I have learned nothing . . . and I don't feel like I walked away with things that made me feel like wow I can really use this in my classroom or wow that is really meaningful. That sort of professional development is a hole in charter schools. You need somebody coming in there who really has a lot of experience.

Another teacher used the word *interesting* with a clear inflection of disapproval. She noted "there was a very common thread that ran through meetings and conversations about the evils of unions." During the roll call of schools at the Summit, each school staff stood wearing their own shirts and did a song or a chant. She described the atmosphere as "frenzied." She also said that when teachers in the auditorium were asked to stand who had less than five years total teaching experience, almost everyone rose.

> [The KIPP Summit] had a part where they would have everybody who has been teaching five years or less stand up, and everybody pretty much in the auditorium stood up—for 5 to 10 years, very few, and there were hardly any over 10 years. That was for teaching in general and not necessarily teaching at KIPP, but that was also very interesting to see it. And [KIPP leaders] didn't seem ashamed of that. They seemed to think that was just fine.

"IT WAS ALMOST LIKE A CULT"

One teacher noted what she called the Summit's "cultish mentality" that others around her saw as well. During the chanting of the KIPP motto, a friend said to her, "I'm not doing this—this is some cult bs." This same teacher likened the conditioning to what she described as a fundamentalist cult. When I asked one teacher how KIPP values affected how she taught, she said,

> You had to have all the KIPP values posted. You had to constantly remind the children of the KIPP values. It was an Orwellian type of teaching. You had to focus on teaching almost like a cult. It was very much brainwashing is how I could describe it. It was like it wasn't you. I mean, believe me, if you didn't have those KIPP values posted in your room, if you did not go over them daily, someone would know and they would remind you, hey, these are the KIPP values, teach them.

This teacher talked about the "language they've created where they just rename things," which she described as "almost comical." When I asked why "almost comical," she replied,

> Almost comical because it's not fully comical, because it's serious. It's just serious. You're working but it's like you're teaching these values and if you

stop and think for a second you're like okay, wait a minute, this is bizarre and ridiculous, but you keep doing it. It's still serious. I don't know. Sometimes you laugh about it. You had to laugh about it because you couldn't stop and think, what am I doing. You just have to laugh because you're like okay, here I am stuck in this situation, and I don't want to quit, so very often you find yourself just laughing at yourself because you fell for it. I don't know.

Another teacher noted, too, the private language and the "different phrases that were used" as "very cultish." It has long been noted among scholars (Lifton, 1961) who have studied thought reform environments that a common characteristic is "manipulation of language in which clichés substitute for analytic thought" (p. 419). A former KIPP teacher who was older and more experienced than most offered this analysis:

They take these young kids and they indoctrinate them into the KIPP way. Whether it works or not doesn't really matter. It works from KIPP's perspective; the teachers who stay are indoctrinated. It's almost, and I hate to use this word, but I'm going to anyway. But it's almost like a cult.

REFERENCES

American Enterprise Institute. (2014, March 3). *From poverty to prosperity: A conversation with Bill Gates.* http://www.aei.org/files/2014/03/14/-bill-gates-event-transcript_082217994272.pdf.

Browne, L. W. (2009). *A character education approach to founding a KIPP college preparatory charter school.* (Doctoral dissertation). Retrieved from Dissertation and Theses database. (UMI No. 3344513).

Chernicoff, D. (2006, October 27). I want you, Yalie, to teach for America. *Yale Daily News.* http://yaledailynews.com/weekend/2006/10/27/i-want-you-yalie-to-teach-for-america/.

Green, E. (2011, February 14). A new graduate school of education, Relay, to open next fall. *Chalkbeat New York.* http://ny.chalkbeat.org/2011/02/14/a-new-graduate-school-of-education-relay-to-open-next-fall/ -.VLGzeyeTDOE.

Horn, J. (2010). Corporatism, KIPP, and cultural eugenics. In *The Bill Gates Foundation and the future of U.S. "public" schools.* Edited by P. Kovacs. New York: Routledge.

KIPP Foundation. (2015d). *Frequently asked questions.* http://www.kipp.org/careers/application-resources/applicant-faqs#Candidate.

KIPP Foundation. (2013). *KIPP: 2013 report card.* http://www.kipp.org/reportcard.

Lemov, D. (2015). *Teach like a champion 2.0: 62 techniques that put students on the path to college.* San Francisco: Jossey Bass.

Lemov, D. (2010). *Teach like a champion: 49 techniques that put students on the path to college (K–12).* San Francisco: Jossey-Bass.

Philanthropy News Digest. (2009, August 21). *Richard Barth, Chief Executive Officer, KIPP Foundation.* http://philanthropynewsdigest.org/newsmakers/richard-barth-chief-executive-officer-kipp-foundation.

Rich, M. (2013, August 26). At charter schools, short careers by choice. *New York Times.* http://www.nytimes.com/2013/08/27/education/at-charter-schools-short-careers-by-choice.html.

Stuit, D., & Smith, T. (2009). *Teacher turnover in charter schools.* Nashville, TN: Vanderbilt University. http://www.vanderbilt.edu/schoolchoice/documents/stuit_smith_ncspe.pdf.

Chapter Six

The KIPP Teaching Experience

It's like you're being used up and thrown out.
—1160

Looking back on it, it just seems crazy that people are willing to do the things that KIPP requires of them without a second thought. You know, you have to have blind obedience, if that makes sense.
—1184

As noted elsewhere in this book, KIPP teachers are at-will employees, which means that the teacher or KIPP can terminate the contract at any time without notice. While this arrangement provides a tangible motivator for teachers to try to keep up with KIPP's expectations, it also allows KIPP to quickly replace teachers who are not producing measurable results in the form of test scores.

This arrangement, in turn, creates higher stress levels among teachers who are already under intense pressure, and the ability to fire teachers at-will creates a negative energy that runs counter to KIPP's advertised face of positivity and widespread "joy factor." Teachers report that job insecurity was a major stressor, which creates negative energy from knowing that termination might come without warning: "I think that KIPP is kind of fueled by negative energy in some ways. You know, it's easier to try to scare people into doing things than to motivate them or encourage them. And I think that was kind of the attitude that I ran into a lot is, you know, you're an at-will employee, so if you don't like it, you can go somewhere else."

Another teacher noted that his lowest points at KIPP were related to his anxiety about job insecurity, which caused him to lose sleep: "A part of the culture among staff at this particular school, and I think at most KIPP schools, because there's no contract, there's this idea of you could go at any time. You could not be rehired next year. You could be let go with absolutely no notice. I felt that pressure a lot, to the point where I was losing sleep."

Another teacher who had worked in public schools before coming to KIPP talked about the downside of KIPP's system of at-will teacher contracts:

> Public schools aren't all perfect. . . . I'm not a wholesale believer in everything that the union has done, because I've seen a lot of ineffective teachers get tenure and things like that. And I've seen a lot of teachers not be protected when they should have been. But I believe that there is a reason for the protections that teachers have. And at KIPP, there is no such thing. You know, you're an at-will employee all the time [and] there's no guarantee that, if you've been there for five years, that year six, they're going to even ask you to come back. And they don't have to give you any notice.

THE TEACHING DAY

Teachers in KIPP Model schools have long days that range from ten to fourteen hours. It is not uncommon for teachers to arrive at school between 5 and 6 a.m. and to leave after 6 or 7 p.m., and all KIPP teachers are on call Monday through Friday until 9 or 10 p.m. for homework tutoring or questions. Some KIPP schools have Saturday school for a half-day, but most have Saturday school every other week. "And then," as one teacher said, "there's the lesson planning and grading" to be done as well.

Most teachers arrive well before 7:00, in order to get their photocopies done before the children begin to arrive at 7:05. School leaders make the rounds checking to see if rooms are ready. At 7:20, children are signaled with a series of hand motions to line up for breakfast, and they are marched silently in single file to the cafeteria. Children return to the classroom for "advisory" at 7:50, where they find the morning work on the board or they are handed a worksheet that may or may not be relevant to the curriculum.

During this time of silent work, teachers check homework folders to make sure all homework has been completed correctly and that the proper paycheck deductions for sloppy or missing work and credits for correct work are made for each child. With as many as thirty students in advisory with four subjects, each requiring written work every night, this task rarely gets completed with complete accuracy in the time allotted. At 8:40, children get the readying hand signals once more and are silently marched to their first class.

One teacher explained the students' transitioning in this way:

> They would move into transition, which was always a stressful time. It's meant to be very routinized. They have a thing called one, two, three dismissal, where they're given about 20 seconds to pack up. Not about 20 seconds; it is an exact 20 seconds. Give them 20 seconds to pack, then they have one, two,

three dismissal, where the teacher raises one finger and that indicates that all students should be tracking them.

When all students are tracking the teacher, the teacher raises the second finger, which shows that all the kids can stand. On three, the students go to line order, which is a very specific, students line up single file. They're meant to have out an independent reading book at all times during this time so that during transition while they're waiting in line, while they're walking, they're reading. Everything is done completely silent. The students line up and then leave the classroom, file out single file to their next class.

Between 8:40 a.m. and 4:40 p.m., teachers have a plan period and a half-hour for lunch, during which time most teachers remain on duty while trying to eat. Because lining up and marching has to be performed perfectly or it must be done again, lunch usually lasts less than the thirty minutes allotted in the schedule. Throughout the day, teachers carry clipboards and spend their time maintaining total compliance and teaching content.

Following the minute details of management, demerit, and punishment plans takes up considerable chunks of class time. One teacher described the "demerit clipboard" this way:

> And I really struggled with this demerit clipboard, because there was a whole, you know, each type of different demerit had a different number from one to nine. And you had to note it in a certain way. And you had to put your initials. And you had to put it next to the student's name. So finding all of this on a clipboard that's legal size with 30 kids on it, while you're in the middle of a lesson on the spot, so you [must] remember to record it—it can interrupt your whole lesson and derail it. I mean, some teachers can just do it quickly. At [another charter school where she taught previously], they have a barcode scanner and they just literally scanned the student's name and the kind of demerit. And they do it instantly. I joked that they should just put the barcodes on the kids' foreheads, you know?

The after-school KIPP teacher experience looks something like this: At 4:40 students begin to get ready for home, and at 4:45 KIPP teachers march their students to the buses. The teachers board the buses with the students to make sure everyone is settled with something to read. Teachers leave the buses and are instructed to wave until the buses are out of sight. Teachers then walk back to the building, where they tutor children until 5:45, except on Mondays and Wednesdays, when professional development meetings last until 8 p.m.

Afterward, teachers compile data for exit tickets that provide "concrete data" that children have learned what was expected of them that day. Then teachers organize their classrooms, prepare lessons for the next day (which must be typed later and turned in to the school leader each Friday), and make sure the independent worksheets are ready for the next morning. By 8 or 9 p.m., it's time to head home to fix dinner and grade papers.

"TRYING TO PUT YOUR FINGER ON EVERY POTENTIAL LEAK"

One teacher, who compared his eighty-to-one-hundred-hour weeks at a KIPP school to "sprinting a marathon for two years," provided insight into KIPP's control strategies and the "intensity" with which they are maintained. At his school, silence was not only maintained at school—it was also enforced on school buses, by teachers. There are no ellipses in this excerpt, as it is verbatim from the audio transcript:

> It wasn't just working on being at the office or something like that. It was we had to create and own an environment that was difficult to manage, and had to do that over a very long period. I'll give you two or three examples that will hopefully illustrate what I'm speaking about. In the mornings, we decided, or the school decided, that kids should be reading as much as possible. The bus drivers picking the kids up and dropping them off wouldn't be able to discipline them or create the same kind of culture that we had expected of our students and that a lot of the culture that we'd created would break down on the way to school and after school. We thought that if kids were unsupervised on those buses, they would inevitably lead to some sort of drama, fighting or conflict of some sort, and that would carry into the school day and distract them from their learning.
>
> Our kids came in performing well below grade level, and we were trying to get them not just on track and caught up, but prepared academically and propel them forward. We felt that was a risk that we couldn't really take in terms of the amount of potential disruption that might come from getting off the bus with fires to put out before 7:30 in the morning. Our solution was to ride the bus with the students. This is actually something that a bunch of schools do. I don't think we were the only ones to do it. What we did on the bus was we had policy that we introduced that kids were not allowed to talk. They could read their books. They could look out the window. They could sleep. They could just relax. But you're getting ready for school—get yourself prepared. Take a moment, gather yourself, read. That was the policy. As you can imagine, that's not something that's very typical for a group of 10, 11, 12 and 13 year-olds to abide by, especially at 6:30 in the morning.
>
> Actually it was certainly harder on the way home from school. It became an exercise in discipline, where the teacher was expected to ride the bus each day, either going out or coming back or sometimes both. The ride would be an hour and you had to sit there and make sure that the kids didn't talk. That's an extra hour or two added on top of the school day that's already extremely intense where as a teacher I felt like I had to be extremely focused. I had to be extremely professional. I had to be extremely consistent.
>
> In retrospect, the benefit of that policy was probably extremely limited. But it was something we decided to do. We were on board with it. We executed to the best of our ability. However, it had a long-term cost of creating

this experience for the teacher that was very intense. And the experience with the kids that was very intense, too. That created, as I mentioned briefly earlier, almost a pressure-cooker kind of environment where you felt—or I should say our strategy was trying to put our fingers on every potential leak. But you'd feel like it's going to explode if you're not putting your hands in the leak.

Upon reflection, this teacher characterized his school's approach as the "far extreme of control," which, for him was "something that creates teacher turnover every two years. It creates kids dropping out of the school. It creates nervousness and stress among parents and students."

SILENCE AND STRESS

Enforced silence is one of the chief sources of stress among KIPP teachers. Failure to meet silence expectations is attributed by school leaders as teachers' shortcomings, rather than any examination of unrealistic expectations of children with real social needs that were not being met:

There is a huge pressure in terms of behavior and the way that kids act in your class. . . . I feel like if there is ever any behavior issue, it is automatically the teacher's fault, when I don't necessarily feel like that is true and those expectations that the kids are supposed to be silent in the hallway, they need to be silent when they are in your room, they need to be SLANTing and tracking you and silent when you are talking—I just feel like it is not realistic, especially developmentally, to expect that from middle school kids.

So it is just frustrating because they are just doing what is natural to them to kind of interact and like play around, and I feel like there is a big pressure for the kids not to be acting that way. Then if they are choosing to act that way, it is your [the teacher's] fault, like "well what should you be doing, you need to be doing more for them to be not acting that way."

As this same teacher noted, the emphasis on silent behavior had so sensitized her to that expectation that more teaching energy was going into enforcement than into offering more effective learning strategies. The result was a focus on constant policing rather than teaching:

In terms of teaching, retrospectively if I look at it, it has made me a worse teacher because now I feel like I am constantly thinking of these expectations that I am supposed to have in terms of behavior—having them be silent and all those things—and I feel like it is making me a bad teacher because it is like constantly looking at the negative, "oh they are not doing good." I feel like it has not helped me to focus on the positive things as much.

FROM STRESS TO DISTRESS

> I feel like there are a lot of really good teachers who did leave and it wasn't
> because they were bad teachers; it was just because they couldn't deal with the
> pressure and the hours and the stress that is kind of put upon people.
> —1177

A former KIPP teacher was headed for a visit to the KIPP school where he
had resigned the year before. He had found a different job since leaving
KIPP, and he was able to sleep again. He had started to gain weight, and his
hair was starting to grow back. While at KIPP, he had made friends with
other KIPP teachers, and he missed the kids that he had come to know,
despite all the organizational rules that discouraged that from happening. He
recalls:

> I was walking down the sidewalk outside of the school, and I ran into one of
> the teachers who was going to the deli on the corner to go grab a Gatorade, and
> he said, "Every time I see somebody who's left this school, they always come
> back looking ten times happier." So when I think about KIPP now, I think
> about how grateful I am that I've been able to get some sleep and have some of
> my hair start growing back.

Other teachers found school time consumed a great deal of personal time,
which brought added stress from a loss of connection with family and
friends. One teacher who had her first child while employed at KIPP placed
the baby with her mother during the four years she spent teaching there. She
supported her mother so that her mother could retire and be the full-time
caregiver for the child. She offered this tearful explanation:

> At the end of the school year in _____ is when I left, and my son started school
> that same year. That's when I realized I just had missed out on one of the most
> important things in my life. He was my first child. I had him late. Yeah, that
> was hard. I realized I didn't know my four-year-old because I had spent four
> years focusing on KIPP. I was a first time parent so I didn't understand. I
> actually I gave him to my mother. My mother quit her job to raise him. I
> supported my mother and myself so my mother could retire from her job to
> take care of my baby so I could work for KIPP. Then I realized it wasn't worth
> it.

Teaching at KIPP has many stressors, but factors related to organizational
policies and practices, time demands, and the weight given to tests figure
significantly to most of the teachers interviewed. The following quote provides insight into how all three of these factors figure into the stress that this
teacher acknowledged:

> There's a lot of stress to do good in terms of making the [state testing] goals, and also for each teacher wanting that group to do at least as well as the teacher the year before, and in a lot of cases because you get a lot of turnover, that's a big thing to hold over somebody. It's like, "Well, this teacher got this [state] scores for her English class," so there's a lot of stress on that, and that's a lot for the English and math departments, which are tested more often. There's also stress that the other departments have to cram stuff into a smaller space in time, because a lot of time is spent on those two subjects, Math and English, because those are the ones that are tested, and so I know that I had to squeeze a lot of curriculum into a smaller space in time that I shouldn't have had to do.

This same teacher said the stress was "more continuous" than in his previous school, where test prep had been restricted to the month prior to the state test. As with the other KIPP teachers I talked with, this teacher's school did not hire substitute teachers for fear of altering the behavioral regimen. Outsiders could not be trusted to maintain the level of academic and behavioral compliance that the KIPP Model demands, and as this teacher put it, "it was hard to get anyone trained to be a sub."

Because other KIPP teachers would have to take up the slack when a teacher was ill or needed to be off for other business, the teachers I talked with only took off for emergencies. Even then, the principal might "call you at home, and say, 'can you possibly come in for part of the day?' And you could be really throwing up, or whatever, and it was like you feel so guilty, and you're trying to get in."

One teacher, who compared KIPP with her other charter school experience, found KIPP less fulfilling and less successful, even though she made between $3,000 and $4,000 dollars more per year at KIPP:

> If you break down how much I am making an hour, I am making way less an hour than a public school teacher is and I am just constantly stressed and worried about school. This is something that I didn't experience in student teaching or when I was at the other charter school in New York: it was a lot more laid back than KIPP, and the day was not as long as a KIPP day, either. And I feel like that school was way more successful than the KIPP that I am at now.

Another teacher, who had landed a public school teaching job in a wealthy community after leaving KIPP, had a similar sense of relief that came when the yelling stopped. She apologized for using the military analogy, but she could not come up with a more appropriate one.

> I felt like I was almost coming out of, I don't feel totally right saying this, but I guess I can, in a minor way, understand how military might feel coming home. And again I don't feel totally right saying that, but that is the only parallel or metaphor I can make right now, but just sort of like this kind of shell shock

sort of feeling and then like coming to a place where you know people are normal and act like humans.

That is kind of how it felt, and I just felt so grateful. I was like wow, we have books, like wow, I don't have to yell at anybody for talking, and I can actually sit down and have lunch. I didn't feel so stressed, and I almost didn't know what to do with that feeling. So it was just liberating, and I felt like I didn't know what to do with all this liberation.

After the grueling work schedule at KIPP Model schools, the time left for family is often consumed with trying to recover from mental and physical exhaustion. One teacher, ironically, pointed to the weekends as her low points while teaching at KIPP:

I was just absolutely exhausted, my body was exhausted. That happened so often, I would just sleep like all day on Sunday. Where most people look forward to the weekend to run their errands, to spend time with their family, that would be my time to sleep. Everyone knew it, like don't call her—she's sleeping. Those are my low points—the weekends.

It is not uncommon for KIPP teachers to have no more than four to five hours of sleep each night during workweeks of twelve-to-fourteen-hour days. One KIPP teacher spoke of a principal whose sleep deprivation while at KIPP had contributed to an inability to get pregnant. Upon resigning from KIPP, "she slept for about a month straight and she was pregnant a month later. So it had a pretty profound impact on other people."

One teacher, who was still under the care of a therapist following her time at KIPP, said that she would leave her house at 4:30 a.m. in order to get to school at 5 a.m. That way she could get her photocopying done before most of the other teachers showed up, and get to her classroom by 6 a.m. so that she should organize for her day, which started at 7:05 with students. Having gotten to bed around midnight after getting home between 9 and 10 p.m., the alarm came earlier each day that she followed this routine. She said of the hours she kept,

I was never the last person in the parking lot, and I was never the first person in the parking lot either. And I worked non-stop. I also have to say KIPP was very isolating when you work those horrible hours. I left my family and my boyfriend in Arizona and I wanted to forge this great life out here. And I wanted to be this great teacher. And I gave it everything I had.

By October, she was getting up at 4:17 a.m. and was out the door by 4:30. It was at this time that she said, "I stopped taking regular showers because I wanted to get 20 more minutes sleep."

While many KIPP educators lose sleep because of the workload and the pace of work life, one teacher found KIPP colleagues who were "very, very,

very much committed," but he said that, because of the workload, he was unsure "how many of them last a long time at KIPP." Sleep is not only an issue for teachers but also for students. One former teacher told me that the first thing he would change about KIPP would be the early start time, which is commonly around 7 a.m.

He framed his argument in terms of test scores achievement: "How much are we harming these kids' scores and their cognitive development by depriving them of sleep because a lot of them are still going to bed at midnight or 1 o'clock in the morning and then getting up at 5 or 6 in the morning? Many of them have the same schedule as the KIPP teachers."

FROM DISTRESS TO OTHER HEALTH ISSUES

> You wind up sacrificing your physical health and most of your social life. . . . I put my relationship with the students before my physical health.
> —1166

With the kind of pressure-filled hours described above, it would be surprising if teachers reported no ill health effects. All the teachers interviewed did report negative health effects from working inside No Excuses pressure cookers. The mental health effects range from PTSD symptoms, anxiety disorders, unusual sadness, nightmares, depression, anger issues, nervous exhaustion, emotional and mental breakdowns, and classic teacher burnout. One teacher spent a week in the hospital in November after a "mental breakdown," and another who was still in treatment described her condition as a "nervous breakdown." A third teacher reported that she saw four teachers have "complete nervous breakdowns."

> I can definitely in my mind right now identify four teachers that I saw unravel that had a nervous breakdown and I would just explain it as crying and shaking and talking and not making sense. Babbling, a lot of babbling. Asking for help. Crying. I felt horrible.

Self-reported physical manifestations included weight loss, weight gain, bad nutrition, more colds and respiratory infections, poor hygiene, and alopecia. One teacher was so unavailable to her partner as life became "completely the job" that her partner began an active job search for her while she was trying to survive the rigors of KIPP. She said, "I lost a lot of weight. A lot of people voiced concern about my weight." The job search proved productive, and she left KIPP for health, relationship, and ethical reasons having to do with the treatment of special education students.

Another teacher who suffered from alopecia and other work-related illnesses resigned from KIPP for health reasons. She talked about not being able to "handle working there," even if it meant not finding another teaching job immediately:

> I am just going to hope that I can find something. I just decided that regardless of whether or not I get another job—I would like to have another job—I just can't handle working there. It is just not worth my health to do that for another year, because even other than my hair falling out, I have had a lot of other health issues. I have had pneumonia, I have had my hair fall out, I have had stomach problems, and I have had a lot of anxiety and it is just not worth it at all. And I am constantly in a bad, bad mood and my boyfriend tells me like all the time that he has noticed a big change in the way I am since I have been working there.

One teacher I talked with came to KIPP after teaching for some time in her home state and winning praise as Teacher of the Year in one of the schools where she worked. She had a noneducation bachelors degree and a prior successful career in her field. Her masters was in education, and it was a short video that she saw during her graduate school experience that sparked her desire to be a KIPP teacher: "I really bought into the mission about helping kids who might not otherwise go to college. And also the video made me think, like, if they didn't go to KIPP, they were going to die. Like it was very drastic. And so I worked really hard. And in the back of my mind, I really just wanted to be a KIPP teacher."

She finally made the decision to apply out of state to a KIPP school, and she was hired to teach middle school. She packed up her car with all her teaching materials, which left room for a single suitcase, and moved to begin her dream job at KIPP. The new KIPP regimen proved brutal. In order to get everything done the KIPP way, she found it necessary to work sixteen-to-eighteen-hour days, which left no time for anything else, including taking care of herself.

> I had no time to grocery shop ever. So my roommate would do all the grocery shopping. She would cook things for me, and she would leave them in the fridge. And if it wasn't for her kindness, I think I would have starved to death. And I'm not exaggerating. I'm so embarrassed that I let my life get like that.

When she told her grade-level supervisor that she was breaking down and thought she needed to see a therapist, she was sent on to the principal, whose first reaction was to ask to observe her class. Following the observation, the principal opened their meeting by saying, "I'm just really worried about you. I hear you have no joy." It was at this point that she "fell apart" and told the school leader that she didn't know how much longer she could "take this."

A distinct lack of joy is not only apparent among many KIPP teachers. One teacher noted that students "look like adults walking down the hallways.

They're stressed. One thing you always notice at the [KIPP] school I was in—you will not see a student smiling. You would not see a teacher smiling. I mean the difference in the school culture from [my] previous school is so different—like the kids were literally breaking down."

Chapter Seven

Teacher Highs and Lows

We had staff meetings that would go past midnight, and I'm glad that's not a part of my life anymore.
—1167

For former KIPP teachers, the high points they remember from KIPP are most often associated with "the kids." Hearing some variation of "the kids were my high points," or "I loved the kids," or "the high point was definitely the kids themselves" was common during our conversations. Another teacher said her high point "would definitely be interactions with students. I mean, there are specific students that I remember very fondly and think about their potential and their kind of stick-to-it-ness when it came to their work, and the things that I admired about them."

High points included projects with children that teachers worked on outside the regular classroom. One teacher talked of a carnival, and another described a history fair on Saturday. One teacher identified her high point as being able to create a special education program at a KIPP school where none had existed before. One teacher talked of teaching children to sing a song in German and "teaching rhythm to my advanced band."

A former KIPP teacher discovered a high point as a result of working with one particular student who "had been diagnosed with several learning disabilities." She had worked one on one with the student on developing "a growth mindset," and as a result the student had "worked her ass off for . . . a 4.0 average by the end of second quarter." This teacher said,

It was one of those success stories that I feel wouldn't have happened at a public school because the support network that this girl had with the [KIPP] teachers who were dedicated to staying until seven o'clock every single day, and she would rotate who she was getting extra help from. She was dedicated.

She was committed. And so to see her work pay off like that and to prove the critics wrong was a highlight for me.

Another teacher had his high point when he found that all of his twenty-two middle school students with whom he had worked with for two years had passed the state test at the end of the second year. He said he remembered "crying and setting up a big party."

One former KIPP teacher experienced her high point near the end of the year after the state test, when her students produced a major writing project that lasted eight weeks that was "really, really beautiful, and very memorable. . . . It was the first time I felt like all year the kids really were enjoying writing class, and what was, you know, hugely frustrating—it was like a high, and a low, because that's how I would have wanted to be teaching all year, but I was told that I need to teach in the five-step lesson plan."

Another teacher's high points came near the end of the year, too, when he and two other KIPP teachers designed a trip for students who had earned enough paycheck points to go on a weeklong trip that included quality time in the outdoors and fun time in a large city in the region. This teacher found that when the lid was loosened on the KIPP pressure cooker, so that teachers let their "guards down," both children and teachers had some profound experiences:

There was very little pressure—there was always some academic thing we would infuse with it, but it was very much a reward. It was fun because it's a reward, and everybody likes rewards. But more than that, we basically let our guards down enough so that we could really stand back and watch and observe the kids be middle school kids in these exciting places. When we took that pressure off and just observed them, not only did we see all of their colors . . . But to see them be interacting with each other in an unsupervised way really, I think, gave them a sense of ownership and freedom to where we were able to create an experience that was theirs.

And then more so because they were allowed to relax and breathe, they were able to reflect a lot easier, and their reflections on the past year, certainly in relation to school and their relationships with each other and their relationships with the teachers, were profound. It's the kind of thing where you feel like you've done your job because you've created an environment for them to thrive as opposed to feeling like you're driving the train.

Another teacher's high point came near the beginning of his time at KIPP "before I got on the radar of the administration," a time that allowed "relative autonomy . . . despite the fact that we were forced to have our doors open at all times" (1170). A former TFA teacher who lasted four months at KIPP had her high point when she was able to set aside the KIPP Model long enough to have a "little Friday afternoon party" for students who had earned a certain level of paycheck dollars for the week. "I felt like someone that they wanted to be around, so that was exciting and it felt good to just kind of be in the chill environment because it's so often so strict and so structured."

Another teacher who struggled "under the weight of guilt" for being part of imposing the harsh KIPP Model on students found her high point, too, in "forging relationships with students, rapport with students . . . [who] were consistently not meeting expectations." These students who "would've been called defiant, questioning authority, questioning the KIPP code" were able to come to trust this teacher:

> I felt like I established a rapport with them, in the sense that I think that over time it became clear to them that they feel secure questioning certain precepts of the KIPP code with me. They felt like rather than respond with either jargon or with accusing them of defiance, and threatening them with some kind of punishment, I felt like they, over time, felt they could come to me and have a real intellectual discussion about some of the rules that they were forced to deal with day in and day out. In terms of a high point at KIPP, those times when I would work with those students, not even work with them but have lunch with them one-on-one and just talk to them about their school and some of the issues they had to deal with in coming to a KIPP school, those were definite high points.

Other teachers found such opportunities rare or unavailable at all. One teacher, whose professional ethic centered on being "on the side of the student all the time" and on caring for each student "as if it was my own," remembered a situation that made it clear to him that his values were not shared by his school leader. In relating his experience, he shines a light on the questionable process used to shed noncompliant students without increasing the low suspension and expulsion statistics that KIPP offers as evidence that its schools do not "dump" problem students.

> One instance that made me feel extremely uncomfortable and I say that in general that as a teacher I want to be and really care about that child as if it was my own. And we're in a parent meeting one student in particular is being someone defiant and disrespectful to some teacher. And so she's been given all these conduct marks and is finally up for suspension, and we sit down with her mother to have this behavior plan meeting because basically the meeting allows us to put the child on a probation status of sorts, which is basically a step away from expulsion. The meeting really is a way to kind of start getting the student either compliant or on the way out. And that's basically said at this meeting with the parent and the principal—the school leader brings up this idea that we're not sure the student is a good fit here.

One former KIPP teacher found her memorable high points in bonding with a small cadre of colleagues who questioned or challenged KIPP rules or mandates that they considered "insane." As she related,

You know, I still talk to these people, and we keep in touch and kind of laugh at the things that happened. . . . Some of the teachers who were there from the years before who had stuck it out obviously are the type of people that can be controlled easily and like things to be in a certain way, kind of like bureaucrats, you know, people who could follow these rules, who are okay with them. . . . We just did not buy in.

Low points while teaching at KIPP were more frequent, more intense, and easier for teachers to recall than the highs. As one teacher said, "I couldn't pick out a single low point because they were so many." She followed up by talking about being "absolutely exhausted" as the low points during the three years she taught at KIPP. The total exhaustion culminated when she fell asleep on her way home and crashed into another car at a traffic light.

Her experiences at KIPP and her subsequent recovery from exhaustion left her with a renewed belief in public education, which she identified as a high point from working at KIPP: "I have not lost faith in the public school system—I've actually gained more faith by working at KIPP. It has tripled my faith in the public school system."

One teacher found her low and high points shifting back and forth as she focused on how other teachers treated, and mistreated, students at KIPP:

The kids . . . for the most part wanted to do well, struggled so hard and worked so hard. Harder than they would have ever worked in a regular public school, and still didn't do well, and seeing them be misunderstood by teachers who didn't understand much. There were a few teachers who thought the same way I did. One of them was let go. . . . Another one, she did her two years and she left there. There were a couple of really amazing teachers who did not need to shout or scream or belittle or berate, and did some amazing things with those kids and seeing that happen was a high point. That is what I thought I was getting into. An organization full of those kinds of people.

One teacher found out she would not be rehired only when she was the lone teacher during a faculty meeting who did not receive a copy of the revamped schedule for the coming year. Another teacher in performance arts who worked four days a week came to school on a Friday to find her computer had been taken away. When she complained, she was given another without a power cord and told the school had no power cords for that computer.

During an interview with Stephen Colbert in 2008, cofounder Dave Levin said that KIPP looks on its teachers as "rock stars" or "star athletes." This contrasts sharply with the way former teachers felt during their time at KIPP, as one teacher explained when she talked about her leaving KIPP to have a home and family, "those things that too many KIPP teachers are not getting." This former KIPP teacher who was in graduate school in education recalled that he "felt like I was not being treated like a rock star at all. I felt like I was a grunt in the military the way I was being treated."

He said that KIPP had been entirely "unwilling to make sacrifices at school to allow for a healthy lifestyle outside of school." He talked, too, of a conversation that he remembered having with a female colleague who also wanted marriage and children:

> We were both commenting on how the KIPP lifestyle was not going to provide us with the opportunity to meet someone and really foster a healthy relationship, and that having kids and working for KIPP are mutually exclusive. They don't go together. The only teachers at KIPP that I know that have kids do not work full time.

For this teacher, this situation was due to a paradox created by placing all KIPP's concern on student test score outcomes and none on teacher welfare, when teacher welfare is key to raising test scores:

> They're kind of creating this paradox or they're contradicting themselves because most schools know and most people know that good teachers raise test scores. Good teachers create good students, and the good teachers are the ones that you need to keep, but if you're not attracting the best teachers to your school and you're not keeping the best teachers at your school, then you're kind of shooting yourself in the foot, and the long hours . . . can only get you so far.
>
> So if KIPP has constant turnover with their teachers, then they're reinventing the wheel every year, and they can't keep those really good teachers that are responsible for the kids making such drastic improvement. . . . That's [the long hours] not what's improving test scores, and it's not the lesson plan. It's the teachers themselves.

One veteran teacher who was hired at one of the Memphis KIPP schools encountered criticism from the outset, when he was shocked to hear that his bulletin boards did not meet specifications. When that had been corrected, he found that school leaders did not like the way he was open with students and engaging them in debate and questioning, even though he had years of high school experience and the school leaders had only taught brief stints in the lower grades.

Criticism of teaching style was quickly followed by a critique of his content, which the school leaders found inappropriate for high school students, even though the readings used are included in most high school curricula for the subject taught. By October, this teacher was demoralized to the point of beginning to feel as if all his prior success and his "entire career had meant nothing."

Angered, he asked the school leaders why they had brought him to Memphis if they did not like what they had seen or heard during his practice teaching and interview. Their reply offered what this teacher considered a deep insult and his low point at KIPP, when they said, "We thought we could make you a KIPP teacher."

One teacher's low point came as a result of being chosen as the new teacher who would get "special help" from a consultant hired by KIPP to help the school better monitor student behaviors that this teacher had never known were so important until she came to KIPP.

> If they had their hands on their desk, or if they were tracking me when I was giving directions, or like, if their backpack was not on the back of their chair, or if they were wearing their sweater instead of their sweater being in their cubby, or on the back of their chair, or if they still were writing when I had said, "pencils down."

The consultant had what he advertised as a sure-fire system based on constant narration of good and bad behaviors that all teachers were to apply. This new teacher admitted she was both skeptical and somewhat resistant, which ended in her having to wear an earpiece as the consultant stood in the back of the room whispering instructions into her ear:

> It just really bothered me that I had to do it this specific way, and it got to the point where he had me wearing like an earpiece, and he was standing in the back of the room, watching me lead my class, and I was so uncomfortable, I was sweating, and then, I had to do this sequence of directions the way that they wanted me to, and he would tell me into my earpiece what I was supposed to be saying to the kids. And it was just really weird, because there were like 27 kids; they were really good kids, but they had to be like perfect, and I—I just—I didn't believe in it, and I didn't agree with it, and [in] meetings with him I was crying, talking to this consultant, saying like I just don't believe in this—I don't get it, and I was just really encouraged, like well, this is how we're doing it, so this is how we need you to do it.

Several teachers related incidents of losing control or of nearly losing control as they tried to keep perfect order while meeting all the expectations of school leaders. One teacher said,

> I personally had an incident in which I lost control with some students in terms of just getting upset with them. And I used a curse word and I got very, very, very, very, very angry. I lost control and so that was probably the low point.

Another teacher's loss of control climaxed in a screaming match with a seventh-grader that had to be broken up by a parent volunteer. It all started when a student "smacked her lips," which was an offense that required a deduction from the student's paycheck:

And if you smack your lips, that was a deduction on your paycheck. I walked around with this clipboard all the time, and I had my pen and everybody's name on it. If someone did something they weren't supposed to be doing, then you'd deduct their paycheck. Which can be done in a nonchalant way or it can be done in a very clear way or it can be done in an escalation manner. I tried very hard to not escalate. . . . I deducted the two points from her paycheck.

She rolled her eyes and started complaining. That leads to another deduction, and she just escalated and I played along with her. Somehow she started screaming; at KIPP that kind of behavior is entirely unacceptable. The typical method, which is something that was somewhat unnatural for me, but something that I employed, was to not let her do that. In front of this whole class we got in this screaming match. I obviously moved her outside, but the kids in the class could hear it until one of the parent coordinators came in with, "Let me take care of this, let me remove her."

I remember going home that night thinking, or I remember in that moment when the parent took this girl away from me, that I had just not only overstepped the bounds of professionalism, but I was extremely embarrassed by my behavior. I think it's probably indicative of some of my experiences, where as much as we loved those kids and we just tried to love them as hard as we could. Everything came from that place of wanting more for our kids. But a hard lesson that I've had to learn over the years is that you can't want more for other people if they don't want that for themselves. As a teacher, you've got to guide them there, but you also have to set high expectations. Again, you've got to meet them where they are and certainly not get into screaming matches with seventh-graders. I felt embarrassed and I think it called into question for me a lot of what we were doing at school.

When asked, specifically, what was called into question for her by this incident, she replied,

This whole notion of extreme discipline. There were some places where we were able to create an environment where there's a love of learning. But by having, exerting, so much control over the environment and the students, I wondered what happened to them when that kind of discipline wasn't instilled, that kind of control wasn't [there], when those reins were taken off when they went to high school, what would happen.

And shouldn't we, as educators, be trying to prepare them to be more independent than we were. I think we felt like a lot of our kids were coming to us in crisis, and they needed stability and they needed somebody who they could trust. I think we did absolutely our best. I can't imagine having done more. But sometimes more is not the answer; sometimes less is the answer. The idea of more rigor, more discipline, more control, more stability, I think, was not appropriate for our kids, over time.

A young teacher who had difficulty adjusting to KIPP Model discipline after two years as a TFA teacher in a public school attributed her struggle to her different style of interactions with students, which had been more persuasive than confrontational. When she was called to a conference with her grade-level chair, who had the same amount of teacher experience as she, she was told that her discipline problems were due to students' lack of respect for her, which derived from her inability to develop relationships with students.

The grade-level chair's advice was for her to follow his lead, which was to drive students home and to buy them food from McDonald's. This teacher found this supervisor's advice "preposterous." "And [to] have this guy my age with the same experience tell me that I didn't know what I was doing or . . . to limit a child's ability to understand a human being based on whether or not they're buying them food at the end of the day just, to me, is so inappropriate."

Another teacher who gave her all to KIPP and found it not enough had received honors in her previous teaching position. Yet at KIPP, she could not seem to ever satisfy the school leader, who had taken her to lunch when she started teaching at the school: "He spent like an hour with me. And I know he's busy. He took that time because he wanted to check on me. And I felt valuable." By December, however, her dream of being a KIPP teacher had turned to nightmare, and she was doing all she could to stay ahead of total exhaustion, while trying to do everything that was expected of her. The low point came during her final conference with the school leader, just days before she was fired:

> He sat down with me. He's, like, "we know you're working hard, but effort does not equal results. And when you look this stressed, not showering," and the way that he looked at me, I felt like he was commenting about my weight and my clothes and my appearance. He's like, "What does it look like to the kids when you're their leader?"
>
> And I think that was the low point because I really had given the kids every single thing that I could think of. I brought every trick with me. And I gave them every minute. And, you know, I felt betrayed by this principal who had sat with me, and he cared about me, I thought, and valued me. And I felt like a complete failure. So that was the low.

The teachers I spoke with were deeply affected by their experiences at KIPP. And while some found points of light that illuminate their stories, for the most part, there remains a darkness that pervaded the narrative spaces that these teachers created as they recalled their time at KIPP.

> I look back at those years, and for that year and a half, it just seems like a dark period. My blue period. And there was some good, but for the most I feel anxious when I think back. It was a very hard time. There were other things going on like I was saying in my private life . . . it was hard because I was never home, it was hard to take care of either the job or my personal life well. It was just a bad time.

Chapter Eight

What Was It Like to Teach at KIPP?

I just feel like KIPP has left this doubt that no matter what I do, I'm just not good enough.
—1183

Most former KIPP teachers expressed grave reservations about recommending KIPP to others as a place to teach. The question I asked all teachers was a variant of this one: *If I were a friend interested in applying for a teaching job at KIPP, and I asked you, "What was it like there?" what would you tell me?* One teacher told me that he loved "the people there," but he did not love the KIPP system that made life hard:

> Ten-hour days with students is definitely taxing on the teacher. You have no life. KIPP is your life. Even when you are done with the children at 5:00, you might have [students] after school or at the same time you are definitely developing lesson plans. . . . Because the way they have it set up, we didn't really get time to plan our formal lessons; we were hired in June, and I started in June. I didn't really get the time to really plan any kind of lessons at all . . . we had a week's worth of planning but that first week before school started we went to a KIPP Summit.
>
> You really don't have a life at all; that is what I would definitely tell them. It's easy for you to get a job with them because you don't have to have education as your major, so I would tell them yes, that's a positive about it and yes you do get paid more than you would in the [public] school system, but it's still a lot of work, a lot of work.

Other teachers were more graphic in their response to the question. A teacher who remained under the care of a therapist when I talked with her said this:

I would say that working at KIPP was the most horrible experience of my life. I would tell people that, I would tell a friend especially, that the message is good with KIPP, that you want to send all kids to and through college, but it is at such great personal sacrifice that it's—it crushed me. I would encourage anyone else to just stop. It wasn't even getting fired that was the worst thing for me. It was knowing that I was told that if the kids didn't go to college, that it was my fault. I just think that anybody else who wants to do good could do better good at their own school rather than destroy themselves by working at KIPP.

Others also experienced the heavy load borne by KIPP teachers who are told that they, alone, must assume responsibility for the success or failure of students. The heavy load of responsibility placed on young shoulders produces pathologies and degrees of burnout, or flameout, uncommon at regular public schools.

Another teacher was particularly eloquent about the guilt that school leaders nurtured at the KIPP school where she taught. She described teaching at KIPP as "hard, draining." When asked to elaborate on how it was draining, this teacher noted that any complaint about unsustainable pressures at KIPP was viewed by the school leaders and colleagues as exhibiting weakness or coming off as "whining." The thought of offering any protestation, then, for unbearable conditions brought with it a sense of guilt for not being on board with "team and family." It also indicated a "sign of a flaw in character," which produced more guilt, and for this teacher, was "almost more exhausting than the work itself."

I hesitate to do this because I feel like it comes off as whining, a lack of work ethic, but then I'll also address that in a moment. Obviously there's the issue of the hours. The school that I was, and I think this is pretty formulaic from most KIPP schools but in my case it was I was at school every day from 6:45 AM until most days 6:00 PM at night, some days later, into 8:00 and 9:00 PM. I would talk about Saturday school. I would talk about the fact that I was on call until 10:00 PM every night for homework questions or for calls from parents. I would talk about two hour classes. Each class that I taught was, three days out of the week each class was usually a two hour and ten minute block. I would talk about all those things.

But for me personally, and I think I addressed this in my original email to you as well, and I don't want to get too much into that—it's a bit too meta-cognitive—but there's this idea in the culture, at least on the staff level, if for any moment you are flagging under that pressure, if you find yourself feeling drained because of the hours or because of the frenzy of work, that's not natural—that's a cause for guilt. That's a sign of a flaw in character, or a lack of commitment to the students or a lack of work ethic. It was draining on all the levels of the particulars in terms of the time, the energy, but it was also draining in that sense of I was always struggling in my own mind with this idea of, "should I feel guilty about the fact that I'm exhausted?" And the guilt was almost more exhausting than the actual work itself.

There was a supreme emotional exhaustion that surpassed the physical exhaustion, that surpassed all the other elements. Had it not been for the emotional exhaustion, I have no doubt that I could have felt more successful in my work. The odd thing is on paper and according to my administrators, I was successful. It's not that I had an unsuccessful year at KIPP and left with a bad record or with a stain across my experience. There was that emotional exhaustion; it was too much.

Other teachers focused directly on the loss of social and family life that comes with teaching at KIPP. One teacher who found KIPP "oppressive" said teaching there is "demanding to the point where you're asked to leave all your family and social aspects behind." Another said, "You had best be ready to give up your social life." Another teacher waved his warning flag, in particular, at teachers with public school experience.

Should I come work at KIPP? I would probably say don't do it. You've already gotten used to life at a public school. You're used to that schedule. You're used to having a life outside of school and it's not an adjustment that's going to go well. If you were somebody who had spent some time in the military, if you were someone who had done TFA or had taught overseas in a third world country, then I might be a little more inclined to recommend teaching at KIPP, but I think for the most part if someone asked if they should work at KIPP, I offer a lot of warning. I say you're not going to sleep at all. It's going to be pretty brutal, real tough. You wind up sacrificing your physical health and most of your social life.

One former KIPP teacher said that others had asked him the "What was it like there?" question in the past.

I told them I wouldn't wish that experience on my worst enemy. That's exactly what I say every time, I wouldn't wish it on my worst enemy. And I have no enemies but I wouldn't wish it if I had an enemy. I wouldn't put anyone through that. Anyone. It was probably—you give up your life and not only do you give up your life you're giving it up for nothing. It's not like you're seeing results. It's not like you're being rewarded appropriately. I mean there's no reward for that type of work. It's just like you're being used up and thrown out. It's like they're going to use you up as much as you can take until you realize okay, I'm being used, and then you get out. My friends quit asking now . . . everybody knows what KIPP is like now so I don't get that question much anymore.

According to one of the former KIPP teachers who served in a number of leadership roles at KIPP, including teacher leader and head of professional development, there are three categories of teachers who "make it" at KIPP:

The teachers that make it at KIPP fall in one of three categories, a) the extremely type A personality. They are dedicated. They love KIPP. . . . They may have a Teach for America background. I can also tell you that 40% of our teachers are Teach for America Corps Members. . . . So, there's those type A's that are just used to this environment and used to self-sacrifice ideology.

The second group is experienced veteran teachers that have been everywhere, public school, private school. They've dealt with the most extreme work environments and the most relaxed, and they genuinely care about the kids and what they do. So they have success because they've had the experience to work on classroom management, to build relationships, they're there.

Then there is the scariest type: those that just stay in it and feel that there is nothing else left better to do. They do not have a life. They don't talk to their family regularly. They don't eat healthy at all. . . . They are at work until 9–10 o'clock at night. KIPP is their life. Anything KIPP, they're there, even on Saturdays, Sundays. So, inside they're there. . . . They're just there because they don't feel a way to get out of it, or it's their life.

Although the prevailing views among the teachers were deeply critical of KIPP, some teachers had positive and negative things to say about teaching at KIPP. Almost all the teachers I talked with missed their students at KIPP, even though most expressed regret that the organizational parameters at KIPP made it difficult to get to know students. Most expressed positive regard for colleagues at KIPP, even though some stories were shared about mistreatment of students and unprofessional conduct by some administrators and, to a lesser degree, teachers. One teacher, in fact, said she would recommend teaching at KIPP, if the school was more established and less dysfunctional than the one from which she had been fired. Another said teaching at KIPP "was worth the dedication at that point in my life," but he also said,

It's work—that was it. I did KIPP and I didn't take days off even when I was sick. So I'd say, yeah, I'm glad you're doing it, you got the fervor, I think you can do amazing things, but understand that your sacrifices are everything from less time to talk to your family, your girlfriend, going out—it's a very single-minded focus.

Self-sacrifice among KIPP teachers sometimes threatens the well-being of others. During a time when another teacher was ill with a fever and flu-like symptoms, he continued going to work at KIPP. When I asked him if he worried about possibly spreading his illness to students, his response offered a glimpse of the paradoxical situation KIPP teachers find themselves in, when "doing whatever it takes" and "putting yourself in harm's way if the job calls for it" can have serious consequences for those who are ostensibly the beneficiaries of such self-sacrifice.

You know I took care of myself and I kind of got myself quarantined in the classroom, and as far as endangering the kids, I was not worried about getting them sick, to be totally honest, because they'd gotten me sick. A lot of them were gone from school already, and a lot of them were already sick and they could take the day off. If they were coming home with something, they could stay home and rest and have some Theraflu or go to the hospital if it was an extreme case.

No doubt parents of children sickened as a result of this unhealthy practice would find little consolation in this teacher's dedication to duty.

One teacher described teaching at KIPP as "kind of soul crushing." He pointed to the anxiety that he developed about going to work, which affected his love for teaching, which began in his teen years. He said "the things I was asked to do," such as enforcing silence, left him with such anxiety that he didn't want to go to work, even though, as he said, "teaching was all I ever wanted to do." When asked to elaborate on how he felt the job was soul crushing, this teacher told me about being "extremely uncomfortable" after a series of meetings that began with a child who was being defiant and disrespectful.

The mother of the child had been called in when the school leader had decided that the child would be placed on probation status, which meant that the mother would know that the next step would be expulsion if the child's behavior was not corrected. During the conference, the mother tearfully shared that her daughter was seeing a counselor, who suspected sexual abuse earlier in the child's life. The child's counselor, too, had thought placement in a KIPP school was inappropriate from the beginning due to her emotional instability.

The response by KIPP administrators was to recommend the child be sent home with a KIPP staff member to live until the child could be "straightened out." At a subsequent meeting with the child's mother present, KIPP's administration "told the mother of the child that this therapist wasn't good for her and that they should get a new therapist . . . because of the therapist's disagreements with KIPP and the effect it was having on the girl." This meeting occurred with no school counselor or school psychologist present.

Another more experienced teacher had a similar experience of anxiety and dread that led him to not "want to go to school." He said that his experience and age allowed him to understand that "what they were doing was wrong."

In terms of browbeating the teachers every day in the meetings, it became more of a process between the administration and the teachers than it did between the teachers and the students. There was very little learning, what I would call learning going on, from what I saw. Anybody can memorize, but they're not doing anything with the material. And if you came to me and said, listen, you know, should I apply, everyone is different. Every KIPP school is probably different, because any time that you have a different KIPP school, you're going to have different administrators. You're going to have different people. I would just tell you to be very careful. You know? The hook is the money. And like I said, they say all the right things.

Another teacher compared teaching at KIPP to being placed every day in a pressure cooker.

> My KIPP experience was extremely intense in a very good way and in a very difficult way. We, to some degree, created a pressure cooker there and that again had some rewards, and then it also presented some challenges to the long-term viability of the school and for the teachers, themselves. . . . Regarding academics, it felt like we really pushed them hard and achieved some tremendous gains with some students. . . . At least according to some measurements.
>
> Exciting, and we almost felt like we were, or felt like I was, doing important work. I felt like this was not just some job that I did from 9 to 5, or 8 to 6 or whatever time. This was a job. This was very much wrapped up with my life and how I saw myself. It became an identity, which just like being part of a family, has some pros and also has some real challenges. From the challenges standpoint, I felt like my experience teaching at KIPP was unsustainable, ultimately.

Another teacher wasn't nearly so nuanced to telling me what teaching at KIPP was like: "I would say it was horrible, that I hated it, and I wouldn't recommend it to anyone, unless you were like masochistic. . . . These are the reasons I really hate it, and I wouldn't recommend: The hours are totally unsustainable, and especially if you're new, and you're developing curriculum. There's not enough hours in the day to get everything done."

Another teacher who shared stories of her and students killing cockroaches and rats in her KIPP classroom responded to the question of what it was like by shouting mock advice to anyone contemplating working at KIPP, "No, run away, don't do that, absolutely not." When asked what it was like teaching at KIPP, she said,

> You know the first word that comes to mind is hell. H-E-L-L, hell it was. There was so much about it that was so good and promising in the beginning, and I got hooked into that from the minute I saw the news piece on them—you know the interview, and coming and seeing the classrooms, it was just so different than what I had seen, but the dirty little secrets are what you don't know until you are in those trenches.

Some teachers focused on logistical or organizational issues when asked what it was like to teach at KIPP. One described her situation as a new teacher in a new school as terrifying: "This is a new school, so imagine every system, every schedule, everything that makes a school run from bell schedules to when to schedule meetings with parents, when to schedule professional development, etc., etc., etc. Imagine everything through the school none of it's established yet, and you're literally creating it as you go."

Another had taught in a temporary facility that was shared by community programs after school. Security and order were real problems, and she found her materials misplaced, disorganized, or missing often.

> Our poor art teacher he had no permanent room. Our PE teacher, the same thing. Actually our PE teacher couldn't even be there every day, so the kids only had PE I think like twice a week, which is ridiculous for middle schoolers, they need it every day. . . . Our Science teacher was in I guess like the arts and crafts room, so there was like paint all over the place that she had to clean up every morning. . . . And there was like dollhouses and toys all over my room that I had to clean up every morning. I had to teach off of a baker's rack where I hung my dry erase board, which really wasn't even big enough for the kids and everybody could lock up their stuff at night and because I was upstairs and there was no elevator I couldn't, so I had to push everything to the side.
>
> There were no textbooks, so you have to make up everything, like your own handouts, your own activities, your own whatever, so I just remember having to copy all the time. And then just the actual day-to-day KIPP mindset or structure was very hard for me to deal with and ultimately that is why I left. Like the kids had to line up in the mornings and there was like no playground for them. It was just like a parking lot and then a gravel place where they lined up and they had to be in a silent line and there was something that we had to give them to do. So like they were reading a passage or they were solving math problems and they were doing it just standing up and there was nowhere for them to sit.

As noted earlier, former teachers found the stress levels at KIPP unsustainable. One teacher who wore a number of hats because of prior experience as a teacher described teaching at KIPP as "like being in a tornado."

> It's just this funnel. It keeps moving. It picks up different things in its path. As a KIPP teacher, every single day is different. You're picking up multiple things in your path. You have multiple hats. Every teacher in my building watches and advises academically and behaviorally 15 to 20 kids in their grade level. They are teaching anywhere from six to eight classes a day. Then, they are sponsoring either athletic events or a club. Then, they lead tutorials in the morning and in the afternoon. Some are not eating lunch. I have gone many days without eating lunch. I have spent until 11 and 12 at night at the school. I have been at the school as early since 4 a.m. in the morning. I have had lesson planning meetings before church on Sunday mornings. I have known some of my colleagues who stay up into 1 a.m. Then not to mention if you're qualified or you have experience, they love giving you additional hats and titles without necessary pay or time to do it, so it's just this big moving tunnel. A revolving funnel of just stuff all the time.

THIRTY CHILDREN IN THE BASEMENT

The disturbing analogies that former teachers used to describe what it is like to teach at KIPP provide further indicators that the picture presented by corporate think tanks and their marketing firms do not focus on the human realities at KIPP schools and the No Excuses emulators. This is partly due to choreographed, deceptive messaging aimed to protect and promote the KIPP brand at all costs.

One teacher said that, in retrospect, KIPP reminded her of the *The Stepford Wives*, the story of a seemingly perfect American neighborhood on the outside, where all the wives, however, have been replaced by total-compliance robots that perform just as instructed by their husbands. Another teacher expressed deep concerns about the repercussions of promoting a false image that is used to mislead the public and to advance an ideological agenda that could further damage communities struggling to remain viable.

This cultivation of an image of perfection is demonstrated in one teacher's recounting of how all the school's students with behavior issues were moved to an empty school basement when important visitors or potential investors were on campus. During visits that lasted as long as three hours, approximately thirty children were rounded up and sent to the basement, while regular classes carried on above them. To make sure that no infractions of rules were visible during visits, class changes were suspended until visitors left the building. Here is our exchange:

TEACHER: My experience was so different from my close friends who were employed at different KIPP schools. But the people that were at my specific school seemed to have a similar experience to me, which is terrible. But I have, like I said, I have a lot of close friends that are still involved in KIPP. . . . but I think that there's a lot swept under the rug as far as things that also aren't so great.

JH: And what do you see as swept under the rug?

TEACHER: You know, there's just cultural things like, I can only speak to what I experienced in my day-to-day, and so that was a lot of yelling, a lot of berating students, a lot of, you know, physically confronting students.

We used to have a special schedule when we had visitors in the building. For instance, sometimes we'd have, you know, investors or bigwigs walking through the building. And so we would have a separate schedule where we would pick out all the behavior issue kids and take them down into the basement for the duration of the visitors' visit, to kind of keep them out of the way. So you know, that's one very, like, clear example of sweeping something under the rug.

JH: Can you tell me how that worked?

TEACHER: Yeah. So in the morning, we would receive an email or a special schedule that said VIB schedule, Visitor in Building schedule. And it would basically list all of the students that needed to be in the basement area, and it would tell us the specific times that they were supposed to be there. And we would also, for instance, we would not transition from class to class if there was a visitor, because the transitions from class to class would sometimes be, you know, kids are kids, and so they would sometimes not listen, or they would run, or whatever the case is. And our administration didn't want the visitors to see anything less than perfection. And so we would hold students in the classroom when normally they'd be transitioning from class to class. So the visitors didn't get the impression that the school was anything less than very well managed.

JH: Right. So what was in the basement? What did the students do in the basement?

TEACHER: That's a great question. I never, fortunately I guess, was never in charge of managing those students. But in the basement, what was down there was just, you know, there was basically nothing. I mean, there was a carpeted area. And I don't know what they did down there, to be honest.

JH: And how many students were sent down there?

TEACHER: I believe our school had about 300 students when I was there. And it probably, you know, less than 30.

JH: And these students were selected how? Based on what?

TEACHER: From my impression, it was that they were, based on their behavior. So if they were a student that acted out frequently, they would be sent down into the basement for the duration of the visitor's stay.

JH: OK, so these were called Visitor in Building days? VIB?

TEACHER: Yeah, VIB schedule.

JH: OK. And what was the longest time that you remember staying in a class, that you weren't allowed to switch?

TEACHER: Two or three hours, depending on the visitors and how long they would be there.

The KIPP Foundation and corporate supporters of the KIPP Model rationalize or ignore the disturbing stories that have come from KIPP's teachers, parents, and students. Too many remain entirely unaware of the darkness beneath the bright smiles that greet visitors at KIPP. Feinberg's and Levin's public pronouncements continue to ignore the fact that former KIPP teachers describe their work at KIPP as "extremely discouraging," "terrifying," "draining," "like sprinting a marathon for two years," "oppressive," "h-e-l-l," "a very high stress place," a "pressure cooker," a "concentration camp," a "tornado," a "soul-crushing" place, the "most horrible experience of my life," the "worst years teaching ever," "something you wouldn't wish on your worst enemy," a "constant surveillance" workplace where teachers felt like they were "being used up" without any opportunity to "replenish" or maintain "family ties."

Though it is not uncommon to find a continuing belief among these former KIPP teachers that they were doing, or attempting to do, important work at KIPP, there remains a consensus among the teachers I talked with that manic organizational parameters, hidebound rules, and inexperienced, hypercritical leaders stood in the way of getting much of that important work done. When one teacher near the end of her second and final year was asked how she would change her KIPP experiences if she could, she said she would have resigned earlier:

> I feel like I tried my hardest and I tried my best, but the thing that is frustrating is that I always felt like no matter how hard I worked and no matter how hard the kids worked, that it was never good enough. Like I am never being like excellent, even though I am working as hard as I possibly can, and I am putting all this energy and effort into it, I feel like I am not appreciated and I feel like it is never good enough.
>
> I think that is just something that I have recently realized is that I will, to their eyes, I will never be good enough, so I just have to not care so much as to what they think and just kind of do things the way that I think they need to be done in my classroom.

Without a constant infusion of new teachers to replace all those who burn out quickly under such grueling conditions and all those who come to believe they will never be good enough to meet expectations, KIPP would have to shut its doors. The role of Teach for America and programs based on Teach for America's hyperabbreviated preparation are crucial, then, for the continued survival of the total-compliance No Excuses charter schools built on the KIPP Model. We turn, then, to an examination of Teach for America's place in corporate education reform's paternalistic agenda for pre-K–12 schools.

Chapter Nine

Teach for America's Socialization and Manipulation

Barbara Veltri

It's like the Peace Corps. But, you know, creepier.
—D. Chernicoff, *Yale Daily News* (2006)

This chapter chronicles the evolution of Teach for America's (TFA) rebranding, from a teaching-as-service nonprofit, to a leadership network with a voracious appetite for expanding and creating new revenue streams. I examine how Teach for America's Corps Members are selected and socialized to support the organization's revamped trajectory away from teacher supply to leadership expansion. Data for this chapter included a range of sources, from insider interviews to TFA annual reports, business plans, tax returns, websites, public records, and other documents. A cautionary tale illuminates how private venture philanthropy and "public good" corporate education reform initiatives are managed and manipulated.

THE MISSION DESIGN OF AMERICA'S #1 EDUCATIONAL NONPROFIT

Twenty-five years ago Princeton University sociology major Wendy Kopp founded Teach for America. Its mission: recruit, train, and place recent college graduates without education credentials into poor rural and urban schools for two-year teaching commitments (Kopp, 2003). The new nonprofit organization, subsequently dubbed America's National Teaching Corps (Veltri, 2010), was charged with addressing the shortage of qualified teachers in underserved regions of the United States (Kopp, 2003; Veltri, 2010). In

1994, Teach for America was granted 501(c)(3) status as a nonprofit organization, which permitted donors to claim exemptions from income taxes, too.

Teach for America targeted areas to field-test the education reform agenda in America's poor communities, where high populations of children of color reside. These urban and rural areas were never properly funded in any way imaginable, and they had gone mostly unnoticed by the business community until Ms. Kopp recruited recent grads from select colleges to begin teaching there.

With substantial financial support from corporations and foundations in hand by the mid-1990s, Ms. Kopp focused her attention on garnering support from the federal government. This ongoing support from the federal government was provided principally through the Corporation for National and Community Service (CNCS), commonly referred to as AmeriCorps (Kopp, 2003). Under an arrangement with AmeriCorps, TFA teachers may receive up to $11,290 during their two-year stints to repay student loans. Too, TFA has received generous federal grants. In 2010, alone, TFA and KIPP (Wendy Kopp is married to KIPP's president and CEO and TFA alum Richard Barth) each received separate $50 million Investing in Innovation grants from the U.S. Department of Education.

THE SOCIALIZATION OF TEACH FOR AMERICA'S CORPS

Socialization of corps members-as-future-leaders in the reform pipeline depends heavily on incorporating a unifying message and philosophy to its incoming teacher trainees (Kopp, 2003; Kopp & Farr, 2011; Brewer, 2014). Teach for America safeguards the training of its recruits at a dozen Corps Training Institute locations across the country. A singular, robust, and paternalistic socialization of its Corps Member teachers remains a foundational element to the mission of TFA.

Toward this end, Teach for America espouses its own brand, image, logo, color scheme, scripted training program, division of labor, sanctions and rewards, and public persona. In 2014, Teach for America accepted 15 percent of its applicant pool (Teach for America, 2014). Corps applicants are selected based upon particular TFA-identified criteria, and principal among them is the crucial measure of "fit" (Dobbie, 2011), a metric based largely on belief and commitment:

> The last TFA measure is fit, which measures whether an applicant believes TFA's goals are attainable through the TFA approach. The fit variable is scored using overall interviewer impressions of knowledge, and commitment to the belief in the ability of children to achieve, and the belief in the TFA focus on raising student academic achievement. (p. 6)

TFA encourages a oneness mind-set that relies upon an expectation that a singular, unifying belief will be commonly held as a prerequisite for success and belonging (Veltri, 2015) within a "community of feeling" that breeds "identical judgment" (Lyotard, 1991). Teach for America's insiders recognize this "community of feeling" as the crux of the enculturation into the TFA philosophy (Brewer, 2014; Sondel, 2014; Veltri, 2010). This socialization most often leads to an ongoing commitment that persists beyond one's two-year teaching affiliation with the organization.

Teach for America's socialization efforts promote (1) corps conformity, (2) corps identity, (3) corps competition, (4) corps collaboration, (5) corps cohesiveness, and (6) corps cliques. Insiders are adept at perceiving contradictions between TFA's official narrative and the methods used to attain its ends:

> TFA is an incredibly hierarchical organization where there is a tremendous amount of leadership by passive-aggressive use of fear. You can really see this at Institute, particularly with the school directors who are under intense pressure from the Institute's managing director to produce "transformational gains" from students in, literally, 10 days of teaching. (Andrew)

Teach for America's "truths" refine, streamline, and reinforce a singular message, and that message speaks often, speaks louder, speaks to a network of supporters in high places, and rarely allows for differing viewpoints. Many TFA insiders face a dualism in how they respond to and/or acknowledge their own self-efficacy as Corps Members and alumni (White, 2013).

Some comply, embrace, or cope during their committed affiliation with TFA, doing what they have to do to get by (Brewer, 2014; White, 2013; Veltri, 2010; Veltri, 2015). Others subvert surreptitiously and are determined not to lose themselves in the TFA enculturation, and these Corps Members "see" through the information presented to the public. Corps Members who assume personae that remain compliant and eager to embrace TFA methods and nonteaching duties during the two-year TFA teaching assignments find favor in post-teaching roles within the TFA organization.

THE ROLE OF THE TFA CORPS MEMBER IN EDUCATION REFORM

TFA adheres to a strategic policy of recruiting young, recent college graduates who generally do not challenge the organization during their first two years, while they "learn the ropes" in order to later reap the benefits of "being a good Corps Member." "Good" Corps Members complete the task at hand with enthusiasm and later recognize financial advantages of their TFA affiliation, post teaching. Teach for America also employs niche recruiters who target evangelicals, dreamers, veterans, Native Americans, and LGBT candidates (Teach for America, 2014).

Teach for America's applicants are not recruited just for the short-term teaching positions they accept but are, in effect, recruited for their future worth to the TFA network and its agenda. Many TFA teachers are groomed by the organization and vetted for leadership positions following their two years of service. Regardless, all Corps Members are expected to remain loyal to the cause:

> So like yes, we're supposed to keep it, education reform, in the forefront and no matter what you do after the 2 years are up, you're supposed to stay focused on education because you've been there. So you can take any influence you may have in your future and use that towards education reform. (Jackie)

A barrage of emails inundates Corps Members with opportunities for leadership and policy roles within the TFA alumni network of charters, including KIPP and other total-compliance schools. Teach for America has become the feeder system (Taylor, 2010) that is crucial to sustaining charter management organizations: "Simply put, Teach for America, Inc. has become an employment agency for charter schools" (p. 1). One TFA teacher said,

> Of the most touted alumni in a particular community, how many work in public school districts in a position that has a direct impact on teaching and learning? Most of the heroic tales of TFA alums come from charter systems, "education reform" groups, and roles in government bodies that are undermining public education. For example, here in _____, the alums who are most held up as examples of the power of TFA are charter school founders and leaders, people who work for the state's charter school association, or head up not-for-profits focused on education reform that are very cozy with those who most threaten our schools. (Caryn)

With five weeks of pedagogical preparation that includes practice teaching time, Teach for America attempts to drive home the message to power constituencies and legislative bodies that TFA novices should be considered as highly qualified and effective beginning teachers. This mantra reverberates as TFA "truth," even as novice Corps Members struggle in out-of-field teaching assignments, special education or resource placements, and other site-based duties for which they are not qualified.

> The program is atrocious—the TFA training is completely worthless and inadequate when it comes to actually preparing people how to teach, they are so full of biased/worthless statistics, the staff is a bunch of cliché-spouting TFA robots, etc., and the list goes on. (Darrell)

Corps Member insiders report that the organization creates lists of those considered for leadership positions, and leadership begets privilege. Elisa Villanueva Beard, co-CEO of Teach for America, states, "Civic leaders call regularly and say, 'We want to know who is available and ready to take on a bigger role' . . . And we will always have names at the ready" (Simon, 2013, p. 2). TFA acts as an incubator for education-industry business and educational governance organizations, political offices, NGOs, nonprofit corporations, foundations, and think tanks.

Tracy-Elizabeth Clay, TFA's General Counsel, addressed Teach for America's alumni at Harvard Law School, focusing on the organization's initiatives to better harness TFA's alumni in law: "The long-term vision is to create a 'talent pool' from which school districts, CMOs and legal advocacy groups can draw from" (Teach for Us, 2012). Corporate education insider Rick Hess predicts, "Five, ten years out, we're going to be talking about hundreds of TFA [political] candidates in all likelihood" (Wieder, 2012).

ALLIANCES WITH FRIENDS IN HIGH PLACES

Teach for America did not work in isolation to achieve its goals. Its "mission" was, and continues to be advanced, by a network of supporters from the corporate, legislative, university, media, and political spectrum. For over a decade, Teach for America has directed its efforts toward expanding the donor pool and to deepening political leaders' commitment to TFA's policies. It has also concentrated on quadrupling leadership placement of TFA alums across the entire political landscape, while protecting the brand and successfully contributing to the stream of alumni-led Charter Management Organizations (CMOs).

TFA has continued to grow by charging fees for teachers it delivers to school districts in poor communities, while urging network alliances to help TFA continue its rhetorical campaign to eliminate educational inequity— even as childhood poverty in the United States of America grows worse (Wieder, 2012; Jehlen, 2012).

Those who capitalize on education innovation propel Teach for America's mission. Quazzo, Cohn, Horne, and Moe's (2012) Global Silicon Valley Advisors report that the global education market is worth $4 trillion and have partnered with Teach for America: "Talent has poured into the sector from leading not-for-profits like Teach for America and elsewhere where bright, talented young people have witnessed educational inequity and can visualize solutions" (p. 24).

Most TFA post-teaching educational careers projectile is classroom based. Evidence suggests that TFA has become less of an alternative pathway to teaching children in poverty and more of an insulated training ground for corporate, media, and philanthropic hierarchies motivated to reform public education across the PK–16 landscape (Kamenetz, 2014; Kovacs, 2006; Simon, 2013; Wieder, 2012; TFA, 2012). Increasing numbers of TFA's alumni are leading large-scale school districts, state education departments, and virtual and charter school networks (Simon, 2013).

With generous support of their alliance of policymakers, corporations, foundations, and philanthropists, Teach for America has remained flush with cash as it has grown its network of teachers and former Corps Members dedicated to the TFA mission. So what happened to America's *teaching* corps? The nonprofit's energies today are more directed toward recruiting potential leaders; building an enduring movement; and seeking and finding funding and favor from corporations, lobbyists, university presidents and deans, the media, philanthropists, and national and state policymakers. As one source reported, "What is happening beyond the 2-year commitment seems to be much more important now than ever before. What has changed is how much emphasis TFA places on this goal (at the expense of the shorter-term goal of developing successful classroom teachers)" (Teach for Us, 2012).

At the same time, TFA has grown increasingly focused on countering document concerns and criticism (Joseph, 2014) through "obsessive PR games to cover up its lack of results in order to justify greater expansion." Teach for America perpetuates a revolving teacher syndrome and "disruptive turnover cycles" (para. 1) that does nothing to limit the educational inequity to which TFA pays lip service. Teach for America is not a solution to what ails education in America's poorest communities, yet policymakers and the public are persuaded to believe so.

From the U.S. Department of Education to Congress to the Office of the President, and across state executive and legislative bodies, TFA finds favor. As one former head of Florida's Office of Evaluation and Assessment told me, "TFA are the sweethearts of education policy. People fall over themselves to support them." That favor translates to a burgeoning financial base. Teach for America reported $1.15 billion in revenue for 2009 to 2013. Teach for America invests millions in public relations to keep its critics at bay.

Teach for America runs a conveyer belt of new teachers in and out of communities who learn to teach on poor people's children (Veltri, 2010). The overwhelming and overwhelmed TFA novice teachers enter communities and schools in underresourced areas, across America, without strategies, support, or training. One mentor of special education said,

> Everyone of our E.D. (Emotionally Disabled) kids is taught by TFA. I went into a class of emotionally disturbed middle schoolers. The teacher is TFA, a very bright, recent grad, top-tier school, TFA. The kids were very quiet when I walked in. I sensed that something was wrong. The teacher imploded on the

kids. They were not permitted to eat in the cafeteria. They are E.D. You cannot threaten the kids, but she was doing that in front of me. So, why is the district hiring them? 43% are new TFA, and 23% are the 2nd year TFA. (Dr. B. mentor, SPED teachers)

Teach for America does not address the pressing demands and needs of its novice teacher-trainees, who are *still* learning on children in the most impoverished and segregated schools in the country. An Atlanta public school teacher (fourth year) was surprised to find a first-year TFA teacher sitting on the floor outside her classroom, crying in the hallway. She asked supportively, "Which one [student] would you like me to take out of the classroom for you?" The novice Corps Member sobbed, "Take them all, I can't do this."

Sadly, rookie CMs (Corps Members) often have to reach out to friends and family in education for help, or go under the TFA radar to seek help from credentialed teachers. Corps Members find fewer veteran educators at their schools, because in far too many classrooms, especially charter-managed urban schools that recruit high populations of minority children of color, TFA rookies are often the *only* teachers hired. As one CM told me, "Those TFA teachers who are doing 'well' are those placed at some of the best charter schools in the area, so their success has nothing to do with the support TFA offers" (Jaqueese).

Sara noted that eleven of the twelve teachers at the Phoenix-area charter school, where she worked as a bilingual teacher, were TFA. The biology teacher shared that she was leaving in May. Unsure of what that meant, Sara asked innocently, "But you just got here last year, right? Where are you going?"

"My plan is to go to medical school," the biology teacher replied emphatically. "I'm not here to be a teacher for more than I have to."

Sara shook her head. "It all makes sense now. They are all going somewhere, and the kids are just a means to advance *their* plan, for *their* life. They might know biology, but they are not really teaching it. It's more like they are commanding the kids to learn it. I'm in their classrooms. I see what's going on. Some of them are trying, and many of them are smart, but they are not really teaching. I can tell that their heart isn't in it, you know?"

Between 1 and 5 percent of Teach for America teachers *are* certified educators who majored in elementary, secondary, or special education in a college or university program.

MANIPULATION OF EDUCATION FOR THE PUBLIC GOOD

The corporate, governmental, and philanthropic supporters of Teach for America publicly claim to advocate for children, but with checkbooks and legislative directives, they choose instead to pledge allegiance to a nonprofit wolf in sheep's clothing that has ransacked the educational landscape. George Soros (2010) cautions,

> The trouble is, that special interests also seek to disguise themselves as protectors of the public interest, and it takes a discerning eye to discriminate between the genuine and the phony, especially since both sides are forced to resort to similar methods of persuasion. (pp. 93–94).

But whose interests does Teach for America protect? My research tells me that veteran educators across the country (particularly those of color), children of color in high-poverty communities, and struggling corps trainees are *not* benefitting from Teach for America's expansion, leadership, and movement building. Corps Members confirm that they are required to lobby their own legislators with scripted correspondence prepared by TFA to ensure the organization's best interests are retained, a duty not advertised by TFA's recruiters when canvassing campuses (Veltri, 2015).

Teach for America's operationalizing strategies lack transparency, and they play fast and loose with the facts. As Duke psychology professor Dr. Dan Ariely (2013) points out, however, "collaborative cheating" is not uncommon among ideological altruists who arrogantly rationalize the misappropriation of both public trust and public dollars: "We found that altruism is a strong motivator for cheating. Based upon these results we could speculate that people who work for ideological organizations such as political groups and not-for-profits might actually feel more comfortable bending the moral rules—because they are doing it for a good cause and to help others" (p. 232).

Teach for America's network hides behind the TINA thesis (There Is No Alternative) (Saltman & Gabbard, 2003, p. 6). The favor granted to TFA is repeatedly justified by those who claim Teach for America *uniquely* addresses educational inequities through recruitment of bright and innovative applicants for service that is tantamount to a civil rights campaign. But the lack of transparency appears to be catching up with America's Teacher Corps.

TFA alumni have interrogated the Teach for America "truths" for a decade and are organized and vocal. The #ResistTFA social media movement deconstructs the organizational rhetoric presented in the public domain, and alumni researchers offer significant and solid evidence of inconsistencies in the TFA "mission" rhetoric and outcomes (Brewer, 2014; Kretchmar, Sondel, & Ferrare, 2014; White, 2015). College seniors at elite universities such as Penn, Harvard, and Berkeley increasingly scoff at being patronized by an organization that dangles a charter network affiliation prize upon completion of teaching for two years in an underresourced school (Jehlen, 2012; Wieder, 2012; Fischer, 2013).

In 2014, the United Students Against Sweatshops (USAS), a nationwide coalition of savvy university undergrads, became TFA's worst nightmare. Operating on college campuses, the USAS traveling program, "The TFA Truth Tour," exposes the dark side of corporate education reform (Ascherman & Li, 2014). USAS seeks to remove TFA from campuses nationwide. They are aware of TFA's promises and rhetoric, and know that their peers will serve as the human capital fueling TFA's pipeline of corps teachers to public and charter schools in poor communities (Ascherman & Li, 2014).

To add to TFA's public relation woes, many stakeholders are no longer willing to give TFA a free pass. District administrators, school boards, parents, students, teachers, researchers, TFA alumni Corps Members, and savvy college seniors (the real game changers) are onto the nonprofit's "hide and seek" schemes and practices. Offering temporary teachers with minimal preparation for poor children of color seems like an inadequate corporate solution to a very public problem, especially when it is funded by hundreds of millions of dollars in corporate and federal charity that could be spent on efforts to end poverty or to create diverse schools. Manipulating a legitimate desire for public good to fit narrow corporate objectives is not meritorious. The time has come; the rules, consequences, and alliances could be about to change.

REFERENCES

Ariely, D. (2013). *The (honest) truth about dishonesty: How we lie to everyone—especially ourselves*. New York: Harper Collins.

Ascherman, R., & Li, K. (2014). "TFA truth tour" to expose the dark side of corporate education reform. United Students Against Sweatshops. http://usas.org/2014/03/23/tfa-truth-tour-to-expose-dark-side-of-corporate-education-reform/ .

Brewer, J. (2014). Accelerated burnout: How Teach for America's academic impact model and theoretical culture of accountability can foster disillusionment among its corps members. *Educational Studies* 50 (3), 246–63.

Chernicoff, D. (2006, October 27). I want you, Yalie, to teach for America. *Yale Daily News.* http://yaledailynews.com/weekend/2006/10/27/i-want-you-yalie-to-teach-for-america/ .

Dobbie, W. (2011). Teacher characteristics and student achievement: Evidence from Teach for America. *Journal of Labor Economics* 9 (25), 95–135.

Fischer, B. (2013). Cashing in on kids: 139 ALEC bills in 2013 promote a private, for-profit education model. *Center for Media and Democracy's Special Report.* http://www.prwatch.org/node/12175.

Jehlen, A. (2012). Boot camp for education CEO's: The Broad Foundation Superintendents Academy. *Rethinking Schools* 27 (1), 29–34.

Joseph, G. (2014). This is what happens when you criticize Teach for America. *The Nation.* http://www.thenation.com/article/186481/what-happens-when-you-criticize-teach-america .

Kamenetz, A. (2014). The end of neighborhood schools: New Orleans is home to the nation's first all-charter district. Is this the future of education? http://apps.npr.org/the-end-of-neighborhood-schools/.

Kopp, W. (2003). *One day, all children . . . : The unlikely triumph of Teach for America and what I learned along the way.* New York: Public Affairs.

Kopp, W. & Farr, S. (2011). *A chance to make history: What works and what doesn't in providing an excellent education for all.* New York: Perseus Books Group.

Kovacs, P. E. (2006). Are public schools worth saving? If so, by whom? *Educational Policy Studies Dissertations.* http://scholarworks.gsu.edu/cgi/viewcontent.cgi?article=1005& context=ep s_diss .

Kretchmar, K., Sondel, B., & Ferrare, J. (2014). Mapping the terrain: Teach for America, charter school reform, and corporate sponsorship. *Journal of Education Policy* 29 (6), 742–59.

Lyotard, J. F. (1991). *The inhuman: Reflections on time.* Stanford, CA: Stanford University Press.

Quazzo, D. H., Cohn, M., Horne, J., & Moe, M. (2012). *Fall of the wall: Capital flows to education innovation: GSV Advisors' white paper.*

Saltman, K. J., & Gabbard, D. (2003). *Education as enforcement: The militarization and corporatization of schools.* New York: RoutledgeFalmer.

Simon, S. (2013). Teach for America rises as a political powerhouse. *Politico.* http://www.politico.com/story/2013/10/teach-for-america-rises-as-a-political-powerhouse-98586.html .

Sondel, B. (2014). My many voices. *Critical Educators for Social Justice.* http://www.cesjsig.org/blog/my-many-voices-by-beth-sondel.

Soros, G. (2010). *The Soros lectures at the Central European University.* New York: Public Affairs.

Taylor, D. (2010). Testimony regarding Seattle education. *Seattle Education.* http://seattleducation2010.wordpress.com/2010/11/08/testimony-regarding-teach-for-america/ .

Teach for America (2014). Teach for America welcomes most diverse talent in 25-year history. www.teachforamerica.org/press-room/press-releases/2014.

Teach for Us. (2012). Has Teach for America's philosophy shifted? http://abcde.teachforus.org/2012/03/10/wendy-kopp-visits-hgse-has-tfas-philosophy-shifted/.

Veltri, B. (2015). Voices of revitalization: Challenging the singularity of Teach for America's echo chamber. In *Teach for America counter-narratives: Alumni speak up and speak out.* Edited by T. Jameson Brewer and Kathleen deMarrais. New York: Peter Lang Publications.

Veltri, B. (2010). *Learning on other people's kids: Becoming a Teach for America teacher.* New York: Information Age Publishers.

White, T. (2015). Beyond dupes, disciples, and dilettantes: Ideological struggles of Teach for America corps members. In *Teach for America counter-narratives: Alumni speak up and speak out.* Edited by T. Jameson Brewer and Kathleen deMarrais. New York: Peter Lang Publications.

White, T. (2013). *Teach for America (TFA) and the "endangerment" of communities: Counter-stories from TFA teachers of color.* Paper presented at the American Educational Research Association Annual Meeting, San Francisco, CA.

Wieder, B. (2012). Teach for America alums take aim at state office. *Pew Charitable Trusts.* http://www.Pewstates.org/projects/stateline/headlines/teach-for-america-alums-take-aim-at-state-office-85899401348.

Chapter Ten

"KIPP is grad school for TFA gluttons for punishment"

If you were in TFA and it wasn't punishing enough for you, then KIPP is right up your alley.
—1166

You cannot teach someone to be a great teacher in twenty days.
—1178

Teach for America and KIPP Model schools maintain a mutually supportive ideological bond and business relationship. Without the 30 to 40 percent of KIPP teachers who are presently or formerly TFA corps members, KIPP and its total-compliance emulators would be hard-pressed to find enough teachers to maintain their operations. At the same time, TFA alums with aspirations for leadership benefit greatly from schools with No Excuses charters. For without KIPP and the other No Excuses charter chains, TFA alumni, with their two years of teaching experience, would have few opportunities to move into school leader positions and be without the requisite administrative and leadership training that is typically required of public school administrators.

Some KIPP Model schools prefer teachers who have matriculated from TFA, while others like to recruit first-year TFA teachers so that they "they don't have to unlearn 'bad' teaching habits." Another KIPP teacher noted that TFA alumni do particularly well at KIPP because they are naïve and have "the mindset of a missionary" who "believes that kids need to be broken before we can build them up."

Seven of the former No Excuses teachers interviewed were former TFA corps members, and all of them had received repeated solicitous emails about

KIPP through their TFA email accounts. One teacher formed specific expectations regarding what KIPP would be like from the emails that she received while working as a TFA teacher in a public school in the Bronx. Not surprisingly, the emails focused on expectations, order, outcomes, team, and leadership:

> I think my expectations going in were that there was going to be some real consistency at a school level regarding expectations for academic achievement and discipline. I was excited to feel part of a larger community. . . . I was excited to be part of a team. From an expectation standpoint, I figured I would be working very hard and that I would be part of a team and that by deploying the KIPP approach, that we would be able to generate some significant outcomes. I also felt like the principal at my school was a really dynamic leader.

Another former TFA member who found out about KIPP during her TFA service was more explicit about the ongoing mythologizing of KIPP that happens during the TFA teaching stint, as well as KIPP's "harvesting" of TFA alumni as they transition out of their TFA-assigned schools. She indicated that TFA, too, engaged in efforts to "funnel" or "channel" those leaving their assigned schools into the KIPP organization or into "TFA staff positions." She said that there was a "constant barrage" of communications urging alumni to "stay affiliated in some way":

> From the very beginning of my experience, from the five week training program that Teach for America employs, all the way through my two year commitment, KIPP was really sort of mythologized as the end-all, be-all, the ideal model for a classroom of high achieving students, from day one of joining Teach for America and seeing videos of KIPP classrooms, up until towards the end of my two year commitment when I was considering next steps, KIPP really actively coming in and harvesting new employees from core members who were finishing up their two year commitment. It was always something that was before me over the course of my two years with Teach for America. I really started to feel like I was being recruited into almost the next phase of my TFA experience towards the end of my second year as I was preparing to transition into being an alumni.

TFA encouraged her to submit a resume to the KIPP database, and soon after she did, she began receiving emails and phone calls from KIPP administrators "trying to gauge my interest in coming on board with a KIPP school." This teacher talked about how she was conditioned at TFA "to believe that if there's any slacking of will at any point—if there's any departure from these philosophies and precepts [of total commitment], which I think are held in common with KIPP (they just look different), then that's a sign of someone giving up."

She talked of regularly feeling tired and of feeling guilty for being tired, as admitting tiredness could be a sign of flagging commitment. "It's almost this idea of a fundamentalist cult. Someone's not allowed to question, someone's not allowed to doubt. If they do, that means that they're fallen; that means that they're out. There's no room for conversation. There's no room for nuance."

When asked how this conditioning was reinforced, she said that because she had "a very positive relationship" with her closest supervisors at TFA, they shared their disappointments with her in regard to her peers who were members of the same TFA cohort:

> I know that the way that they would talk to me about certain peers of mine, who were the same year in the program, the way that they would talk about some of those peers who were less committed, or some of those peers who were starting to balk under some of the expectations, or thinking about doing something after the two year experience that had nothing to do with education, had nothing to do with Teach for America, there was always a tone, an undercurrent.

This teacher said she found a similar insistence on staying connected to KIPP in the plaque she was given when she left. "The only reason I have it on my wall is because all my students signed it and I appreciate looking at what they had to say. But the centerpiece of it [says] 'once a KIPPster, always a KIPPster.'"

Another former KIPP teacher referred to how a "self-sacrifice ideology" was common among successful TFA and KIPP teachers. To her this represented the "scariest type" of successful KIPP teacher. "Those that just stay in it and feel that there is nothing else left better to do. They do not have a life. I have some teammates; they don't talk to their family regularly. They don't eat healthy. . . . They are at work until 9 to 10 o'clock at night. KIPP is their life. Anything KIPP, they're there, even on Saturdays and Sundays."

One teacher talked of a type of TFA-KIPP synergism that had devastating effects on one of her colleagues at KIPP, who was also an active TFA enlistee at the time.

> We have a Teach for America corps member, who is an outstanding English I teacher from the region. She was denied leave after having several anxiety attacks. The ambulance actually came to our school to pick her up. She has been neglected by our instructional coach in the school. She has been told that she has to model our instructional coach and the other powers that be. She has had bronchitis on many different days. She has been yelled at and told, "Oh you look fine," even though she was about to pass out and eventually collapsed that same day, from not taking off. She is going to quit Teach for America. She is going to quit KIPP and between the two, they have run her ragged.

Chapter Eleven

Special Needs Students and the KIPP Model: "A Lawsuit Waiting to Happen"

Research (Miron, Urschel, & Saxton, 2011; Miron, Urschel, Mathis, & Tornquist, 2010) consistently shows that the majority of total-compliance charter schools have significantly fewer English-language learners and special education students. The charts (figures 11.1 and 11.2) show trends of students served by KIPP schools and public school districts for 2005 through 2009 (Miron, Urschel, & Saxton, 2011, p. 14).

More recent research (Weber & Rubin, 2014) shows that, when comparing the types of disabilities found at charters with regular public schools, the disabilities of students enrolled in charter schools are ones that require fewer time-consuming and costly accommodations and individual education plans (IEPs). Based on interviews with former KIPP teachers, these findings become more understandable.

Schools that follow the KIPP Model use predominantly large-group, direct instruction, with the teacher expected to be in complete command of behavioral and academic tasks. Most school leaders and teachers at KIPP have not completed traditional teacher education programs, and their understanding of special needs children's learning modalities is most often scant or nonexistent. This reality presented itself for one former KIPP teacher, who had never been consulted regarding his students' IEPs.

The lone special education teacher was a faculty member he had seen "once or twice" during his two years at KIPP. He spoke of the inexperience, isolation, and lack of collaboration at his school that he blamed for a dangerous event involving a special needs student:

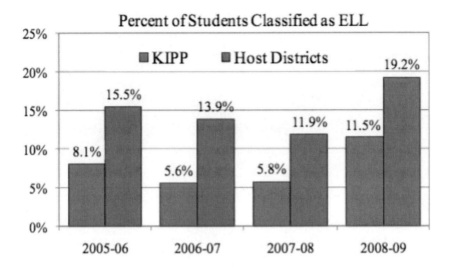

Figure 11.1.   KIPP schools have fewer English-language learners

So many times I felt like I was just working in isolation. And again, I liked my colleagues and I never felt like there was anybody who was against me or didn't like me, but I didn't feel a sense of unity or collaboration there, and I think that is something that has to come from the top. . . . I don't think that charters are evil and the people who run them are evil, but I think they are incredibly misguided.

I think our principal was very young. I think she was without a lot of experiences, and I think when you have those combinations you are not going to guide your faculty with wisdom, and so I think that is why there is just so much miscommunication. There wasn't a lot of bringing the faculty together. There wasn't a lot of quality professional development. I think that is why I am like scratching my head like, "where is the special education teacher," like we need to talk.

One day one of my kids, and I don't recall exactly what all of his issues were, but he had some academic and emotional disabilities, and one day he just like freaked out, pushed this other kid and threw a chair across the room. And I was just like what the heck just happened, and so I had like one of the kids run downstairs and grab someone from the office, and I come to find out later that he has an IEP. Well, I didn't even know that.

So I didn't even know like what things were going to be triggers for him, and after I read his IEP, I could see like okay this and that set him off, and now I know not to let that happen, but you know you can't throw your teachers under the bus like that. And that's how I felt. Just moment after moment there was something happen[ing] that just made me feel alienated or unsupported or out of the loop.

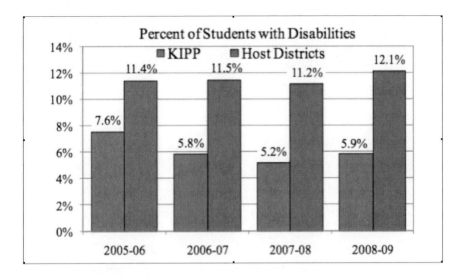

Figure 11.2. KIPP schools have fewer special education students

Some KIPP schools ignore IEPs for special needs children they enroll, and at other schools IEPs are adjusted to fit the KIPP Model, which disallows or discourages differentiation. At another school, a teacher who had previously taught in an urban public school with large numbers of special needs children did not get to see the IEPs for the third-grade special needs children in her class, thus making it impossible to address the special needs of children as mandated by law.

The IEPs, she said, "were in the office with the special education coordinator," who was the only trained special education teacher for the school: "She would come once a week maybe, and take the kids out. I honestly have no idea what she did with them. I never saw an IEP." This teacher noted, however, that seeing the IEPs would not have been very helpful to her, since there was only one way to teach at KIPP:

> Even if I had seen them, we literally weren't allowed to differentiate. We had to teach every single lesson in the same exact format. Every kid. There was no concept of accommodating. There was no concept of maybe having this one group work on something a little bit different. It was the most rigid way of teaching.

She became very familiar with the "rigid way" during the fall term after the school's third-graders did not do well on the "mock exam," which resulted in school leaders concluding that "third-grade instruction was off." She became one among four teachers new to KIPP that year who were called in over winter holiday break for "professional development" based on KIPP's most used instructional manual, *Teach Like a Champion*, by Doug Lemov (2010). When school started back after the holidays, she and her new colleagues "were constantly being observed," videotaped, and measured against checklists from Lemov's teachings. She found any variation from Lemov's method was not allowed:

> I used to present a question for the kids to ponder. I like to start lessons like that from time to time. Not all the time, but sometimes. Let's look at this problem on the board. Let's brainstorm some ways about how we might solve this. We were not allowed to do that. That was an inefficient use of the time. I had to go right from, Teacher shows the kid how to do it, to We Do, to You Do. Which I hated. I couldn't get over how superficial it was. I didn't understand how nobody seemed to be saying anything about it. It was like, "No, this is just how things happen here. We've got to get them ready for the tests."

This teacher was assigned a self-contained room with between twenty and twenty-five of the lowest-performing third-graders, and she was assisted by a "floating teacher" who "would teach some classes." Seven of her students she knew had IEPs, even though she did not know what their individual plans stipulated. Four of the seven she knew "had diagnosed ADHD," even though the diagnosis brought no alterations to the SLANT requirements that demanded all children to sit with hands folded while tracking the teacher.

> These poor kids just had to sit there with their hands folded, and they would rock and they would tap. Every time they would rock or tap or talk, you would have to mark it on the chart. If you had to mark it three times, then they had to go to time out. If they had to go to time out twice, they had to go to the Dean. There was about five, six or seven kids who were constantly either in time out, or in with the Dean because they just physically were struggling to sit that still. I don't blame them at all.
>
> The kids that I had taught up in _____ [prior school], they also had ADHD. Part of what I thought as my job was to find ways to make it so that even though they still had a lot of energy, and needed to move, and talk, and be active they could still learn. There are so many things that you can do, I think, to keep active, so that they can still learn. Instead of this, they just got sent to the Dean. I had one little boy who got suspended probably once or twice a week. He wanted to talk, and he wanted to tap, and he didn't want to have to sit completely still. He couldn't sit completely still like his peers. It was really, really sad.

This third-grader's parents became angry with the school when school leaders put "enormous, enormous pressure on them to have him medicated for ADHD" so that he could remain enrolled at KIPP. The teacher said,

I'm not anti-medicine, but I have worked with special kids that are way, way more extreme than this little boy was. The fact that everyone was pushing meds for him so hard—it just didn't seem right to me. He was the kind of kid that if I had been given the opportunity, I really feel confident that I could have found ways for him to succeed in the classroom. I don't think he was a kid that needed medication. I'm not an expert for that, obviously, but I know that his parents were getting very frustrated and had stopped showing up for the meetings.

When this teacher was asked what other parents thought about the services they were receiving for their special needs children, she replied:

I don't really know because I don't really know if they were aware of what actually happened in the school. I never saw a parent actually come in and observe a classroom. I never once saw a parent actually in the school during school hours. I don't think they really knew what their kid was being expected to do, and why they kept getting in trouble. They just kept getting these phone calls saying, "So and so was talking during class. We had to mark it down four times. It disrupted everyone. Now you have to come pick him up." I don't think they really knew.

Another teacher found that her KIPP school attempted to use "inclusive methods," even though there were too few special education teachers for this strategy to work. She noted that during the first days of the new school year when KIPP-notizing was the sole priority, protocol did not allow for special education teachers to be in the classrooms: "You would start off trying to condition them and definitely that is when the special education teacher wasn't in the classroom."

One KIPP teacher I interviewed had been hired as a special education teacher after years in public schools as a special education teacher. When I asked her to describe KIPP's way of doing special education, she said, "This is a question I've answered many times—a lawsuit waiting to happen." She said that when she began, "There was no special ed program, so I did start it and I ran it the way I wanted to, which was according with all the [state] laws and the federal laws . . . but I worked day and night."

Complicating her tasks with special needs students were the many other hats she was forced to wear, which included school nurse, "because the nurse who was not a certified teacher was teaching science because the science teacher was on maternity leave." She also served as school counselor, mentor, compliance officer, and classroom teacher of various subjects, thus giving the term *inclusion* a whole new meaning, perhaps.

You didn't have to be good at that subject or have it as your specialty or what you were certified in, but since I'm certified in special ed, I can teach all subjects. I can teach any subject—I would just have to read up at night. In

20___, I was teaching math, which is not my strength so I would just study at night.

She explained how the Admission, Review, and Dismissal (ARD) meeting, which determines the supports and services for the special needs child, more often worked to serve the needs of KIPP, rather than the special needs child.

> When I talk about it, it's scary because having experience in special ed . . . before I arrived at KIPP—that's why I was hired—to make it to where it looked like we had a special ed program. Let's say if we had a student come in who had severe behavior problems, there were no counselors—I was the counselor. Whatever need that the student had in his ARD meetings, I served as that person: a tutor, a small group instructor. There is no small group instruction at KIPP, so basically what we would do is eliminate that modification or accommodation and tailor it to KIPP's program.

Parents would sometimes be told during ARD meetings that a requested service "is just not here, ma'am" or "we don't have this." When asked what happened if the IEP did not fit the KIPP program, she said,

> We tailored the IEP to meet the KIPP program, therefore, we could remain in compliance. But, let's say the child was required 30 minutes of one-on-one instruction in math, well, we would just take that out and say we don't offer 30 minutes of individual instruction in math—so we would just say no accommodation. We would say "sit in front of the classroom," something that we had that could provide some type of help to that student, but it would not be what was required from the previous ARD at a different school.

How effective was this kind of program for special education students? She said that special education students "were not successful," and that "they didn't stay very long." When asked why she stayed on more than a year at this school, she said,

> I felt very bad for them. Back to that question why did you stay, I did form a bond with some parents and some students, and I felt like if I left I would leave them. And you kind of do get that feeling like you're helping them somehow. It's like if you leave, then they're gone. They're going to lose them. Which I'm sure that that's what happened to the few that I was very close to.

This teacher remembered fondly the one success she recalled at KIPP, when she discovered a child was dyslexic and was able to devise some interventions for him that worked. Most of her memories, however, were associated with the many lost weekends when she was recovering from her week of work at KIPP.

Another teacher had also been hired to teach special education. Since this KIPP school had previously used part-time special needs teachers from the district, she was the first full-time special education teacher at her KIPP school. At the beginning of the school year during the faculty's KIPP-notizing, she was inundated with information from "a giant binder" that the school leaders reviewed with new teachers, page by page. Oddly, she found there was nothing at all about special education in the giant binder.

> No, no. I was asked later—I was asked to give a presentation to the staff about that, which I did, but at that point there was nothing that was specific to special education or to my role or how the gen ed teachers needed to be in compliance, either.

She said, "They had no clue about what a special education teacher did or how to use me or anything at that point, but I was still involved in the entire training, which was good because I got a good understanding" [of the organization]. She found the status of KIPP's special education students "horrific." She said, "Their accommodations were not being met. Their IEPs were out of date. It was just bad. It was shocking to me." She said the principal did not know about the "IEP process," nor did she understand "compliance and the ramification of being out of compliance."

This teacher had previously worked with severely emotionally disturbed children, where she had two assistants most of the time, and at least one instructional assistant all of the time. During her hiring interview at KIPP, she had asked "what sort of assistant situation would there be," and the school leader replied "we don't do that," but that if the need arose, it would be "something we can talk about" and "go from there."

With approximately twenty special needs students in different classes, the need did, indeed, arise, but requests for an instructional assistant were denied. This teacher found herself stretched beyond her capacity to help students and to remain in compliance with state law.

> Even if I were to hit all of those classes every period, I still couldn't get to everyone, and what it turned out to be is, I would go in, make eye contact, make sure they were there and working, and then move on. I was covering my butt in terms of fulfilling what the accommodations were.
>
> I began using a system where I had a sheet for every student in a binder, and I would go in and write the day and the time and my observation about what was happening with that student because if for some reason we had a litigious parent, I wanted to at least say I am doing this. . . . So I wanted to do whatever I could. . . . I wasn't doing anything that those kids needed. If someone had a meltdown or something like that while I was in the class, I could take care of it, and often students who are more disruptive due to attention difficulties and things like that, teachers would send them to me. So if I

had students sent to me, that is great, but then I can't roam around to all the classes.

After several attempts to sway the school leader, this teacher stopped asking. Around midyear, however, a leadership shake-up ended with a new school leader being installed. The new leader was a colleague who had previously served as a part-time teacher at the school, and she had neither teacher nor administrator certification. The special education teacher tried again, this time focusing on "compliance, compliance, compliance," but to no avail. She was told by the new school leader, "No, we really can't do that."

Another teacher said that IEPs were being met for reading and math students at her school, but not for other classes. This teacher, however, focused her remarks on the absence of accommodations for the "English-learning students" at her school, for whom, she said "there was absolutely nothing." When she talked at school about two core concepts for English learners, Basic Interpersonal Communications Skills (BICS) and Cognitive Academic Language Capacity (CALP), she was met with "blank stares" from her colleagues: "My coworkers had no idea what I was talking about, which is like Teaching English Learners 101. . . . There wasn't opportunity for English learners to practice oral language in a low-stakes environment, and because there is so much whole-class instruction, the opportunity just to talk was infrequent."

One former KIPP teacher who had no experience with or preparation for working with special needs children felt he was pressured out of his position at KIPP for expressing concerns and complaints regarding the treatment of special needs children in his class. The situation involved his last class of the day, which he had trouble controlling. The class began at 3:30 in the afternoon after three hundred minutes of instruction and "all day of being silent." Fifteen of his twenty-one students had IEPs. Even though the students "were receiving some access to special education resources" earlier in the day, this teacher had no assistance during this final period.

During a one-on-one meeting that the school leader had requested on Friday afternoon, he pointed out his lack of special education training, and he shared his concern that it could be "illegal to have so many special education students in one classroom because the law states they have to be educated in the least restrictive environment available to them." The school leader responded by asking him a series of rapid-fire questions: What kind of structure was he providing, did he believe all children could succeed, if children were not successful, was it the fault of the child or the teacher, and "Do you believe that students fail or teachers fail?"

He felt cornered by the school leader "putting things in these dichotomies." He said he felt as though his answers were "digging my own grave." He was told that he would be observed every day of the next week. In the meantime, the school leader suggested a book on classroom management. Considering his mental state, his weight loss, and his stress-related alopecia, he decided that weekend he should cut his losses. On Monday morning, he sent his resignation by email. It was Labor Day, and he had been a KIPP teacher for six weeks.

REFERENCES

Lemov, D. (2010). *Teach like a champion: 49 techniques that put students on the path to college (K–12)*. San Francisco: Jossey-Bass.

Miron, G., Urschel, J., Mathis, W., & Tornquist, E. (2010). Schools without diversity: Educational management organizations, charter schools, and the demographic stratification of the American school system. East Lansing, MI: The Great Lakes Center for Educational Research and Practice. http://greatlakescenter.org/docs/Policy_Briefs/Miron_Diversity.pdf.

Miron, G., Urschel, J., & Saxton, N. (2011). *What makes KIPP work: Study of student characteristics, attrition, and school finance*. New York: National Center for the Study of Privatization in Education. http://www.ncspe.org/readrel.php?set=pub&cat=253.

Weber, M., & Rubin, J. (2014). *New Jersey charter schools: A data-driven view, part 1*. Rutgers Graduate School of Education. http://www.saveourschoolsnj.org/save/corefiles/wp-content/uploads/2014/10/NJ-Charter-School-Report_10.29.2014.pdf.

Chapter Twelve

The Final KIPP Interview

My first interviews with former KIPP teachers began in 2011, and the last ones for this project were conducted in 2014. The very last one was with a young woman who contacted me to tell her KIPP story, which had ended just a few days before our interview. Like other former KIPP teachers, she stepped out of the darkness to speak, even though she feared reprisals and "harassment" from KIPP employees if her identity could be assigned to her words.

As with so many other former KIPP teachers who left damaged by their experience, she is a former Teach for America corps member who taught two years in a poor public school before coming to KIPP. She had suffered through her first TFA year finding out all that her college double major did not teach her about children and teaching, but by the second year she felt as if she had hit her stride. She had, nonetheless, decided to leave teaching when her two-year TFA commitment was up, when she was contacted by KIPP.

KIPP had acquired her name as a prospective teacher from her first-year teacher mentor, who previously had spent her first year as a teacher at a KIPP school. Her mentor, she explained, was looking to cash in on large finder fees for new teachers hired from his leads if the new hires stayed at KIPP for at least thirty days.

She was invited for an interview in an urban area large enough to have its own KIPP network, and she received a guided tour of the "most beautiful classrooms" and "perfectly arranged classrooms." She was taken to lunch and to dinner, and twenty-four hours later she was offered a teaching job. Since this KIPP school seemed to "have it together more" than the public school she was leaving, she took a risk and decided to give teaching one more try.

Like other KIPP teachers, she started to work in early July. On the first day of her second week at KIPP, she was part of a team-level meeting that included two program chairs and several other teachers, none of whom was new to KIPP. At that meeting she heard this: "Because you're hired here doesn't mean that you're anything more than a warm body. Until you prove yourself worthy of my trust you will not have it." The colleague who offered this warning, she found out later, had students with the highest test scores in the school, which provided him with great a deal of latitude for his words and actions, regardless of how callous or foolish they might be.

This was her first exposure to what she called "an adult culture of negativity," one in which she "felt bullied every single day." She was told, too, "by multiple people [at KIPP], 'I'm so sorry, but you don't have any of the skills that it takes to be successful here in terms of management.' It was just constant negativity." At one point, a grade-level fellow teacher told her, "You're the weakest link, but you're not the weakest link of the school, so at least appreciate that."

In what she described as a poisonous and unprofessional environment, group messages flew back and forth with cutting remarks, jibes, and bad-mouthing of school leaders, other teachers, and students as well:

> I have saved text messages of them complaining about the fact that our princi-pal can never show up to school on time. I have saved text messages about teachers actually making fun of students and their disabilities . . . a child who has special ed needs. He was caught playing with himself a couple times in school. They started making fun of him via a group message about the fact that "finally we taught this child how to use his right brain and his left brain at the same time." And some absolutely horrific things about that child. Things that should never be spoken at any school anywhere.

Having heard some KIPP teachers make negative comments about other teachers and school leaders when they were not present, she began to wonder if these same teachers were talking about her. She found herself walking unannounced into group meetings that would go suddenly silent, where "you know people are complaining about you." She had suspicions that students had overheard remarks about her from teachers. She said she felt as if she and the kids were "surrounded by a culture of negativity day in and day out" that served as a vitriolic variety of behavioral hazing.

She quickly worked into a schedule that had her arriving at school at 5:45 to make copies and to get her board and other materials ready before the 7:10 start. Like many KIPP teachers, she usually worked through lunch, and she had her first break at 2:45. Although a plan period was in her daily schedule, meetings and other commitments consumed that time except for one day of the week, so that she was left with eighty minutes during the week, as she said, "to myself." She insisted on leaving school just after 6 p.m., even though school leaders "chastised" her and said, "You would have better relationships with the people you work with if you stayed here past 6 p.m."

Having never been seriously ill or hospitalized, her family was alarmed when she was hospitalized early in the fall with a "bleeding cyst in [her] reproductive system." She was prescribed morphine and kept in the hospital for three days. Her mother, who suspected work stress as a major factor, flew in to be with her and to take her home, and doctors ordered more pain medication and three more days of bed rest. As with most other KIPP schools, substitute teachers were not part of the culture, and her biggest worry during her recovery was the other teachers who were having to cover for her.

> The doctor told me I couldn't be at work while I was on morphine because it would just be a disservice to the whole world. I couldn't drive a car. God knows I shouldn't have been in front of children. . . . I did come back. I [still] had a little bit of pain, but more I had so much anxiety about screwing these other teachers over because of my own illness that caused even more stress.

She came back to work for several more weeks before resigning prior to Thanksgiving, when she became the sixth out of ten newly hired teachers to leave that KIPP school before midterm. Two of those were new teachers, and four had prior experience.

Before she resigned, other teachers were falling ill, too. Two colleagues on different occasions required treatment at an emergency clinic, where both were prescribed antianxiety medication and antidepressants. Two weeks before she resigned, another teacher was treated for hives that covered most of her body. The weight of the negative pressure was taking a toll. When I asked the purpose of all the negativity, she replied without hesitation, "I think it's to get every teacher working at that school to give every single thing they have until they can't give anymore."

A bit later in the interview, she said, "I don't think that that's what the [KIPP] administrators want. But I think that they're so focused on these test scores that they don't see teacher satisfaction. They don't see the benefit of long-term teacher relationships or the benefit of maybe seeing a student struggle and realize that there's more to a child than hitting a certain number on their math test. They just haven't figured it out yet."

A few days after leaving KIPP and returning to public school teaching, this teacher found herself in a psychological space that she had forgotten during her four months at KIPP. The day of our interview she had called her boyfriend to chat, and it occurred to her to ask him, "Is there something different in my voice?" He reminded her that she sounded "really happy" again. She said that during her time at KIPP a "dark cloud was cast" on her and that she "had become a shell" of the confident teacher she had been prior to coming to KIPP. "They successfully stomped out any type of confidence or this feeling I had about my abilities—and made me feel like this person who was just failing students every day."

In reflecting on positive aspects at KIPP, she found the focus on professional development for "making the teacher look more effective" commendable, but she noted that "you can't get a teacher to be more effective if she feels unhappy at work every day." She estimated that fewer than one in five KIPP teachers at her school appeared to be happy. She said that those who realize working conditions are unfair would quit, and she described the teachers who remain at KIPP as "impressively resilient but also very passive."

She said they are the ones "who will just take hit after hit after hit," and she described one "beautiful young woman" who came to KIPP as a new teacher without knowing that teaching in other schools can be very different from KIPP. "It's really hard for me to see her because . . . she's actually been physically assaulted by students, but they don't want to suspend students because it makes the school look bad."

Finally, this teacher agreed with KIPP's focus on trying to motivate children for college, even though she found their approach "a little bit . . . overbearing." She noted, too, the countervailing influences that work to neutralize KIPP's stated goals. On the one hand, KIPP optimistically hastens children toward college, yet on (or with) the other hand, students are gripped in a negative behavioral vice that detracts from learning how to become autonomous and thinking young adults.

> When we talk about KIPP and its limitations on getting kids to college, it makes sense . . . [and yet] we taught at this middle school how to have kids walk in a straight line and how to open a textbook and rewrite a problem silently with the proper notation. We're not teaching them how to be young, free-thinking, independent adults. I think that's really a disservice that's happening at those schools.

Chapter Thirteen

The Reach of the KIPP Model

During the early years of charter schools, policymakers who were eager to see the types of charters expand emphasized the philosophy of "let a thousand flowers bloom," which led to new charter school growth with a variety of pedagogical approaches and organizational options. By 2009, however, Secretary of Education Arne Duncan was looking to discourage the proliferation of models and to replicate and scale up the test score successes among the charter school industry's "biggest brands" (Toch, 2009, p. 26).

With most of funded charter research focused on the test score successes of KIPP, the influence of the KIPP Model reaches far beyond the seventy thousand students who attend KIPP's 183 schools. For the 6,700 other charter schools with 2.89 million students in 2015, the KIPP Model has been and remains the charter school system to emulate.

With billions of dollars in federal Race to the Top (RTTT) grants available in 2009 to 2010 to fund new charter schools to replace as many as five thousand low-scoring public schools nationwide, highly touted charter models like KIPP suddenly became even more prominent. Even in 2009, the short list of highly regarded charter chains, which included Aspire, Green Dot, YES Prep, and Uncommon Schools, all sought to emulate the longer hours, high expectation, and No Excuses of KIPP.

By 2014, there were more than a dozen other highly touted charter networks emulating the No Excuses and "joyful rigor" of the KIPP Model. These charter chains and those that share their commitment to the No Excuses ideology received the lion's share of RTTT grant money designated to charter schools in 2010 and 2011, as well as from other federal charter grant programs in those years and since. In October 2014, for instance, the U.S. DOE Charter School Program (CSP) announced $39.7 million in grants to "expand high-quality charter schools," with almost $36 million of that total going to KIPP and the charter networks listed below. KIPP received more than a third of the total ($13,789,074):

Achievement First Public Charter Schools (twenty-nine sites NY, CT, RI)
Alliance College-Ready Public Schools (twenty-six sites CA)
American Quality Schools (eight sites IL, IN)
Aspire Public Schools (thirty-eight sites CA, TN)
Ascend Learning (eleven sites NY)
Concept Schools (thirty-two sites OH, IL)
Gestalt Community Schools (four sites TN)
Green Dot Public Schools (twenty-two sites CA, TN)
Harmony Public Schools (forty-three sites TX)
IDEA Public Schools (eighteen sites TX)
LEAD Public Schools (five sites TN)
Lighthouse Academies (eighteen sites AK, IL, IN, MI, NY, OK, WI)
Mastery Charter Schools (seventeen sites NJ)
Noble Network of Charter Schools (seventeen sites IL)
Partnerships to Uplift Communities (sixteen sites CA)
St. HOPE Public Schools (four sites CA)
Success Academy Charter Schools (thirty-two sites NYC)
Uncommon Schools (forty-one sites NY, NJ, MA)
Uplift Education (thirteen sites TX)
YES Prep (fourteen sites TX, TN)

The federal Charter School Program (CSP) was funded at $253 million in 2014, and President Obama's 2015 budget requested $375 million for 2015. A powerful charter advocacy group, the National Alliance for Public Charter Schools, announced its goal, however, of $500 million per year for the CSP.

Outside the charter movement, the KIPP Model has also had an impact in how school is conducted. With increasing frequency, the public schools in urban areas that are fighting to survive the next round of school closings have taken to emulating KIPP's unrelenting focus (Dillon, 2011b) on test scores, the harsh behavioral codes, the inculcation of performance character traits, and the marginalization of subjects and activities that are not tested. Even if KIPP were to disappear overnight, its influence would likely continue for some time, as the grammar, syntax, and tone of urban schooling have taken on a number of KIPP's more antediluvian aspects disinterred from previous generations.

Along with interviews conducted with former KIPP teachers, three teachers from two other No Excuses charter networks shared their stories for this book. One was from Ascend Learning, Inc., and the other two were from St. HOPE Public Schools, Inc. These teachers were asked the same questions asked of former KIPP teachers, and the overlap of their responses was striking. This should come as no surprise, perhaps, since both charter chains share organizational and pedagogical features derived from the KIPP Model. At Ascend Learning (2015), for instance, their website states,

> At Ascend, teachers assertively shape students' habits, values, and aspirations. Teachers hold stark convictions: knowledge is the ticket to a better future. Effort, not talent, is the determinant of success, and students are the masters of their own destinies. They can beat the odds, there are no shortcuts, and the goal for every child is college.

At St. HOPE Public Schools, KIPP's Five Pillars provide the schools' philosophical and strategic orientation, even though no credit or citation is offered on St. HOPE's website (St. HOPE, n.d.):

These basic principles form the five pillars are responsible [*sic*] for the success of St. HOPE Public Schools.

1. **High Expectations** St. HOPE Public Schools has high expectations for academic achievement and conduct that are clearly defined, measurable, and make no excuses based on the background of students. Students, parents, teachers, and staff create and reinforce a culture of achievement and support, through a range of formal and informal rewards and consequences for academic performance and behavior.

2. **Choice and Commitment** Students, their parents, and the staff of St. HOPE Public Schools choose to participate in the program. No one is assigned or forced to attend. Everyone must make and uphold a commitment to their school and to each other to put in the time and effort required to achieve success.

3. **More Time** St. HOPE Public Schools knows that there are no shortcuts when it comes to success in academics and life. With an extended school day, week, and year, students have more time in the classroom to acquire the academic knowledge and skills that prepare them for competitive colleges, as well as more opportunities to engage in diverse extracurricular experiences.

4. **Focus on Results** St. HOPE Public Schools focuses relentlessly on high student performance through standardized tests and other objective measures. Just as there are no shortcuts, there are no exceptions. Students are expected to achieve a level of academic performance that will enable them to succeed in the nation's best colleges and the world beyond.

5. **Power to Lead** St. HOPE Public Schools strongly believes the measure of a person's success is in what he or she gives to others. Through community service, students develop a strong sense of civic responsibility and establish the foundation for a lifetime of meaningful community involvement. Students also deepen and demonstrate their learning, are empowered to become leaders, and impact the community in which they live.

As at KIPP, St. HOPE depends heavily on Teach for America teachers. At St. HOPE's middle school, PS7, fifteen of the eighteen teachers were active TFA corps members in 2014, and one other teacher was a former corps member. One of the former St. HOPE teachers noted, "Our principal, our deans, our superintendent, our HR people, our teachers that get recognized frequently, are all Teach for America alumni." She said that with St. HOPE's embrace of TFA, the "culture completely shifted. And it turned into a teach-to-the-test type environment. And you know, suddenly all of our administration, there were tons of turnover, and then there were tons of turnovers as far as teachers are concerned—so St. HOPE now is just a completely different place than it was three or four years ago."

Whether we are examining teaching strategies, curriculum, stress levels, management, discipline, attrition, school environment, parent relations, or intended outcomes, similar issues and problems are encountered by No Excuses charter schoolteachers, whether at KIPP or one of the many KIPP knockoffs. The teacher from Brooklyn Ascend, for instance, found that questioning the school leader's decisions "wasn't tolerated," and that "teachers were treated with the same total-compliance attitude as the children were."

After a teacher was denied a day off near the end of the school year to help a friend who had injured himself in an accident, the audacity to "question things" earned him a blunt invitation from the school leader to resign:

> My friend had fallen down the stairs. I needed to take the day. It was the third day that I'd asked to take off the whole year. The other two times I was sick. I didn't feel like I was screwing anybody over by taking that day. My friend needed the help, [but] our school Director, he didn't want to hear it. He told me that it seems that I had recently stopped being part of their mission, and that it wasn't helpful to have somebody on the team that wasn't part of the mission. He said that I should resign.

Another teacher said the first-year teachers from TFA "got the least grief" because they did not ask questions and were good at following directions: "If they had to read a script that says, 'now watch while I show you how to do this,' then they'd do it." As with many KIPP schools, Ascend Learning's strict use of Doug Lemov's *Teach Like a Champion* provides justification for total compliance for both students and teachers: "There is one acceptable percentage of students following a direction: 100 percent. Less, and your authority is subject to interpretation, situation, and motivation" (Lemov, 2010, p. 168). Translated into practice, Lemov's "Technique #36" became part of an authoritarian mandate that crippled this teacher's capacity to be an effective teacher:

> Lemov's idea is that if you don't have one hundred percent compliance—one hundred percent authority—then others will think they can question. There's

something to that, maybe, but I think that idea just got taken way, way too far at the school I was at. If a kid even giggles. The kids weren't even allowed to giggle. If a student giggled too loud, we had to mark it down that they were being disruptive. If I'm reading a story aloud, I'm okay with my kids giggling every now and then. That's what kids do. That shows that they're listening. It shows they're interested. We had to mark it because any little misbehavior was a threat to the one hundred percent authority, and one hundred percent compliance. It was just so exhausting, and it left no time. I was there for a year, and I feel like I never got to know the kids.

As at KIPP, much of the school day was silent; even whole-class trips to the bathroom followed the HALLS dictum:

Hands by your sides

Attention forward

Lines straight

Lines together

Silent always.

When asked if there remained an image of Brooklyn Ascend that stands out to her, she said:

The image that comes to mind is this kid with mouth closed, with hands by his side, and really not looking happy. There wasn't a lot of happiness there. The image that comes to mind is kids with either their hands folded, or their hands by their side, with their mouths shut. Also, really unhappy teachers. I should have picked up on that, and I wish I had picked up on that before I ever started working there. The teachers at that school—everybody just seemed annoyed and frustrated all the time. There was so much scowling. I got the impression that the kids were pests. That's what comes to mind.

Another teacher who had worked at both KIPP and St. HOPE had similar reactions to the total-compliance enforcement. She said she had learned a great deal working in a charter school before quitting to go to work in a public school, and that she was grateful for the experience. However, she said, "I wouldn't wish it on anyone who wanted to be a teacher for the long term." When I asked why not, she said, "It's exhausting. It's demoralizing. And it's just, there are parts of it that are kind of a joke, you know, as far as principals being promoted [from] within, after being teachers for two years, and things like that. You know, totally unqualified people running every aspect of the school."

In comparing the two charter school environments, she found St. HOPE a "step down" from KIPP. When I asked for specifics, she said:

It's a step down from KIPP as far as the commitment, because they didn't require us to host Saturday school, which was a requirement at KIPP. I had to be at school, you know, every Saturday. So PS7 did not require us to do that.

PS7 did not require us to host students after school and provide them with dinner. You know, we didn't have to do that. Whereas, at KIPP, we did.

The other St. HOPE teacher had previously served as a teacher, teacher coach, and public school administrator at both the building and central office levels before returning to middle school teaching at St. HOPE. She echoed a number of the concerns that I had heard from former KIPP teachers. She felt pushed into an unfamiliar "mold" that she felt was "disrespectful to the students." As someone with a background in research, she found the school's student expectations "very contrary to what research says about adolescent kids' need to be able to grow and mature." When I asked her to be specific, she said,

> All of student movement and activity is controlled—I mean completely controlled by the adults. And by that I mean the expectation is that students aren't supposed to be talking in the classroom, where my belief system says that children can't learn if they can't talk—and that structured opportunities to practice language are critical for all kids.

She was visited on a regular basis, and was told she was "too nice to the kids" and "too soft on them." She found "the behavior that they modeled was, you know, very militaristic screaming at the kids—I mean, shouting." She found that all the students in the school "were expected to line up in silence, facing front, and accompanied by an adult for every transition in their day." She said,

> We'd waste 10 minutes [at every transition] lining kids up to meet these expectations, making them, you know, stand silently for a few minutes, walk in silence. If they didn't, stop them and, you know, do it again. And it just seems bizarre to me. And I tried to meet the expectations of the school, to behave in the way that I was expected to behave, but it just felt awful. I mean, it felt wrong in every way. And when I found myself shouting at kids I just said, this is not right. This is not who I am, and this is, I can't do this.

As at KIPP, St. HOPE uses the student paycheck as a way to control student behavior. Students start the week with one hundred dollars in their paycheck and must end the week with at least seventy dollars. During the week, teachers must carry the clipboard with them at all times and record additions and deletions to student paycheck totals for any offense. Students who got to Friday with less than seventy dollars on their checks were subjected to "culture reboot." The offenders were escorted to lunch, where

> they would get their food and go eat lunch in silence in a large room that they had, and some of them would have to turn and actually face the wall, but they

weren't allowed to talk. So they had to eat their lunch in silence and then just sit there and do worksheets for the 90 minutes that was this electives period.

She said that everything about the control of movement and control of thinking left her with the sense that "everything about it was cultlike," and the emphasis on team and school identity could not disguise a school environment where "kids do not feel connected to their school." Her realization that her first year with St. HOPE would be her last came on one of her many late evenings at school, as she tried to finish all the work that had be done the St. HOPE way:

> I actually tried to drink the Kool-Aid for a while. And so I think there was really a moment where, you know, one of the many, many, many evenings that I was at the school site at nine o'clock trying to finish up what we were supposed to have done, just thinking, this is insane. This is certainly not good for me, and I really don't think it's good for them, and I just, I can't drink the Kool-Aid anymore.

When asked what she would tell a friend who was thinking about applying at St. HOPE, she said, "I'd say, don't do it. Don't do it. Let me help you get a job somewhere else. I've helped three teachers leave there since I left. What I would tell them is to expect untenable work expectations that are very discouraging."

New York Times Magazine reported in 2006 that KIPP, Achievement First, Uncommon Schools, Amistad Academy in Connecticut, and North Star Academy in New Jersey consistently shared strategies and methods aimed to produce the high test scores. That list of KIPP emulators has proliferated since then, and the emulation of KIPP methods with it. For instance, KIPP's SLANT model for classroom behavior (sitting up, listening, asking questions, nodding, and tracking the teacher) is a widely shared strategy among No Excuses charters. *New York Times* reporter Paul Tough (2006) noted that David Levin believes that, unlike KIPPsters, "Americans of a certain background learn these methods for taking in information early on and employ them instinctively" (para. 39).

Because KIPP students or the hundreds of thousands of other segregated charter students in No Excuses lockdown schools are not among those "Americans of a certain background," they "need to be taught the methods explicitly." Perhaps more eyebrows would have been raised if No Excuses charter operators like Levin did not have gifted writers like Paul Tough to make the paternalists' condescension at least vaguely couched.

If Tough had stated explicitly that Levin and Feinberg believe that brown and black children of poor parents must be explicitly programmed to sit up, listen, nod, and track the teacher in order to avoid chaos in the classroom, then the KIPP Model's ideology of the "Broken Windows" paternalism would have been clear for all to see. This would surely require the reframing of the civil rights rhetoric of No Excuses schooling, at least from those elites not entirely sanguine about corporate missionary work aimed to isolate and treat, by behavioral and neurological alteration, the defects of poor children.

REFERENCES

Ascend Learning. (2015). *The Ascend culture.* http://www.ascendlearning.com/about/culture/.

Dillon, S. (2011b, March 31). Study says charter network has financial advantages over public schools. *New York Times.* http://www.nytimes.com/2011/03/31/education/31kipp.html?_r= 1&.

Lemov, D. (2010). *Teach like a champion: 49 techniques that put students on the path to college (K–12).* San Francisco: Jossey-Bass.

St. HOPE Public Schools. (n.d). *Five pillars.* http://sthopepublicschools.org/five-pillars/.

Toch, T. (2009). Charter-management organizations: Expansion, survival, and impact. *Education Week* 29 (9), 26–27, 32.

Tough, P. (2006, November 26). What it takes to make a student. *New York Times Magazine.* http://www.nytimes.com/2006/11/26/magazine/26tough.html?pagewanted=print&_r=0.

Chapter Fourteen

A Model Whose Time Has Past

Since its beginning in 1994, the KIPP Model has focused on getting economically disadvantaged students to and through college. As the first KIPP schools were grades five through eight, the long-term goal of college makes some sense as a motivator, even though higher education means high school for most fifth-graders, KIPP or no KIPP. Most often college remains a distant dream for children whose poverty levels have excluded them and their families from that experience in the past.

With KIPP now expanding its reach into early elementary grades and even pre-K, the focus on college may make for attractive classroom posters, but the value of college can hardly be viewed as a realistic motivator for children in these early grades. In fact, KIPP's insistence of the singular goal of attaining a college education in some "remote future" (Dewey, 1897) serves to distract from the integration of young children's experiences or the healthy development of empathetic understanding. Working to make children's schooling more in-tune requirements for working and playing together may have a greater moral force than any of the "performance character" regimen designed by "positive" psychologists in search of interventions to alter children's neural landscapes to fit the compliance requirements of the KIPP Model.

The festooning of KIPP Model school hallways with university pennants and the labeling of classrooms with college names may serve to motivate adults in the school, but elementary-age children are less likely to be affected by these memorabilia, as Dewey (1897) astutely noted over a century ago:

> Much of present education . . . conceives the school as a place where certain information is to be given, where certain lessons are to be learned, or where certain habits are to be formed. The value of these is conceived as lying largely in the remote future; the child must do these things for the sake of something

else he is to do; they are mere preparation. As a result they do not become a part of the life experience of the child and so are not truly educative. (Article II, para. 10)

Like many of Dewey's insights, the ones related to limits of children's abilities to conceive a distant goal have been borne out by research (Scott & Steinberg, 2008; Eccles, 1999). Adolescents' capacity in this regard is based on developmental schedules and environmental realities, rather than adult insistence. The total failure of drug education programs like DARE (Lynam et al., 1999) and the common failure of sexual abstinence programs are not due to the lack of commitment of the programs' instructors, but to the failure to acknowledge the limited capacity among children and adolescents to reflect on and base present conduct on potential future outcomes.

In considering the effects of KIPP's remonstrations on the 80 percent of children who begin fifth grade at KIPP and never finish college, we must question the rigidity of the non-negotiable goal of college graduation for every KIPPster. When combined with KIPP's behavioral strategies aimed to have students internalize all responsibility for shortcomings or failure to attain KIPP's adult goals, whether now or in the future, the unrealistic college goals place enormous stress on already stressed KIPP children. For the eight out of ten KIPP children who begin fifth grade at KIPP and never graduate from college, we can imagine the debilitating effects when many KIPPsters come to weigh their success or failure in life on the basis of a life outcome chosen for them by KIPP.

A dramatic example of the importance of KIPP's college graduation indoctrination was provided during the 2014 KIPP Summit in Houston (KIPP Foundation, 2015e), when an aspiring teacher and former KIPPster, Juanita Davis, recounted a violent episode in her life when she thought she was going to be killed by the father of her child: "If you ever wonder what will go through your head before you think you're about to leave this earth—it's an experience I hope no one has to have, but I remember staring down the barrel of that gun, experiencing the most traumatic event of my life—and the only thing I could think of was that I never earned a college degree."

Considering the sad fact that a disproportionate number of nonprivileged students who attend college end up, if they graduate, with bottom-tier college degrees from online or for-profit colleges, we may ask who is being advantaged by insisting on college for those who must borrow heavily to obtain degrees that may or may not be worth the years of indebtedness and sacrifice that former students cannot escape. In a study by Education Trust (Lynch, Engle, & Cruz, 2011), the authors examined 1,200 colleges with comparable data to determine

1. how many colleges enroll a proportion of low-income students that is at least as high as the national average
2. how many colleges ask these students to pay a portion of their family income no greater than what the average middle-income student pays for a bachelor's degree
3. how many colleges offer all students at least a one-in-two chance at graduation (p. 3)

Researchers found five colleges and universities of the 1,200 that met the three criteria.

Of more concern, still, are student experiences with for-profit colleges of questionable academic reputation and documented histories of preying on the poor and vulnerable (Golden, 2010; U.S. Government Accounting Office, 2010). These "diploma mills" enroll a larger percentage of low-income students like KIPPsters than any other type of college, whether private or public. In 2012, 46 percent of students enrolled at for-profit colleges were from families making less than $30,000 per year, whereas the percentage of low-income students at private nonprofit and public four-year colleges was 18.1 percent and 21.9 percent, respectively (Choi, 2014).

KIPP students who do manage to graduate from legitimate institutions with large debt burdens must face stiff competition in tighter job markets for most college majors. Since 2010, in fact, the demand for noncollege jobs outpaced jobs requiring college degrees. In 2012, over one million Americans with four-year college degrees who were heads of household earned less than $25,000 per year (Eichelberger, 2014).

We may wonder if the facts will catch up with the non-negotiable No Excuses ideology, or if the KIPP Foundation and its philanthropic supporters will remain undeterred by facts as they attempt to compel teachers and students to superhuman feats in order to further burnish the KIPP brand and the other No Excuses brand names. Will support for KIPP's lucrative colonization of urban schools be redirected by the knowledge that "the number of [U.S.] households with children living on less than $2 a day per person has grown 160 percent since 1996, to 1.65 million families in 2011" (Eichelberger, 2014)?

Or would such facts, if known, simply underscore for KIPP's corporate missionaries and their backers the vital need for their mission? Will the unwavering insistence on the college-degree solution for segregated KIPP students be influenced by data that show a college degree "does not significantly reduce racial disparity" (Cohen, 2014), or that the demand for college jobs is flat as the demand for noncollege jobs is on the increase (see figure 14.1)? Will the decided disadvantage of black college graduates in the job market influence the KIPP Modelers' implacable insistence that working hard and being nice is enough to counter the racism and classism that KIPP-sters will surely face if they are fortunate enough to earn degrees?

In 2015, Nobel Prize–winning economist Paul Krugman (2015a) provided the following chart (figure 14.2), which shows shrinking earnings beginning in 2000 for the shrinking numbers of college jobs. Krugman (2015b) casts doubt on the common claim by KIPP supporters that "achievement gaps" are fueling a "skills gap," which must be addressed by improving education so that more raw knowledge more widely dispersed can be transformed into usable power that will solve the problem of inequality.

Krugman (2015b) suggests, instead, that believing, or pretending to believe, that inequality as simply an education problem is an "evasion" that represents a "deeply unserious fantasy" (para. 13): "As for wages and salaries, never mind college degrees—all the big gains are going to a tiny group of individuals holding strategic positions in corporate suites or astride the crossroads of finance. Rising inequality isn't about who has the knowledge; it's about who has the power" (para. 11).

In light of shifting economic and workforce trends, we must question the choice among policymakers who insist that disadvantaged children grow up attending total-compliance "choice" schools where their future has been chosen for them. It would seem to make more sense to develop school programs and learning conditions that acknowledge that we cannot "foretell definitely just what civilization will be twenty years from now," as John Dewey (1897) pointed out back before automobiles replaced horse-drawn carriages.

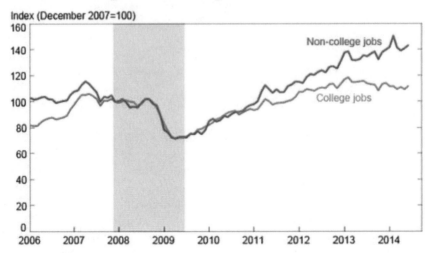

Figure 14.1.   Shrinkage of college jobs and growth among noncollege jobs

Figure 14.2. **Falling incomes for men with college degrees**

No doubt it would be more practical, humane, and rewarding for both children and society alike to have schools that prepare children for uncertain futures by putting them in "complete possession" of all their intellectual, moral, and emotional powers and skills, rather than emphasizing the refinement of a new batch of psychological gimmicks aimed to make poverty more palatable to the poor while offering a fantasy version of social justice.

Clearly related to KIPP's assumptions about children's capacity to be motivated by distant goals beyond their immediate or intermediate horizons are the ill-advised total-compliance policies and practices that further inhibit possibilities for healthy development among disadvantaged children and adolescents. We know, for instance, that children from high-poverty environments often exhibit attachment anxiety more so than children in socioeconomically sound environments, and we also know that the less securely attached children are least able to tolerate frustrating situations or to be able to delay gratification.

Moore (2006) found that "a secure attachment promotes a sense of trust in the future as well as a sense of trust in others" (p. 200). The constant churn created by teacher attrition and replacements in KIPP Model schools only adds to the impermanence and attachment anxiety that children already feel. Child stress is exacerbated, and self-blaming displaces chances for self-efficacy when "zero tolerance" punishment schedules, "straightjacket" behavioral expectations, and demands for more self-control and grit are imposed by temporary teachers whose educational and cultural histories are entirely detached from urban realities.

The KIPP Model schools defy or remain unaware of these evidence-based realities, and the No Excuses formulae exacerbate the problems that the KIPP Model purports to solve. Emotional support cannot occur where teachers are allowed and encouraged to yell and scream at children or to be "militant" in their demeanor. Student autonomy cannot survive where children are harshly punished for even minor infractions of rules and forced to remain silent, on guard, and docile. Students cannot trust or form relationships with important adults where the adults are being replaced every year or two.

Without the active help from those who are able, yet unwilling, to help end poverty, demanding more from children who have the least will never make them the most they might be.

It is doubtful that entrenched reformers with paternalistic agendas will be rerouted by either logic or compassion from their long-standing mission. As long as generous public funding continues to support corporate reform school endeavors and/or as long as the same reformulated reforms result in the initiation of new ideologues convinced that public problems are best addressed by "market based" solutions, we will see a continuing push for more No Excuses urban chain gangs that pursue their inhumane and miseducative ends by "any means necessary."

What we can expect from the new (and old) paternalists is a renewed crusade, in fact, to alter the children of the poor in ways that will encourage further shrinkage of our social and ethical infrastructures and the growth of new, more lucrative revenue streams for publicly funded and privately operated education.

REFERENCES

Choi, L. (2014, January 10). *For-profit colleges and the student debt crisis.* San Francisco: Federal Bank of San Francisco. http://www.frbsf.org/community-development/blog/for-profit-colleges-and-the-student-debt-crisis/.

Cohen, P. (2014, December 24). For recent black college graduates, a tougher road to employment. *New York Times.* http://www.nytimes.com/2014/12/25/business/for-recent-black-college-graduates-a-tougher-road-to-employment.html?_r=0.

Dewey, J. (1897). *My pedagogic creed.* New York: E. L. Kellogg & Co. http://dewey.pragmatism.org/creed.htm.

Eccles, J. (1999, Fall). The development of children ages 6 to 14. *Future Child* 9 (2), 30–44.

Eichelberger, E. (2014, March/April). 10 poverty myths, busted. *Mother Jones.* http://www.motherjones.com/politics/2014/03/10-poverty-myths-busted.

Golden, D. (2010, April 29). Homeless dropouts from high school lured by for-profit colleges. *Bloomberg.com.* http://www.bloomberg.com/news/2010-04-30/homeless-dropouts-from-high-school-lured-by-for-profit-colleges-with-cash.html.

KIPP Foundation. (2015e). *KIPP school summit 2014.* http://www.kipp.org/our-approach/sharing-and-collaboration/kipp-school-summit-2014.

Krugman, P. (2015a, February 27). Rip van skillsgap. *New York Times.* http://krugman.blogs.nytimes.com/2015/02/22/rip-van-skillsgap/?_r=0.

Krugman, P. (2015b, February 23). Knowledge isn't power. *New York Times.* http://www.nytimes.com/2015/02/23/opinion/paul-krugman-knowledge-isnt-power.html.

Lynam, D. et al. (1999). Project DARE: No effects at 10-year follow-up. *Journal of Consulting and Clinical Psychology* 67 (4), 590–93. http://homepage.psy.utexas.edu/HomePage/Class/Psy394Q/Behavior%20Therapy%20Class/Assigned%20Readings/Substance%20Abuse/DARE.pdf.

Lynch, M., Engle, J., & Cruz, J. (2011). *Priced out: How the wrong financial-aid policies hurt low-income students.* Washington, DC: Education Trust. https://edtrust.org/resource/priced-out-how-the-wrong-financial-aid-policies-hurt-low-income-students/.

Moore, C. (2006). *The development of commonsense psychology.* New York: Taylor and Francis.

Scott, E., & Steinberg, L. (2008, Fall). Adolescent development and the regulation of youth crime. *Future Child* 18 (2), 15–33.

U.S. Government Accounting Office. (2010, August 4). *For-profit colleges: Undercover testing finds colleges encouraged fraud and engaged in deceptive and questionable marketing practices.* Washington, DC: U.S. Government Accounting Office. http://www.gao.gov/new.items/d10948t.pdf.

Chapter Fifteen

Another Generation of the KIPP Model?

As we have already established, the No Excuses KIPP Model schools are concerned with measuring student test performance and student performance character, which provide the sought-after evidence of both student and teacher production values. Despite the consensus among researchers and statisticians that teachers are responsible for a small percentage of the differences in student achievement (the American Statistical Association [2014] puts the number between 1 percent and 14 percent), KIPP's policies are predicated on the assumption that teachers are the primary influence on student test performance.

Student scores, then, become the metric for determining the worth of a teacher. Consistent, too, with reformers' derogation of evidence for the effects of poverty and discrimination on KIPP students' test and character performance, the leaders of KIPP have set into motion a schooling machine that processes both students and teachers through a system sustained by the conversion of human energy sources into academic and character test scores. These scores, then, function to define and predict human capital outcomes. Those students and teachers whose energy cannot be converted into higher scores are extracted before they weaken the system.

Even though academic test performance remains the primary production function at KIPP, David Levin in recent years has worked with positive psychologists Martin Seligman and Angela Duckworth at the University of Pennsylvania to further develop strategies to better instill performance character traits. Not surprisingly, the development of performance character assessments has preceded the elaboration of a performance character curriculum, as witnessed with the example below of a character progress card that is meant to accompany the academic report card.

Ostensibly aimed to measure performance character in a handful of KIPP schools, most of the traits evaluated on the "Character Performance Report" (see figure 15.1) serve to undergird the academic program outputs at KIPP, which are measured by tests, either standardized or teacher made. Because students have come to understand that their results on standardized tests or the "formative" tests that are used to prepare for the summative standardized tests provide the evidence of learning that counts for their grades, they have

KIPP:CHARACTER
REPORT CARD

Jane Smith, Grade: 8	KIPP Imagine, Date: 01/28/11	Q2	Q2					
	OVERALL SCORE	4.30	Teacher 1	Teacher 2	Teacher 3	Teacher 4	Teacher 5	Teacher 6
Zest		4.28						
1	Actively participates	4.50	4	5	5	4	4	5
2	Shows enthusiasm	4.17	5	4	3	4	4	5
3	Invigorates others	4.17	3	4	5	4	5	4
Grit		4.11						
4	Finishes whatever he or she begins	4.00	4	5	3	4	4	4
5	Tries very hard even after experiencing failure	4.17	5	4	4	3	4	5
6	Works independently with focus	4.17	4	4	3	4	5	5
Self Control – School Work		4.33						
7	Comes to class prepared	4.50	4	5	5	5	4	4
8	Pays attention and resists distractions	4.50	4	5	4	5	4	5
9	Remembers and follows directions	4.17	4	5	5	4	3	4
10	Gets to work right away rather than procrastinating	4.17	5	4	4	4	3	5
Self Control - Interpersonal		4.54						
11	Remains calm even when criticized or otherwise provoked	4.50	4	5	4	5	5	4
12	Allows others to speak without interruption	4.83	5	5	5	4	5	5
13	Is polite to adults and peers	4.50	4	5	4	5	4	5
14	Keeps his/her temper in check	4.33	4	5	4	4	5	4
Optimism		4.25						
15	Gets over frustrations and setbacks quickly	4.33	5	4	4	4	5	4
16	Believes that effort will improve his or her future	4.17	5	4	4	3	4	5
Gratitude		4.25						
17	Recognizes and shows appreciation for others	4.17	4	4	5	4	5	3
18	Recognizes and shows appreciation for his/her opportunities	4.33	5	4	5	3	4	5
Social Intelligence		4.33						
19	Is able to find solutions during conflicts with others	4.17	4	4	3	5	4	5
20	Demonstrates respect for feelings of others	4.50	5	4	4	4	5	5
21	Knows when and how to include others	4.33	5	4	4	4	5	4
Curiosity		4.28						
22	Is eager to explore new things	4.17	5	4	3	4	5	4
23	Asks and answers questions to deepen understanding	4.50	5	4	5	4	4	5
24	Actively listens to others	4.17	4	4	5	4	5	3

SCALE
1= Very much unlike the student
2= Unlike the student
3= Somewhat like the student
4= Like the student
5= Very much like the student

Figure 15.1. KIPP Character Performance Report Card

come to understand, too, that other areas of measured performance are tertiary.

As may be expected, most KIPP students give attention to the demands of the testing regime and little else. As one former KIPP teacher noted, "They were really good performers on tests . . . but they had figured out that they didn't need to perform in class. And so the teachers were not satisfied with the performance in class, but they still would perform well on the standardized test."

Supporters of the KIPP Model insist that self-regulation and self-control must prevail if disadvantaged children are not to be carried down a future road to ruin by their bad habits that focus on satisfying present needs. According to a new breed of psycho-paternalists (Steinberg, 2014), future-oriented self-control behavior must overcome present-oriented self-rewarding behaviors. Schools that serve poor children, then, should introduce social and emotional learning (SEL) strategies that are sequenced, active, focused, and explicit (SAFE).

Steinberg calls for less socialization and more training of "executive functions," which remain, as they were in the eighteenth century, tied to memory capacity. Improving memory works to raise test scores and grades, which are largely dependent upon the ample presence of "executive function." Delayed gratification, grit, self-control, and the rest of the performance character traits must be imposed and assessed in order to mediate the internal warring impulses between self-reward and self-regulation systems within the brains of adolescents.

Based on what we have learned of KIPP's compliance demands, the KIPP Model would seem to offer the optimal environment for dredging the new neural channels required by the paternalist psychology. However, the available research does not show any kind of character transformation happening at KIPP. In the widely disseminated Mathematica study (2008–2013) for which KIPP patrons paid almost $4 million, we find significant test score gains at KIPP when compared to local public schools, but the same cannot be said for improvements in performance character strengths. Steinberg (2014) offers this sobering summary of the Mathematica findings that "were not so widely broadcast":

> They [students] weren't more effortful or persistent. They didn't have more favorable academic self-conceptions or stronger school engagement. They didn't score higher than the comparison group in self-control. In fact, they were more likely to engage in "undesirable behavior," including losing their temper, lying to and arguing with their parents, and giving teachers a hard time. They were more likely to get into trouble at school. Despite the program's emphasis on character development, the KIPP students were no less likely to smoke, drink, get high, or break the law. Nor were their hopes for their educational futures any higher or their plans any more ambitious. (p. 153)

According to that same Mathematica study, KIPP students were significantly less well adjusted, did much more homework, and reported much less involvement in extracurricular activities than non-KIPPsters (Steinberg, 2014, pp. 144–45). With two hours of homework per night on average, and with the extended day, week, and year, little time remains for extracurricular activities that are, after all, in shorter supply at KIPP than at public or private schools.

KIPP's No Excuses methods emphasizing silence and minimal peer interactions offer clues as to the growth of problem behaviors reported by the Mathematica researchers. KIPP rules appear to assume that performance character can be improved without the need for interactions with others. With the exception of just one criterion on KIPP's performance character rubric (KIPP Foundation, 2015c), "Asked questions to help s/he [*sic*] learn better," we find that there is no need for a KIPPster to ever verbalize at all.

Even so, former teachers that I interviewed saw enforced silence as a big organizational mistake, a pedagogical shortcoming, and an oppressive fixation that was not in the best interests of students or teachers. One teacher offered important insights into the effects of the limited opportunities for isolated and disadvantaged children to learn how dialogue works:

> Well, some of these students come from broken homes and they've experienced trauma, which is essentially untreated in many cases. And there's not a whole lot of socialization at KIPP, and so it's a lot of silence and frustration, I imagine, for some of the students who are further behind academically, as was the case here for this class. Because they were expected to basically be these all-star students and there's the No Excuses mentality that's driven in throughout the entire school year, there's just all this frustration throughout the day.
>
> And they're not allowed to really bond with each other throughout the day, so there's a lot of conflict amongst each other. And so some of the disrespect that I see between my students there at KIPP—I think had to deal with the fact that they didn't have a real good opportunity to bond. But it was due to the fact that many of them have had traumatic lives or continue to experience trauma and are punished instead of really being cared for and listened to, even. The big thing at KIPP was no talking back no matter what—I don't want to hear it. You could receive a harsher punishment if you even utter a word of talking back in response [to a] punishment.

Among the teachers interviewed for this book, there was a shared anxiety with regard to what KIPP's lockdown environment will eventually produce. As student success entails a sense of empowerment, or the ability to not only control but also to affect or transform one's world, these former teachers understood the danger that the KIPP Model poses to that purpose or aim. The resulting anxiety is represented by the statement below, which expresses concern that the KIPP influence would continue to reach beyond the 183 KIPP franchises:

> I am worried that if the KIPP motto starts to spread that it will end up going into public schools as well and then because KIPP is so test-focused, other schools are going to be that way. I feel like we are just going to be creating robots, like people who aren't really able to think for themselves and be creative and expressive and be able to have their own personalities. I am just worried that it is just going to create a society of people who are going to be complacent and just kind of do whatever people tell them to do because that is what they have learned their whole life.

Growing interest among corporate foundations and their think tanks (Center on Children and Families at Brookings, 2014) for "character" building through social-emotional learning (SEL) interventions suggests the KIPP Model is likely to be repackaged for another generation of No Excuses schools. Once again, psychologists of the developmental variety are coming to dominate this social and emotional learning (SEL) niche (Steinberg, 2014; Farrington et al., 2012), and they are joined by new paternalists who are fixated, as they always have been, on self-regulation and self-control.

As a solution to their character deficiencies among the disenfranchised, SEL will likely have a dominant role in the next phase of the crusade to fix the poor. In a recent research review (Dweck, Walton, & Cohen, 2014) sponsored by the Gates Foundation, the authors examine studies that support the Duckworth thesis that noncognitive, or motivational, factors like "academic tenacity" can have more effect than "cognitive factors" on "core academic outcomes such as GPA and test scores" (p. 2):

> At its most basic level, academic tenacity is about working hard, and working smart, for a long time. More specifically, academic tenacity is about the mindsets and skills that allow students to . . . look beyond short-term concerns to longer-term or higher-order goals, and withstand challenges and setbacks to persevere toward these goals. (p. 4)

The philanthrocapitalists and their think tank scholars quote liberally from the work of Walter Mischel (1989; 2014), whose experiments with delayed gratification among preschoolers provide the dominant metaphor for another generation of paternalist endeavors. In Mischel's experiments, children were offered a single marshmallow immediately or two marshmallows later if they could delay their reward. The test, which came to be labeled "The Marshmallow Test," represents the potential to delay gratification in order to gain a larger reward later on.

At many of the KIPP, Aspire, Achievement First, and YES Prep schools, children wear T-shirts emblazoned with "Don't Eat the Marshmallow." Mischel's (2014) latest work, *The Marshmallow Test: Mastering Self-Control*, acknowledges KIPP's prominent role and places it within the context of recent research on improving self-control. David Levin has made Mischel's book a central component in his Coursera massive open online course (MOOC), *Teaching Character and Creating Positive Classrooms*, which was first offered with coinstructor Angela Duckworth in 2014.

Levin and Duckworth are two of the cofounders of Character Lab, which uses Duckworth's experimental work at the Upper Darby School District near the University of Pennsylvania to fine-tune the character performance interventions that Levin initiated at KIPP schools in the early 2000s. Interestingly, much of the research that is used to justify the use of the Seligman-Duckworth resiliency improvement methodology is the same data offered to justify the Seligman deal that cost the U.S. Army $145 million (see chapter 1) for interventions that brought no benefit to GIs suffering from the stresses of war. We may wonder how much these alleged remedies for children might cost federal and state education departments, whose bankrolls are much smaller than those at the Pentagon.

A related character approach that operates under the trade name *Brainology* claims that one thousand schools are now using its "growth mind-set" based on Carol Dweck's book, *Mindset* (2006). Dweck's work is included on the suggested reading list used by Levin and Duckworth for their online course mentioned above. Brainology cites unpublished research that shows teaching the growth mind-set "boosts motivation and achievement" and narrows both the gender and racial achievement gaps (Mindset Works, Inc., 2008–2012). A license for three hundred students is available for $5,250, or the program may be purchased for $79 per student. A separate site license for professional development is sold for $1,500.

The Brainology website has links to a handout that summarizes findings for a short list of preliminary studies showing Brainology's effectiveness in increasing motivation, although none of the findings has appeared in refereed journals. Even so, the enthusiasm among reformers is strong and growing stronger as the debilitating stresses from poverty rise, and the spread of educational austerity measures calls for the ramping up of strategies that might mollify those affected children whose promised rewards become even less certain.

THE NEXT GENERATION OF NO EXCUSES PATERNALISM

Just as the appearance of the Thernstroms' (2004) *No Excuses* announced the delivery of a new paternalistic script for schools that serve poor, black, and brown children, the publication of another book (Tough, 2012), *How Children Succeed: Grit, Curiosity, and the Hidden Power of Character*, brought news of the next act in the school-based morality tale plotted to save the poor from themselves. Tough provides a popularized survey of the psychological theory that underpins the KIPP Model's character education program, and as such it moves the focus away from the Thernstroms' conclusions regarding cultural deficits among the poor to a fixation of character shortcomings.

Tough's book examines the justifications and methods for neurologically altering children in order to improve their "performance character" and to enhance their human capital potential, as measured by grades and test scores. Instead of directly assaulting the cultural shortcomings of the poor, as the Thernstroms had done, Tough's book centers on the possibilities for fixing flawed character.

Within the new paternalist plot outline, performance character is viewed as a collected demonstration of noncognitive and significantly alterable traits that greatly influence cognitive outcomes. Supporters contend that if cognitive outcomes (grades and test scores) among poor children are going to equal those of privileged children, then deficient performance character has to be zeroed in on. Even if the target's label has changed from "culture" to "character," the destination of the arrow has not; it remains the psychology (attitude, motivation, and behavior) of the child that must be altered, rather than any sociocultural or socioeconomic contexts.

Tough (2012) provides a compendium of enthused speculation and scanty research findings on the capacity to alter the malleable brain chemistry and functions of children traumatized by poverty. Tough explores the grand, or grandiose, hope for a scientific way to take advantage of the neurological plasticity of children in order to program good discipline and character. With an enthusiasm reminiscent of the heady days of eugenics when Stanford's president, David Jordan, talked of the potential for "Burbanking the human race" (The American Practitioner, 1912), Tough (2012) quotes pediatrician Nadine Burke Harris, who excitedly discusses the possibility of changing children's behaviors in order to alter brain chemistry and, thus, permanently modify performance character:

> When we look at these kids and their behavior, it can all seem so mysterious. . . . But at some point, what you're seeing is just a complex series of chemical reactions. It's the folding of a protein or the activation of a neuron. And what's exciting about that is that those things are treatable. When you get down to the molecules, you realize, that's where the healing is. That's where you're discovering a solution. (p. 26)

In a *New York Times* article that preceded the publication of *How Children Succeed*, Tough (2012) conceded that the earlier reform strategy of ignoring the effects of poverty on children had been a mistake. But rather than advocating for interventions that would alter the structural conditions that enable the continuation of poverty, a new generation of KIPP Model supporters influenced by writers like Paul Tough now appears focused on behavioral-cognitive interventions to alter the body's reactions to the stress that poverty creates.

These alterations are to make it possible for "executive functioning," or conscious memory, to proceed uninterrupted, despite poverty-induced distractions such as noise, danger, hunger, or any of the other life-altering annoyances with which the poor must contend. To change the body's reactions to stress, of course, gets us back to the need to change the brain, which must be done, it is argued, by strengthening behaviors, specifically those behaviors that signal healthy "academic mindsets."

The flawed mindsets brought on by the body's capitulation to stress are to be successfully altered, then, with activities and habits that increase *grit, self-control, zest, social intelligence, gratitude, optimism*, and *curiosity*. To carry out this child improvement agenda, teachers will be trained in a new pedagogy that places as much emphasis on performance character calisthenics as it does on exercising the executive functions, where memory occupies the position of the brain's CEO.

WHERE'S THE BEEF, OR THE MARSHMALLOW?

When white, middle-class corporate education reformers talk about the need to have brown and black poor children learn to "delay gratification," who can help but wince, at least just a little? After all, black children were being trained to accept the same message over a hundred years ago, when white teachers funded by Northern philanthropists taught the children of former slaves that moral inferiority required them to wait until their race could catch up to the morally superior white race, whose history as Christian people provided a two-thousand-year divine advantage that clearly justified their superior status.

Booker T. Washington was one of those youngsters taught this lesson of inherited moral depravity at Hampton Normal and Agricultural Institute, and the brainwashing he received lasted him a lifetime. He was the first black man to have lunch at the White House, and he served loyally throughout his life as a spokesman for white Northern philanthropists who wanted their message of unforced gradualism in civil rights and economic servitude to dominate discourse among black citizens whose parents and grandparents were America's only involuntary immigrants.

When Washington admonished African Americans to "dignify and glorify labor," for "it is at the bottom of life that we must begin, not at the top" (Bacon, 1986, p. 14), he was anticipating a later version of the same message to work hard, be nice, and be patient. Or as some may say, "Work hard, be hard, and don't eat the marshmallow."

Today's white reformer philanthropists are the planners of another century of authoritarian, paternalistic schooling models for the children of the black and brown poor, and though some of the tools and techniques have changed from the late nineteenth century, the aim and the purpose clearly echoes down to us from the heyday of the Hampton Model (see introduction). Today, black children are told that it is not their moral inferiority that holds them back but, rather, their character defects.

And if white reformer icons like Mike Feinberg and David Levin can come up with ways to improve black and brown children's character, compliance, grades, and test scores, then all the poverty in the world cannot hold them back as long as they remain patient. Or so they are told. In the meantime, the poor children who are having their characters altered and their cultures cleansed so that they are immunized against the effects of poverty must wait. How long must they wait to eat that marshmallow? What kind of threats, punishments, and humiliations will be required for them in the meantime? Will unending patience be required until policy reformers and pedagogical technicians can discover another more compelling explanation for the failure of the oppressed?

In his best seller, *Outliers*, Malcolm Gladwell (2008) offers KIPP as an example to support his premise that *most* people achieve success with hard work and the help of others. Gladwell views KIPP and KIPP supporters as providers of the "helping-hand" solution that is aimed to close the gaps between the haves and have-nots. It would seem, then, that if success in life is achieved with the help of others and some good luck, rather than from personal advantage or a special gift (as Gladwell argues), then it makes sense that failure should abide by the same law. That is, if we are to no longer believe in self-made successes, as Gladwell clearly does not, then can we really continue to believe in the self-made failure?

Apparently, Gladwell can, as he attributes the educational disadvantages of the poor to the failure of the poor. Gladwell offers us the example of twelve-year-old Marita, whose "[poor] community does not give her what she needs," and, as a result, she is placed into the KIPP school so that she can be helped:

> Marita's life is not the life of a typical twelve-year-old. Nor is it what we would necessarily wish for a twelve-year old. Children, we like to believe, should have time to play and dream and sleep. Marita has responsibilities. . . . Marita has had to ["shed some part" of . . . [her] own identity] because the cultural legacy she had been given does not match her circumstances . . . not when middle and upper middle class families are using weekends and summer vacation to push their children ahead. Her community does not give her what she needs. So what does she have to do? Give up her evenings and weekends and friends—all the elements of her old world—and replace them with KIPP. (p. 266)

Are we to believe, as Gladwell obviously does, that poverty and its debili-tating effects are the faults of the poor, which must be remedied, then, by KIPP-like character and cultural interventions that require children to sacri-fice "all the elements" of their worlds—except for that most striking element of being poor? Must Marita and the rest of the KIPPsters give up everything for KIPP except their poverty?

It doesn't seem to occur to Gladwell or to any of the other No Excuses culture and character fixers that providing the needed resources for Marita's community to "give her what she needs" may be a more responsible and sustainable kind of intervention than resorting to psychological and neuro-logical manipulations by clueless amateurs, who demand Marita's childhood in exchange for some far-distant and questionable path to economic salva-tion.

This modern-day example of blaming the poor for their poverty follows a long lineage of patronizing ideology that goes all the way back to our Puritan forefathers, who viewed poverty as clear evidence of the poor's own moral depravity and wickedness. For the twenty-first-century KIPP Model's pater-nalist patrons and apologists, the poor's depraved culture and weak character must be addressed with precision interventions, so as to overcome the condi-tions that corporate and governmental enablers of *in absentia* poverty contin-ue to silently support with their colossal passivity. Today's public punish-ments of the children of the poor come in doses of brain-altering classroom interventions that are meted out by unwitting nonprofessionals, yet they re-main inspired by the rigid catechism of working hard and becoming harder, still, for even the slimmest chance one day to be among the Economic Elect.

In an influential report (Farrington, Roderick, Allensworth, Nagaoka, Keyes, Johnson, & Beechum, 2012) from the University of Chicago's CCSR, which provides a schematic for moving forward with the kind of character education that will produce greater human capital formation, there is figure 15.2 from page 13 of the report. I offer it here near the close of this book, for I think it encapsulates the uniquely insular framing that has remained so remarkably persistent over the decades of reformulated education reforms of the new paternalist era.

In figure 15.2 we see all sorts of connections from the "School and Class-room Context" on down to the bottom line of "Academic Performance," which then feeds back into the "Academic Mindsets." On the side and dis-connected from the flow of influences is "Student Background Characteris-tics." And even though all of this active interplay of influences occurs within a "Socio-Cultural Context," that context would appear to have no influence on, or to not be influenced by, anything that goes on at the school and classroom level.

Now it is not as if the authors (Farrington, Roderick, Allensworth, Nagao-ka, Keyes, Johnson, & Beechum, 2012) did not know of the interplay of

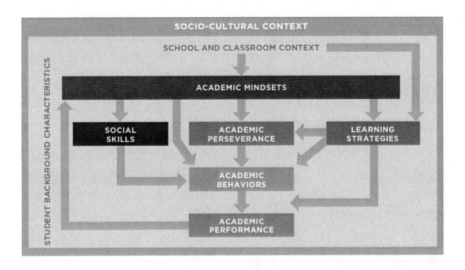

Figure 15.2.   A model showing interactions of five noncognitive factors without influence to or from sociocultural context

structural factors and student background outside of school with the pedagogical factors inside. In fact, they admit that the "interrelationships between cognitive, psychological, and structural variables and school performance are exceedingly complex."

> We situate the model within a larger "Socio-Cultural Context" that shapes the structural mechanisms of schools and classrooms, as well as the interactions and subjective experiences of the human beings within schools. Opportunity structures in the larger society; economic conditions that shape employment opportunities as well as schooling costs; the presence of racism, sexism, and other types of discrimination that give rise to stereotypes and prejudice; and stark inequalities in resources across neighborhoods and schools all contribute to the larger context in which American students learn. (p. 13)

The authors' expansiveness in the consideration of the problem is, in the next sentence, neutralized, for reasons that those preferring psychological solutions to psychosocial problems readily explain: "We offer this model as a simplified framework for conceptualizing the primary relationships among these factors, for the purpose of framing our discussion" (p. 13). With that cleaving caveat, then, the discussion is severed from the complexity of "primary relationships" that have to be understood and acted upon for social and economic wounds to be effectively remedied.

In doing so, the attempt at healing begins even before the cutting stops, which will, in turn, require increasingly advanced bandages to staunch the bleeding, even as the social and economic wounds deepen and the infection advances. The result is a corporate education reform discussion framed once again for the benefit of a failed solution with a new pseudoscientific twist. Those who engage in it actively fortify the boundary between the psychological and the sociological sides of the human enterprise, even though history is replete with grim examples that "neither can be subordinated to the other or neglected without evil results following" (Dewey, 1897, p. 4).

IF NOT THE KIPP MODEL, THEN WHAT?

In defending schooling practices for disadvantaged, urban children that middle-class parents would never allow for their own children, corporate education reformers like to talk about achievement inequities that cannot wait for utopian social plans to be enacted or for perfectly fair solutions to be found. Whatever-it-takes kinds of action, they argue, are needed now. Secretary Duncan (U.S. Department of Education, 2012) expressed this sentiment in 2012 when he said, "We can't let the perfect become the enemy of the good. We can't let the utopian become the enemy of the excellent. And we can't let rhetorical purity become the enemy of rigorous practice" (para. 22).

Ironically, it is the kind of consistent inaction with regard to child poverty and social injustice that has created the presumed emergency status that reformers argue now justifies the jettisoning of fair, effective, professional, and democratic schooling practices that were once the ideal of American public education. One has to wonder, too, what price this new rigor and grit agenda will demand.

Will it require of Marita and other children at total-compliance schools more than their childhoods, which have already been claimed as a necessary cost to helping them to become the behavioral equivalents of middle-class children with the stamina to sit quietly and wait for the marshmallow? If more social-emotional learning treatments are required, what else will be paved over as new neurologic road maps are excavated and built in the brains of children who, otherwise, would be traumatized by the effects of poverty?

We have to wonder, here, which is more utopian in nature and concept: a) to expand into schools the "learned optimism" and "resiliency training" practices from the Seligman/Duckworth self-control and grit movement that have been demonstrated to have little empirical basis and no practical value in the prevention of suicide, violence, and other antisocial behaviors associated with post-traumatic stress, or b) to strategically set about the business that justice and honesty require of a democratic society by

- incentivizing (at the federal level) and investing (at the corporate level) in research-based efforts to create and sustain economically and culturally integrated classrooms, schools, and communities
- instituting an ongoing Race to End Childhood Poverty, which will provide adequate funding and human resource assistance to states for developing and piloting initiatives that, if successful, can be scaled up in communities with similar cultural and social characteristics
- developing a national plan to recruit and professionally prepare the most diverse and competent teacher and administrator force in the world, which will be thoroughly schooled in the history and implementation of best practices, effective policy planning, multicultural community relations, and the social science and art of teaching
- incentivizing and investing in institutional capacity to develop, implement, and study curriculum and assessment practices that address the entire learning spectrum within a variety of cultural contexts, from the simplest repetitive learning tasks to the most complex and contextually demanding tasks
- mandating by regulation and statute fair and adequate systems for funding public education that are subject to public oversight and accountability at all levels
- building a sense of shared mission, trust, and mutually shared accountability among policymakers, educators, political leaders, the business community, and the general public
- instituting a system of research and public sharing that will provide needed guidance for education policy decisions
- creating cross-disciplinary teams of researchers and practitioners from the sciences, technologies, arts, and humanities to focus on novel ways of addressing social, economic, cultural, and health issues to benefit all citizens
- constructing democratic governance structures at the local, state, and federal levels that are proactive as well as responsive in making sure that equal educational, economic, and cultural opportunities are provided to all citizens
- protecting children, parents, and teachers from miseducative, abusive, misguided, and/or developmentally inappropriate schooling practices

As some readers will dismiss this list as more advocacy for "utopian social change" (Tough, 2011), closer consideration will hopefully show that much of the infrastructure in already in place to move forward with some of these initiatives. The U.S. Department of Education (USDOE), for instance, has the capacity to direct and connect researchers from around the nation and the world toward projects that could be initiated from current levels of discretionary funding.

The Education Resources Information Center (ERIC) could expand its online reach to serve scholars, educators, and the general public, alike. Rather than incentivizing more resegregation and ill-prepared teachers with generous federal allocations for more No Excuses charter schools and Teach for America and TFA emulators, the Department could shift funding to research and development of magnet schools, controlled choice plans, and development of teacher preparation and credentialing systems that have worked in countries such as Finland and cities such as Shanghai.

Ironically, some of the foreign countries who do well on international tests lean heavily on the decades of research and shared thinking by American educational icons (Sahlberg, 2011; Asma, 2014) such as Jerome Bruner, Ralph Tyler, John Dewey, Maxine Greene, and John Goodlad—rather than a Harvard MBA (Lemov, 2015) with sixty-four foolproof ways to "teach like a champion."

Rather than making excuses for more school segregation by continuing to point to failed desegregation efforts of the past, unions, businesses, and governments could commit to uphold the 9–0 Supreme Court ruling over sixty years ago that declared separate schools are inherently unequal. And rather than cheerleading for myopic and unaccountable corporate solutions to educational issues that have deep roots in economic and social inequality, political leaders can and must be forced to confront the problems that they would rather contract out to the well-connected for temporal corporate non-remedies.

I offer a final example of the kind of program that, if studied, fine-tuned, and expanded, could begin to operationalize some of the ten options presented above as preferable alternatives to paternalists' neoeugenic schemes to correct the "noncognitive" defects of poor children. In Baltimore, a program called Promise Heights provides a number of wraparound services to a handful of inner-city Baltimore schools and in part of Baltimore's first African American community.

Initially funded by a modest $500,000 grant from USDOE in 2012, program services are coordinated by the School of Social Work at the University of Maryland, which partnered with churches, schools, community groups, and Baltimore's social workers to "test out ways" to help the children in neighborhoods plagued by poverty and violence (McDaniels, 2014): "The goal of the multiyear initiative is to combat the cycle of poverty by wrapping children and families in supportive services from cradle to college. Dealing with trauma is a major focus of that work" (para. 13).

Trauma comes in the form of post-traumatic stress disorder (PTSD), which affects as many as a third of Promise Height elementary and middle school children who have been exposed to violence inside or outside the home.

Some students bit classmates, leaving teeth marks on hands and cheeks; a few threatened to hurt staff members. Other children, dubbed "runners," darted out of the building and down barren city blocks, with frantic teachers on their heels. The encounters exhausted Johnson and other teachers, who began to see the children as troublemakers.

Studies have piled up showing that in the tangle of tough, intractable issues like poverty and drug addiction, exposure to violence is a major factor damaging children's health. The stress that fills their little bodies breeds anxiety and depression, making it hard for them to concentrate in school. In fact, research has found that such experiences hurt the development of crucial areas of their brains—those involving attention, memory and behavior control. In the worst cases, children walk around with symptoms of post-traumatic stress disorder no different from those plaguing soldiers who have fought on the front lines. (para. 3, 7)

Strategies used in the Promise Heights program, however, do not focus on behavioral lockdown or experiments to build self-control and grit among children with little capacity for either. Instead, social workers are in the schools and in homes to work with teachers and parents to understand what is going on and to provide interventions that preserve the dignity of children, parents, and teachers alike. No one is asked to sacrifice her childhood: The University of Maryland team has embedded social workers in neighborhood schools. They make home visits and coach adults on parenting. Teachers learn that instead of asking a misbehaving child, "What's wrong with you?" they need to ask, "What happened last night?"

Other services include psychological services, parenting courses, wellness programs, prenatal childcare, asthma treatment, GED classes, job counseling, and a "parent scholar program," which puts parents in classrooms to assist teachers. In the first year of the parent-scholar program that had five parent scholars embedded in one school, school suspensions fell by 43 percent.

Results for Promise Heights are encouraging, and it provides but a single example—a beginning point to address the many inequalities that consistently produce achievement gaps, which are the obvious symptoms of the growing child poverty that paternalist reformers and supporters of the KIPP Model ignore. There may have been at one time an excuse for such disregard, but with what we know and can no longer deny there can be no excuse for imposing tried-and-failed remedies from previous centuries that exacerbate the problems, now grown epidemic. Surely the very notion of education reform deserves something better if it is to escape the long shadow cast by a patronizing and racist education policy.

REFERENCES

American Practitioner. (1912, September). Burbanking the human race. *The American Practitioner* 46, 458.

American Statistical Association. (2014). *ASA statement on using value-added models for educational assessment.* https://www.amstat.org/policy/pdfs/ASA_VAM_Statement.pdf.

Asma, S. (2014, June 8). From China, with pragmatism. *New York Times.* http://opinionator. blogs.nytimes.com/2014/06/08/from-china-with-pragmatism/.

Bacon, A. (1986). *The Negro and the Atlanta Exposition.* Baltimore: Trustees of the John Slater Fund.

Center on Children and Families at Brookings. (2014). *Essay series on character and opportunity.* Washington, DC: The Character and Opportunity Project of the Brookings Institution. http://www.brookings.edu/~/media/multimedia/interactives/2014/ccf_characterseries/characterandopportunityessays.pdf.

Dweck, C., Walton, G., & Cohen, G. (2014). *Tenacity: Mindsets and skills that promote long-term learning.* The Bill and Melinda Gates Foundation. https://web.stanford.edu/~gwalton/home/Welcome_files/DweckWaltonCohen_2014.pdf.

Dweck, C. (2006). *Mindset: The new psychology of success.* New York: Ballantine.

Farrington, C. A., Roderick, M., Allensworth, E., Nagaoka, J., Keyes, T. S., Johnson, D. W., & Beechum, N. (2012). *Teaching adolescents to become learners. The role of noncognitive factors in shaping school performance: A critical literature review.* Chicago: University of Chicago Consortium on Chicago School Research.

Gladwell, M. (2008). *Outliers: The story of success.* New York: Little, Brown and Company.

KIPP Foundation. (2015c). *Character strengths and corresponding behaviors.* http://www.kipp.org/our-approach/strengths-and-behaviors.

Lemov, D. (2015). *Teach like a champion 2.0: 62 techniques that put students on the path to college.* San Francisco: Jossey Bass.

McDaniels, A. (2014, December 13). Collateral damage: Advocates aim to save Baltimore children from impact of violence. *Baltimore Sun.* http://www.baltimoresun.com/health/bs-md-health-violence-121114-story.html -page=1.

Mindset Works, Inc. (2008–2012). *Mindset works: Spark learning.* http://www.mindsetworks.com/webnav/whatismindset.aspx.

Mischel, W. (2014). *The marshmallow test: Mastering self-control.* New York: Little, Brown.

Mischel, W., Shoda, Y., & Rodriguez, M. (1989). Delay of gratification in children. *Science* 244, 933–38.

Sahlberg, P. (2011). *Finnish lesson: What can the world learn from educational change in Finland?* New York: Teachers College Press.

Steinberg, L. (2014). *Age of opportunity: Lesson from the new science of adolescence.* New York: Dolan/Houghton Mifflin Harcourt.

Thernstrom, S., & Thernstrom, A. (2003). *No excuses: Closing the racial gap in learning.* New York: Simon and Schuster.

Tough, P. (2012). *How children succeed: Grit, curiosity, and the hidden power of character.* New York: Houghton Mifflin Harcourt.

Tough, P. (2011, July 7). No, seriously: No excuses. *New York Times.* http://www.nytimes.com/2011/07/10/magazine/reforming-the-school-reformers.html?pagewanted=all&_r=1&.

U.S. Department of Education. (2012, November 8). *Remarks of U. S. Secretary of Education Arne Duncan at the Education Trust conference.* http://www.ed.gov/news/speeches/remarks-us-secretary-education-arne-duncan-he-education-trust-conference.

Chapter Sixteen

The KIPP Fresno Story

In the KIPP schools and the schools that emulate the KIPP Model, whether they are regular public or charter, we find the arbitrary separation of cultural factors from socioeconomic class continues to draw attention away from the effects of poverty and discrimination on school performance. This, in turn, encourages the kinds of depersonalized crustiness among KIPP staff who are focused only on behaviors and attitudes that improve measurable test results. The No Excuses ideology, then, not only ignores the documented effects of poverty on the poor but also becomes, ironically, an inadequate excuse for justifying morally hazardous acts.

Young, privileged, beginning teachers like the ones recruited by Teach for America and other alternative preparation programs are particularly prone to imposing the kinds of psychological manhandling that No Excuses schools demand. Many of these young teacher aspirants grew up enjoying the advantages of economic privilege, while expecting and knowing personal success in school and social life, with little understanding of failure. The threat of failure, then, sometimes initiates a fear that is played out by fear's twin sister, anger, especially when KIPP school leaders encourage their teachers to be more "militant" in their approach to discipline and to low test performance.

Many of these middle-class neophyte teachers, too, share the same missionary zeal that often motivates well-meaning privileged individuals into the service of those less fortunate. Whether one labels this phenomenon liberal guilt, advantaged idealism, or simply the desire to do good, it is a mind-set that is easily manipulated by administrators who are, most often, survivors of the pedagogical gauntlet that TFA Corps Members must go through.

Having gone through it with their hardness made harder, still, empathy or sympathy for those who are struggling cannot be allowed to become another excuse for not accomplishing what they, themselves, have proven to be possible. The dominant demeanor of hardness, however, masks an underlying brittleness that becomes visible in emotional meltdowns, nervous exhaustion, explosive anger, physical deterioration, and high attrition.

This detached hardness often yields a moral callousness by school leaders that is regularly too harsh for teachers to endure, but when it is applied to children, as it is in KIPP Model schools, it takes on an even darker specter. Such is the case in the KIPP story that follows. Names are used in this section because the following incident is a matter of public record.

During the 2007 to 2008 school year, California's Office of Child and Protective Services notified Fresno Unified School District, the charter authorizer for KIPP Academy Fresno Charter School, that a student at KIPP Fresno had threatened suicide following a punishment administered by KIPP Fresno's CEO, Chi Tschang. Although complaints against Mr. Tschang had been lodged by parents as early as 2004, the threatened suicide by a punished student proved to be the culminating factor that launched a third-party investigation paid for by Fresno Unified School District. The independent investigation by Dan Brake culminated in a sixty-four-page "Notice to Cure and Correct Violations," a document (Horn, 2014) that recounts in harrowing detail the students' punishments between 2004 and 2008, all of which were authorized or meted out, personally, by Mr. Tschang.

The KIPP Academy Fresno Charter School was founded in 2004, and Chi Tschang was its first school leader. Like many of KIPP's school leaders, Tschang had graduated from an Ivy League school and never studied education or educational leadership prior to teaching. After earning a degree in history from Yale in 1998, Tschang tutored low-income children in Providence, Rhode Island, for a nonprofit corporation, City Year.

The following year, he moved to Boston and taught for four years at the No Excuses charter middle school, Academy of the Pacific Rim. There he earned the reputation as a hard worker, strict disciplinarian, and public admirer of KIPP and KIPP's methodology. He also started a blog called *Chi Unplugged*, where he wrote about professional and personal issues. In one of his first blog posts from December 2000, Tschang complained about his deep frustrations with women who did not want to date him but who, more often, wanted to tell him about being mistreated by other men.

Describing himself as less exciting than other more aggressive men that women seemed to prefer over the hard-working and loyal nice guy type, Tschang (2000) described himself as "a bitter, unsportsmanlike sore loser since not one single woman in America under the age of 35 wants to date my kind" (para. 4). In 2004, Tschang applied for and was selected as KIPP Fresno's first CEO.

According to a "Notice to Cure and Correct" issued in December 2008, complaints about harsh treatment of students at Tschang's school began during the 2004 to 2005 school year. Based on parent complaints about Tschang's disciplinary actions against students, the Fresno branch of NAACP visited the school during that year, which led to Tschang's counseling by the Fresno Unified School District for "inappropriate behavior." Other complaints followed the same year, which led to a meeting of KIPP Foundation officials, the district, and Tschang.

The following year, KIPP Fresno received training from the district on its roles and responsibilities regarding student discipline and reporting. Complaints against Mr. Tschang resumed, however, during the 2007 to 2008 school year, and the Board of KIPP Fresno decided to call for Mr. Tschang's resignation. The KIPP Foundation communicated to the unelected KIPP Fresno Board that it had no authority to demand Mr. Tschang's resignation. The Board resigned shortly thereafter.

During that same year, the District grew increasingly concerned for student "psychological and emotional health" (Fresno Unified School District, 2008, p. 2). As a result, the district offered KIPP Fresno's staff training to deal with emotional and psychological problems. Tschang refused, even though KIPP teachers there and elsewhere regularly lack child development or child psychology coursework and training. The culminating complaint that year came when Child and Protective Services notified the Fresno Unified School District that a child who had recently undergone one of Mr. Tschang's punishments had subsequently threatened suicide. Mr. Tschang had failed to notify the parents of the child's threat.

On December 11, 2008, the district's chartering authority issued KIPP Academy Fresno Charter School a sixty-three-page "Notice to Cure and Correct Violations" (Fresno Unified School District, 2008). The report detailed alleged violations of state law and of KIPP's charter that focused mainly on Chi Tschang's behavior toward students, but other serious violations were cited as well. They included charges of impropriety with regard to

- board composition
- credentialing
- criminal background checking
- state mandated testing
- right to privacy
- transporting students off campus
- copyright
- failure to report child sexual abuse

Among the fifteen particulars in the section on "State Mandated Testing" (pp. 43–46) are these noted ethical breaches and unlawful acts:

- In 2006, completed state tests were stored in a location where students and parents had access to the tests. Two of the . . . former teachers, Kim Kutzner and Marcella Mayfield, stated that they witnessed violations of the testing procedures. They stated that tests were not placed in a secure environment. State tests were stacked in boxes around the school's office, tests were not returned promptly by teachers after the closing of that day's testing, and tests were left in classrooms, the principal's office and the school's office.
- Kim Kutzner [a KIPP teacher] and Marcella Mayfield [a KIPP office employee] stated that the school adopted a policy that students were required to check their answers again and again after they had finished their tests and were not allowed to do other activities.
- Ms. Kutzner also witnessed teachers record students' answers during testing, review students' tests, and tell students which page to correct.
- Chi Tschang [subsequently referred to as T], as the test site coordinator for 2006, also admitted that in a couple of cases, teachers forgot to bring tests back.
- In a staff meeting in May 2006, Ms. Kutzner, who had five years of experience as a test site coordinator, reviewed with the entire staff the violations that she had witnessed during testing and presented the written testing protocol materials to T. The staff actively opposed any changes in procedures that would potentially lower test scores, and T and Mr. Hawke stated that the legal and ethical requirements for testing were, in fact, only guidelines that could be ignored.
- The violations were knowingly in disregard of state testing procedures in that T signed the STAR Test Security Agreement and the charter school's teachers signed the STAR Test Security Affidavit in which they agreed to the conditions designed to ensure test security. T also failed to report the testing irregularities to the District STAR coordinator.

Other administrative and technical breaches can be found in the "Fresno Unified Notice to Cure and Correct" report. More troubling, however, are the descriptions of how Tschang treated students at KIPP Fresno. And more troubling, still, are the similarities between Tschang's behaviors as described in the "Notice to Cure" and the descriptions of the disciplinary regimen by former KIPP teachers interviewed for this book. At KIPP Fresno and the schools described by former KIPP teachers, we find common practices that include screaming at children, enforced silence for most of the day, harsh punishments for minor rule infractions, isolation, ostracism, labeling, and public humiliation. Below is a sampling (Horn, 2010, March 15) from the dozens of allegations against Tschang and his faculty for mistreating children. The entire report is archived (Fresno Unified School District, 2008) online and may be downloaded from http://www.pdf-archive.com/2015/01/05/kipp-report-fresno/.

2004–2005

- In her interview, Kia Spenhoff [school employee] stated that she witnessed Mr. Tschang put his hands on students. She witnessed Mr. Tschang pick up a student off the ground, hold the student by the neck against a wall, and then drop the student. When asked about this incident, Mr. Tschang stated, "I don't remember picking up and dropping a student, I do remember shaking a kid."
- _____ also reported witnessing Tschang push another student's face against the wall and saying, "Put your ugly face against the wall, I don't want to see your face."
- Student _____ reported witnessing Mr. Tschang draw a circle on the ground and force a student to stand in the circle for two hours in the sun during the summertime.
- _____, a student at KIPP from 2004 to 2007, stated that in the 2004 to 2005 term he saw Mr. Tschang pick students up and drop them. If a student wasn't sitting correctly he would pick them up by their shirt, move the chair, and drop them on the floor.

2005–2006

- Vincent Montgomery, former Chief Operating Officer for the school, reported that he observed several incidents in which he felt Chi Tschang was emotionally abusive toward students, such as requiring students to stand outside in the rain. Mr. Montgomery also stated he felt any gains made by kids were offset by the emotional abuse they experienced.
- Richard Keyes made a comment to Mr. Tschang that he thought Mr. Tschang needed training in child growth and development because there were things going on that were psychologically damaging.
- Students stated in an interview that Mr. Tschang would make kids stand in the sun while he yelled at them, and that _____ had to stand there for an hour.

2006–2007

- Marcella Mayfield witnessed Mr. Tschang grab a backpack off a student and then repeatedly kick it.

2007–2008

- In December 2007 the police reported several students for shoplifting at a _____ store. As punishment, Mr. Tschang had them sit at their desks outside in the cold for two days. Diane Gutierrez, an employee at the charter school, stated that Mr. Tschang took away their shoes on one day to let them know how it feels to have something taken away from them. Marcella Mayfield stated that it was bitterly cold in December and the students were only allowed to wear sweatshirts. She also stated that Mr. Tschang screamed at the students during the entire day. She told this investigation, "I lost count how many times he could be heard from the classroom. When there was a quiet spell in the class, you could hear him outside screaming at them."
- _____ reported that [KIPP teacher] Mr. Ammon admitted to intentionally humiliating her son and that in a meeting between Mr. Ammon, Mr. Tschang, and _____, Mr. Ammon said, "I thought he needed to be humiliated, that it is my job to do this," and "I just really think he needs to be humbled, he reminds me of me at that age, and I know he has no dad at home." When asked about the incident, Mr. Tschang stated, "No, I don't remember this. What I do remember is that _____ was repeatedly acting in a defiant and disrespect [*sic*] way to Mr. Ammon and other teachers."
- Diana Gutierrez stated in her interview that Mr. Tschang raged and screamed at students on several occasions. She stated that he "has thrown backpacks belonging to students in a manner that the contents fell out. He has grabbed papers out of students' hands and yelled at them. He yells at students right in their faces. The children are so afraid of him that they do not want to look at him. He will just yell louder and say things like 'Look at me,' 'Listen to me,' and 'What's wrong with you?' 'Do you want me to kick you out of school?'"
- Former Board member Steve Hopper stated that Mr. Tschang was so focused on peer accountability that he would lose track of the moment. Mr. Hopper said, "When he yells or throws books, and you confront him, he calls it 'strategic.'"
- When asked about his yelling at students, Mr. Tschang stated, "If parents are not happy with the school program, it is a school of choice."

Chi Tschang was eventually replaced as KIPP Fresno's school leader on February 20, 2009, and the school closed at the end of the 2008 to 2009 school year under the shadow of unresolved allegations of numerous irregularities, illegalities, and ethical breaches. Tschang, however, was not unemployed for long. In the fall of 2009, the No Excuses charter chain Achievement First hired Tschang as assistant superintendent at an Achievement First charter school in New York.

A year later in November 2010, Tschang was back in the news (Cartright, 2010), as New York parents reported Mr. Tschang had "aggressively grabbed an 11-year-old boy he was kicking out of class" (para. 2). Achievement First's co-CEO, Doug McCurry, responded with a six-page letter to parents that "qualified Tschang's move as a misunderstanding of school policy" (para. 6). McCurry also took the opportunity to blast the Fresno report that detailed Tschang's KIPP offenses as a "bogus" attack by a school system hostile to charter schools.

It is hard to imagine an administrator from a regular public school surviving such charges over such an extended period. It is even harder to imagine a public school leader under such a cloud of charges provided new employment with a promotion. As if to underscore the fact that the No Excuses community was ready to forget the KIPP Fresno incident entirely, on February 13, 2011, Tschang and McCurry presented a session at the annual Teach for America Conference in Washington, D.C. Their session was titled "Bringing the 'Joy Factor' into Your School." Tschang has since been promoted to regional superintendent for Achievement First Charter Schools. In 2015, the Achievement First website (Achievement First, 1999–2015) stated, "Mr. Tschang is responsible for driving high student achievement by overseeing a portfolio of schools and supporting Achievement First principals in developing and implementing rigorous academic programs and positive school cultures."

REFERENCES

Achievement First. (1999–2015). *Achievement First leadership team.* http://www. achievementfirst.org/about-us/leadership-team/ -ChiBio.

Cartright, L. (2010, November 1). School big "bullies" kids. *New York Post.* http://nypost.com/2010/11/01/school-big-bullies-kids/.

Fresno Unified School District. (2008, December 11). Notice to cure and correct violations. http://www.pdf-archive.com/2015/01/05/kipp-report-fresno/.

Horn, J. (2014, December 15). The Fresno KIPP report that has been scrubbed from the web. [Blog post]. http://www.schoolsmatter.info/2014/12/the-fresno-kipp-report-that-has-been. html.

Horn, J. (2010, March 15). The KIPP Fresno horror story that the national media won't tell: Part I. [Blog post]. http://www.schoolsmatter.info/2009/03/kipp-fresno-horror-story-that-national.html.

Tschang, C. (2000, January 8). *Confessions of a twenty-something single Asian male.* [Blogpost]. http://chi.blogspot.com/2001_01_07_archive.html -1898968.

Chapter Seventeen

The KIPP Model and the Media

Much of the humiliation and public shaming of KIPP students and teachers remains out of public view. When such events do occur, as in the case of the KIPP Fresno episode, they are either ignored or underreported by the mainstream media. Coverage of the KIPP Fresno story was limited to the *Fresno Bee*, with nothing appearing in any regional or national newspaper or news aggregator. The story did reach the attention of education writer and KIPP supporter Jay Mathews, who downplayed the allegations in his *Washington Post* column.

Without the benefit of an investigation, Mathews wrote that, based on a conversation with Tschang, the allegations "were either false or ripped out of context" (Mathews, 2009b). We may wonder if media elites would have remained as sanguine if a state authority issued a sixty-four-page report based on an independent investigation with detailed accusations of ethical breaches and law breaking by an official in a regular public school.

While there are no exposés or critiques of KIPP on record by the mainstream media, a number of adulatory stories on KIPP are noteworthy, beginning in 1999 with a *60 Minutes* segment reported by Mike Wallace. Known for his propensity to challenge his interview subjects, Wallace offered nothing of the sort with Dave Levin and Mike Feinberg. Without benefit of any data to back him up, Wallace offered this assessment at the beginning of the fourteen-minute segment: "KIPP is proving that with hard work and the right kind of discipline that children from poor minority neighborhoods can perform just as well as children from the most privileged middle schools from across America."

The normally hard-boiled Wallace left the KIPP cofounders' accounts unchallenged, and what viewers came to know of KIPP that evening they were told by Feinberg and Levin. Following Wallace's introduction, the camera pulls in for a close-up of Mike Feinberg, who states, "What KIPP proves is that there are no more excuses."

Two weeks after the *60 Minutes* KIPP story, David Grann (1999), writing for *New Republic*, wrote a feature on KIPP, noting that KIPP's "teachers are willing to do something other schools are increasingly afraid to do: teach morality and decorum" (para. 12). Contrasting KIPP to other schools that celebrate cultural diversity, Grann approvingly states, "There is a conscious effort at KIPP to transform the students' culture into that of the mainstream" (para. 11) of the business or corporate culture.

While the school uses the "paycheck" system to teach youths to earn rewards and manage their money, it also serves as an introduction to the working world. Every Friday, even the ten-year-olds dress like corporate executives, in suits and ties or full-length skirts, their long cornrows often tucked under their blazer collars, their braids pulled into buns. "The rest of the world goes casual," says Levin. "We go professional" (para. 15).

"Professional," one might say, except for this juvenile justice touch: "Between classes, the students are required to stand in neat rows, backs ramrod straight and mouths closed, and march along the black lines that bisect the corridors" (para. 10).

Following the initial airing of the *60 Minutes* segment on KIPP, the *New York Times* (Goodnough, 1999) also published an article on October 20, 1999, featuring KIPP's first middle school in New York that was opened by David Levin. In the first paragraph, reporter Abby Goodnough notes that KIPP's "impressive results" that "won praise from left and right and is helping shape the national debate on how the most disadvantaged students should be taught" (para. 1).

The impressive results to which Goodnough refers are test score results, which were reported by KIPP to be "66 percent above the national average in reading and 70 percent in math" (para. 5). Goodnough provides no information as to how these comparisons were made or what data were used, despite the fact that no benchmarking method is available for making such determinations, either then or now.

Though the *Times* reporter notes that KIPP teachers "are unusually devoted to their jobs" (para. 13), she does not report any contact with KIPP teachers there. Instead, Goodnough spoke with KIPP's recruiter and trainer Fred Shannon, who said, "We get tired, but it's the kind of exhaustion that comes from having a good time and making a difference" (para. 13). The only clue that Goodnough got the story that KIPP wanted to have reported comes near the end of the piece, as she notes,

> Students rarely diverged from KIPP's party line. Asked whether she minded
> the structure, Juanita Ramos, 13, sounded as if she were launching into one of
> KIPP's chants. "The structure that we have builds us up as people, so we can

be leaders as well as followers," she said. "Sometimes it's important to follow, because you might not always know how to lead." (para. 15)

Just days after KIPP students performed a skit on the opening night (Wilgoren, 2000) of the Republican National Convention in August 2000, *60 Minutes* repeated the 1999 segment, once again introduced by Mike Wallace. Following the rerun, Wallace closed by noting that following the initial broadcast, Don and Doris Fisher had given $15 million to KIPP to open new schools.

Even though the mainstream media could find only praise for KIPP during those initial heady days for Feinberg and Levin's new experiment in No Excuses schooling, skepticism could be found if one looked for it. Five days after the initial *60 Minutes* airing of its KIPP feature, the online *Daily Howler* (Somerby, 1999) had this criticism of Wallace's claim that "KIPP is proving that with hard work and the right kind of discipline children from poor minority neighborhoods can perform just as well as the most privileged middle school students from across America."

> Given the drop-out rates and academic performance of urban school systems in the past thirty years, such "proof" would be revolutionary. Unfortunately, *60 Minutes* makes no effort whatever to show that its statement is true. There is no attempt to describe the measured achievement of the KIPP students, or to compare that achievement with suburban norms. There is, however, plenty of boilerplate, straight from the script for these stories. (para. 7)

In 2005 PBS provided another video feature on KIPP similar to the *60 Minutes* piece in its soft focus and promotional tone. Reported by Hedrick Smith (Smith, 2005a) and funded principally by three corporate foundation sponsors—the Ford, Broad, and Carnegie foundations—the PBS feature presents a tightly controlled version of what life is like for KIPP students. Smith, with cameraman in tow, records Feinberg offering a firm, respectful behavioral intervention at a KIPP middle school.

As in the *60 Minutes* segment six years earlier, there are no voices offered to cast any doubt on the value of the KIPP Model, and Smith provides no evidence to either substantiate or disprove the claims presented by KIPP spokesmen Feinberg and Levin. While no doubt is presented as to whether or not KIPP schools are unqualified successes, New York City schools chancellor Anthony Alvarado clearly signals who will ultimately be at fault if schoolchildren do not learn: "All children can learn *if* adults provide high quality instruction" (Smith, 2005a).

In 2006, Oprah Winfrey's highly rated television program contributed to KIPP's official story line by introducing Mike Feinberg and David Levin to the afternoon television audience. In offering a segment on her widely viewed program to Feinberg and Levin, which included remote video clips

produced by CNN and reported by Anderson Cooper, Oprah helped under-
gird in the public mind the KIPP narrative and product image that the KIPP
Foundation had carefully crafted. Following the appearance by Feinberg and
Levin, the segment was posted on Oprah's Facebook page in 2008, and the
KIPP Foundation has posted the segment on Vimeo (KIPP Foundation,
2014).

After eliciting a recitation of KIPP's main talking points from Feinberg
and Levin, Oprah closed with this:

> Look, I'm African American, everyone can see that I am. And when I see what
> the stats are for African American males—for what's happening to young,
> black boys. And then I see this young [KIPP student from video clip] boy say,
> I love being smart, I just want to weep, because that is what needs to happen
> more and more and more in this country, and what you guys [Feinberg and
> Levin] saw is that every kid wants a chance, they just want a chance, so thanks
> for giving it to them.

Notwithstanding her tearful sentiment about giving all black boys a
chance, Oprah and her research team could not have known then that more
than half of the boys who start KIPP in fifth grade never finish eighth grade
at KIPP.

REPORTING THE NUMBERS

Journalist Jonathan Alter's columns for *Newsweek* stand as exemplars for
aggressive support of corporate education ideology and policy, which have
been embraced by the editorial boards of the *Wall Street Journal*, the *Washington Post*, and the *New York Times*, just to mention the most prominent
national newspapers. When Alter railed against "Paleolithic teachers unions"
in 2008 as the real reason the achievement gap has not been closed, he
expressed a widely held view that has been promulgated by both neoliberal
and conservative think tanks, and one that continues to be featured in education policy best sellers like the one by former New York City schools chancellor Joel Klein (2014).

Alter (2008) also represents a common problem among these policy
thought leaders, too, who regularly get opinion far ahead of fact. Here is an
example from 2008:

> The irony is, we know what works to close the achievement gap. At the 60
> KIPP (Knowledge Is Power Program) schools, more than 80 percent of 16,000
> randomly selected low-income students go to college, four times the national
> average for poor kids. While KIPP isn't fully replicable (not enough effective
> teachers to go around), every low-income school should be measured by how
> close it gets to that model, where kids go to school from 7:30 a.m. to 5 p.m.

and part of the summer, and teachers are held strictly accountable for showing student improvement. (para. 4)

Notwithstanding Alter's claim that 20 percent of poor kids who graduate high school enroll in college, he is simply wrong.

In 2007, 58.4 percent of low-income high school graduates entered college. In 2012, the National Center for Education Statistics (NCES) reported that 50.9 percent of low-income high school graduates enrolled in college upon graduation (DeSilver, 2014). Alter's sixteen thousand KIPPsters going to college in 2008 is wrong, too. In 2008, KIPP had a total of sixteen thousand students enrolled in its middle schools, but only a few hundred had graduated from eighth grade, completed high school, and enrolled in college. In an email obtained by Caroline Grannan (2008), KIPP shed some light on how, perhaps, a sloppy or misleading Jonathan Alter came up with the "more than 80 percent" figure for former KIPPsters attending college in 2008:

> We have been tracking KIPP middle school alumni (i.e., KIPP students that completed the eighth grade at KIPP) since the fifth grade class that entered KIPP in 1995. Since that time, 546 students have completed the eighth grade at KIPP, and 447 of those students have matriculated to college for an average college matriculation rate over five years of roughly 81 percent. (para. 9)

There is a good reason that KIPP would prefer tracking those students who completed eighth grade at KIPP, rather than students who enroll at KIPP. After all, between 40 and 60 percent of children who begin at KIPP in fifth grade never finish eighth grade. Those who complete eighth grade at KIPP represent smaller, more able cohorts of survivors. In the SRI study (Woodworth, David, Guha, Wang, & Lopez-Torkos, 2008) of KIPP schools in the Bay Area, researchers found that 60 percent of fifth-grade students in Oakland's KIPP schools who began KIPP in fifth grade did not finish eighth grade:

> Together, the four schools began with a combined total of 312 fifth graders in 2003–04, and ended with 173 eighth graders in 2006–07. The number of eighth graders includes new students who entered KIPP after fifth grade. (p. 12)

If KIPP were to divide the number of students eventually entering college (447) by the number of former KIPPsters old enough to have finished eighth grade if they had remained at KIPP (approximately one thousand), then the percentage of students entering college would be around 45 percent, which is lower than the national average for low-income students matriculating to college.

Another fact unreported by the media involves the percentage of former KIPP students completing college. In 2011, KIPP released a study stating that 33 percent of former KIPP students who graduated from eighth grade at least ten years prior had gone on to earn four-year college degrees. This number was updated in 2013 to 44 percent of KIPP graduates eventually graduating from college, even though more recent KIPP research is very limited to the same small group that KIPP was following in 2008: "These results reflect over 550 students from the two original KIPP academies only" (KIPP Foundation, 2014). We know nothing, in fact, about the college attendance rates for students in KIPP's twenty-two high schools.

Indeed, if 44 percent of those eighth-grade KIPP graduates from the two original academies have now graduated from college, that represents less than 25 percent of all former KIPP students from that group (since more than half never finished eighth grade). KIPP's misleading use of statistics to publicize its numbers of college graduates remains unmentioned by media commentators or news outlets, but the resulting "fuzzy math" was understood and explained during an interview with a former KIPP teacher who had recently read a piece in *Time* (Rotherham, 2011) that reported KIPP's finding that 33 percent of KIPP students that graduate from a KIPP middle school end up completing college. As the former KIPP teacher pointed out,

> *Time* published an article or a column in early May [April 27] that asked the question if KIPP is successful enough. It said KIPP is being successful, but is KIPP being successful enough, and one of the figures that they used was 8% versus 33%: in the neighborhoods where KIPP schools [are located], 8% of the students in those neighborhoods graduate from college, whereas 33% of KIPP schools' [students] graduate from college. I take issue with that because at the real KIPP schools where there is no lottery process, where the attrition is so terrible, where a fifth grade may be 85 students and by the time those kids have reach eighth grade, it's been whittled down to 40 students.
>
> If you're looking at the kids who have graduated from KIPP, that's not even half the kids that started at KIPP, so how positive an influence is KIPP really having if they're only sending 33% of their graduates [to college], which is only half the kids that started at that school. You have to question how much of that 33% would have been included already in the 8% of kids that would have gone on to college [with or without KIPP]. How many kids is [KIPP] really saving? It's a valid question, and while there are undeniably teachers at KIPP today who will tell you I was a KIPP student and KIPP saved my life, there's a hundred other kids who didn't make it through middle school at KIPP because their parents pulled them. (1166)

Given the winnowing of KIPP students between grades five and eight, and given the fact that KIPPsters spend 60 to 70 percent more time in school than their public school counterparts, KIPP's college completion rate begins to appear less miraculous, and its vaunted status among the mainstream media outlets appears even more dubious. Facts, however, have not prevented the media from continuing to parrot Alter's original incorrect information that "more than 80 percent [of former KIPP students] go to college."

In January 2015, for instance, Paul Solman reported on the *PBS News Hour*, "Almost all KIPP students meet federal poverty guidelines, and yet an overwhelming majority—82 percent—go to college, with nearly half completing a four-year degree. That's nearly five times the rate for the average low-income student" (*PBS News Hour*, 2015).

In a more recent example of KIPP-friendly reporting in both the education and mainstream media, the *The Hechinger Report* and *The Atlantic* jointly published a feature news story (Monahan, 2014) on KIPP's efforts to stem the hemorrhagic loss of teachers in Houston (36 percent in 2013 to 2014) by providing on-site childcare to teachers. The article was just over 2,700 words, and the first 1,800 words outlined the problem from KIPP's perspective and offered Mike Feinberg space to promote KIPP's planned remedy to staunch the outflow of teachers from KIPP. Twenty-four KIPP schools in Houston, ten in New Orleans, and five in Arkansas have established on-site day care for KIPP teachers, providing $1,000 to each teacher family to help defray the approximately $7,000 that KIPP will charge teachers for each child they enroll.

In the last part of the article, reporter Rachel Monahan (2014) blends into her piece on KIPP some information on another charter, Boston's Collegiate Charter School. Boston Collegiate is very different from KIPP with regard to demographics and program parameters, even though Monahan does not mention these differences. Instead, the reader is left to assume that what is happening at Boston Collegiate is happening or likely to happen at KIPP schools:

> Like KIPP, Boston Collegiate has something to offer its teachers who become parents, and by at least one measure, the charter school has succeeded in establishing its reputation as a family-friendly place to work: A dozen staffers were pregnant last school year, something of a challenge for a school with a 65-person teaching staff. "Everyone here is so excited for everyone else when they're having a baby," said Sarah Muncey, director of family and community relations. "It's a real community of moms and dads." With so many babies arriving, there's been competition for the daycare. (para. 38)

Both KIPP and Boston Collegiate (BC) do, indeed, have on-site day care (at least for 39 of the 183 KIPP schools), but they have many differences, not the least of which is the percentage of imminent deliveries of new babies. Monahan does not report, for instance, that pregnant or married teachers at KIPP are extremely rare.

Nor does she mention that the high-performing Boston Collegiate's school day does not follow KIPP's 7:15 a.m. to 5 p.m. schedule but, rather, runs from 8 a.m. to 3 p.m. with no Saturday classes. In addition, BC's percentage of low-income students is 43 percent, as compared to KIPP's 88 percent, and unlike KIPP's miniscule number of non-Hispanic or African American students (less than 5 percent), Boston Collegiate's student population is 54 percent white non-Hispanic, 15 percent Hispanic, and 25 percent African American.

Could it be that ethnic diversity, social capital sharing, and economic integration patterns make it easier for Boston Collegiate to maintain their high test scores, all the while allowing time for its teachers and students to have lives outside school that include getting married and having children? We cannot tell, of course, from Monahan's article, but we are left with the impression that it is simply the on-site childcare that brought the big changes in family structure at Boston Collegiate—and, therefore, we may expect the same at KIPP. We cannot tell, either, if this neglect of social and economic differences between these two very different school environments is planned or unintentional. In either case, the misleading effects on readers are likely to be the same.

AWAKENING TO THE "MISERY"

On April 6, 2015, the *New York Times* published a 4,800-word news story (Taylor, 2015) on the front page of its New York edition that reported for the first time some of the extreme charter school practices that are detailed in this book. The *Times*'s groundbreaking feature was aimed at Success Academy Charter Schools (SACS), which operates forty-three No Excuses charter schools in New York City. Taylor's investigative reporting could mark a turning point in media coverage, even though the *Times*'s Editorial Board has remained committed to the corporate education reform agenda.

SACS's Board of Directors is comprised largely of Wall Street equity and hedge fund managers, and it shares many of the same funding streams, values, and methods of KIPP and its emulators. Along with huge injections of philanthropic and investor cash, SACS selectively enrolls students, enrolls fewer special education students and English learners, engages in active weeding of problem students that are not "backfilled" with new students, imposes longer and more school days, and maintains a laser focus on tests and test prep. And like other KIPP Model schools, SACS produces high test scores among its surviving students.

SACS also has a huge teacher attrition problem. Untrained teachers fresh out of college work eleven-hour days, with unceasing stress to produce higher test scores and perfect student behavior. All test and quiz data go into a shared database that provides the basis for surveillance and monitoring by inexperienced principals who have been promoted after a couple of years of teaching:

> One consequence of the competitive environment is a high rate of teacher turnover. Some teachers who left said that the job was too stressful. Others said they left because they disagreed with the network's approach, particularly when they believed it was taken to extremes. In an internal email that some former teachers said typified the attitude at some schools, one school leader said that students who were lagging should be made to feel "misery." (para. 15)

Pressure is unrelenting. When a group of students failed to use approved test-taking strategies, or the approved "plan of attack," a leadership resident sent an email to her fourth-grade teachers that included this:

> We can NOT let up on them. . . . Any scholar who is not using the plan of attack will go to effort academy, have their parent called, and will miss electives. This is serious business, and there has to be misery felt for the kids who are not doing what is expected of them. (para. 98)

THE MEDIA AND KIPP RESEARCH

In 2008, Columbia University professor Jeffrey Henig (2008) examined seven previous KIPP studies, and based on his analysis of previous findings, he offered the following recommendations:

- Policymakers at all levels of government should pay attention to KIPP and consider it a possible source of information and guidance for their decisions.
- Although KIPP may yield useful information, policymakers and others should temper their interest in the operation with wariness and realistic expectations. There are significant unanswered questions about how expansion might affect outcomes, especially in relation to the difficulty of sustaining gains dependent upon KIPP's heavy demands on teachers and school leaders. Moreover, it is not realistic to think that the KIPP Model is a panacea for distressed systems. It is possible that only a small proportion of students and families will be able to meet the demands KIPP imposes on them; even those enthused when they begin the KIPP regimen tend to leave in high numbers.
- Policymakers, accordingly, should treat KIPP schools as potential tools that may contribute to—but not substitute for—systemic improvement.
- Policymakers should be aware that KIPP has prompted some district interest in longer school days, weeks, and years. However, an extended schedule sometimes brings parental objections as well as potential taxpayer

objections to the additional expense. With no strong evidence yet linking extended scheduling to KIPP success, policymakers might best encourage it as a school-level (rather than district-wide) option while concurrently promoting a combination of experimentation and careful analysis of consequences.

• Researchers should help provide better data on patterns of movement in and between charter schools and traditional public schools, including information on why students leave and how their mobility affects student and school-level performance. (p. 22)

The Great Lakes Center for Educational Research and Practice published Henig's paper online on Monday, November 10, 2008. Three days before the paper was published, however, Jay Mathews (2008) dedicated his education column at the *Washington Post* to preempting the Henig paper with his own interpretation, while taking the opportunity to promote the imminent publication of Mathews's *Work Hard, Be Nice* (Mathews, 2009a). Mathews included this in his gloss of Henig's recommendations:

> He [Henig] says that "policymakers at all levels of government should pay attention to KIPP and consider it a possible source of information and guidance for their decisions" but "should temper their interest in the operation with wariness and realistic expectations." He says policymakers "should treat KIPP schools as potential tools that may contribute to—but not substitute for—systemic improvement."
>
> That makes sense to me and the KIPP officials I have been interviewing the past seven years. (Mathews, 2008, para. 7–8)

Mathews does not mention in his column Henig's other caveats and reservations, and no other news outlets, including the *Washington Post*, carried news stories on the publication of Henig's research.

The situation was quite different, however, when Mathematica Policy Research, Inc., published the final piece of a study commissioned by KIPP and paid for by The Atlantic Philanthropies in 2008 at a cost of almost $4 million. Not only did Jay Mathews (2013) devote a lengthy post to a piece, "Biggest Study Ever Says KIPP Gains Substantial," but the *Washington Post*'s Editorial Board (*Washington Post*, 2013) went on the record a few days later to announce "KIPP Doubters Proven Wrong":

> Officials of KIPP (Knowledge Is Power Program) have become accustomed to the doubters who think the success of the fast-growing charter-school network is too good to be true. . . . A study conducted by the independent firm Mathematica Policy Research, which analyzed data from 43 KIPP middle schools, found that students in these charter schools showed significantly greater learning gains in math, reading, science and social studies than did their peers in traditional public schools. The cumulative effects three to four years after

entering KIPP translated, researchers found, into middle-schoolers gaining 11 months of additional learning growth in math and social studies, eight months in reading and 14 months in science. . . . Debunking claims that KIPP's success is rooted in "creaming" the best students, researchers found that students entering KIPP schools are very similar to other students in their neighborhoods: low-achieving, low-income and nonwhite. (para. 2, 3)

Indeed, both KIPP (the study included 43 of KIPP's 125 schools) and the neighborhood students in this study are similar in terms of family income, achievement levels, and ethnicity. In their eagerness to make a case for supporting KIPP, however, the Editorial Board remains mum about differences acknowledged by the Mathematica study (Tuttle et al., 2013) that influence test outcomes. For instance, the Mathematica researchers note characteristic differences that are common in examining charter school and public school demographics: the forty-three KIPP schools enrolled significantly fewer male students (52 percent compared to 49 percent) and fewer limited English proficiency (15 percent compared to 10 percent) and special education students (13 percent compared to 9 percent) (p. xiv).

Conducted over five years, an earlier part of the Mathematica study was presented at an annual conference of the American Education Research Association (AERA) in New Orleans in 2011. There, researchers presented findings related to attrition rates that were not included in the final summary findings. Researchers (Nichols-Barrer, Gill, Gleason, & Tuttle, 2012) found that when attrition rates were compared between middle school KIPPsters and public middle school students from the same feeder elementary schools (rather than comparing to the entire district), KIPP's attrition rates were significantly higher than comparison schools for fifth grade (16 percent compared to 11 percent), not significantly different for sixth grade, and significantly lower at KIPP than comparison schools for seventh grade (9 percent compared to 13 percent).

Researchers found, too, that while KIPP maintained stable populations in grades seven and eight, the public comparison schools were receiving large numbers of new students in grades seven and eight. The chart below (see figure 17.1) was part of the 2011 AERA presentation and was not included in Mathematica's final report.

In effect, KIPP schools replace, or "backfill," fewer students in grades six, seven, and eight than the surrounding public schools, and the late arrivals that KIPP schools generally have scores above the mean for the district (Nichols-Barrer, Gill, Gleason, & Tuttle, 2012), whereas the late arrivals at the public schools have scores below the mean:

KIPP schools differ from district comparison group middle schools in how late arrivals compare with on-time enrollees. Students who enroll late at KIPP tend to be higher achieving than those who enroll on time, as measured by their

Average Number of Attriters, New Arrivals, and Total Enrollment by Grade								
	Grade 6			Grade 7			Grade 8		
	Prior Attrition	New Arrivals	Total Enroll.	Prior Attrition	New Arrivals	Total Enroll.	Prior Attrition	New Arrivals	Total Enroll.
KIPP	11	13	69	9	7	60	5	3	53
Comparison	N/A	N/A	N/A	20	29	228	24	35	246

KIPP schools replace more students than they lose in grade 6, but fewer in grades 7 and 8

District comparison schools replace more students than they lose in both grades 7 and 8

Figure 17.1.   KIPP schools replace fewer students than they lose

grade 4 test scores, whereas the reverse is true at district comparison group schools (see Table III.2). At KIPP schools, on average, late arrivals scored 0.16 and 0.15 standard deviations above the mean for the local district in math and reading, respectively, at baseline (or the 56th percentile). . . . Conversely, late arrivals at district schools had significantly lower average baseline test scores than on-time enrollees. In district comparison schools, late arrivals scored 0.29 standard deviations below the mean in both subjects (or the 39th percentile); on-time entrants scored 0.03 and 0.01 above the mean in math and reading, respectively (the 51st and the 50th percentile). All of these differences are statistically significant. (p. 15)

In short, late arrivals at KIPP are significantly stronger academically than the average district students who arrive late, while the larger influx of late arrivals to public comparison schools in grades seven and eight are significantly weaker than the district mean. The same paper reported that KIPP's late arrivals were significantly less likely to be black males or in special education, and they were more likely to make the KIPP schools less disadvantaged over time. The opposite was found to be the case for the late arrivals at district comparison group schools. All of these important facts escaped the attention of the *Washington Post*'s Editorial Board and its principal education writer, Jay Mathews.

While the Mathematica study (Tuttle, Gill, Gleason, Knechtel, Nichols-Barrer, & Resch, 2013) found significant test score increases among KIPP students (pp. 31–40), questions remain as to how much better KIPP school test scores would be without the known advantages such as 50 to 60 percent more time in school, test preparation focus, fewer and higher-achieving replacement students, fewer black male students, higher attrition among low performers and problem students, fewer special education and ELL students, and large funding advantages from both public and private sources.

To its credit, the *New York Times* (Dillon, 2011b) reported in 2011 that Western Michigan University researchers found

> the KIPP network received $12,731 in taxpayer money per student, compared with $11,960 at the average traditional public school and $9,579, on average, at charter schools nationwide.
>
> In addition, KIPP generated $5,760 per student from private donors, the study said, based on a review of KIPP's nonprofit filings with the Internal Revenue Service. (para. 8–9)

Another study (Baker, Libby, & Wiley, 2012) also found large budgeting advantages at KIPP, as well as at two other KIPP-inspired charter chains, Achievement First and Uncommon Schools:

> We find that in New York City, KIPP, Achievement First and Uncommon Schools charter schools spend substantially more ($2,000 to $4,300 per pupil) than similar district schools. Given that the average spending per pupil was around $12,000 to $14,000 citywide, a nearly $4,000 difference in spending amounts to an increase of some 30%. In Ohio, charters across the board spend less than district schools in the same city. And in Texas, some charter chains such as KIPP spend substantially more per pupil than district schools in the same city and serving similar populations, around 30 to 50% more in some cities (and at the middle school level) based on state reported current expenditures, and 50 to 100% more based on IRS filings. Even in New York where we have the highest degree of confidence in the match between our IRS data and Annual Financial Report Data, we remain unconvinced that we are accounting fully for all charter school expenditures. (pp. i–ii)

Mathematica researchers acknowledged, too, the potential positive influence on KIPP scores that results from built-in parental self-selection bias, even though Mathematica (Nichols-Barrar, Gill, Gleason, & Tuttle, 2014) was not asked to investigate this important aspect.

> A potentially important limitation of this study is that there could still be unmeasured differences between the students attracted to KIPP and those enrolling in other schools. We analyze the peer environment at KIPP as measured by demographic characteristics and prior achievement, but we do not have direct measures of parent characteristics, prior motivation, or student behavior. (para. 31)

Finally, the enthused Editorial Board of the *Washington Post* did not mention the following significant findings from the Mathematica study (Tuttle, Gill, Gleason, Knechtel, Nichols-Barrar, & Resch, 2013) that raise serious questions related to KIPP's inability to increase student "good behaviors," as well as KIPP's negative effects on the behavior of children in KIPP's total-compliance environments where "grit" and zest are valued over honesty and compassion:

> KIPP has no statistically significant effect on several measures of student behavior, including self-reported illegal activities, an index of good behavior, and parent reports of behavior problems. However, KIPP has a negative estimated effect on a student-reported measure of undesirable behavior, with KIPP students more likely to report behaviors such as losing their temper, arguing or lying to their parents, or having conflicts with their teachers. (p. 68)

REFERENCES

Alter, J. (2008, July 11). Jonathan Alter on Obama and education. *Newsweek*. http://www. newsweek.com/jonathan-alter-obama-and-education-92615 .

Baker, B. D., Libby, K., & Wiley, K. (2012). *Spending by the major charter management organizations: Comparing charter school and local public district financial resources in New York, Ohio, and Texas*. Boulder, CO: National Education Policy Center. http://nepc. colorado.edu/publication/spending-major-charter.

Desilver, D. (2013, December 19). *Global inequality: How the U.S. compares*. Pew Research Center. http://www.Pewresearch.org/fact-tank/2013/12/19/global-inequality-how-the-u-s-compares/.

Dillon, S. (2011b, March 31). Study says charter network has financial advantages over public schools. *New York Times*. http://www.nytimes.com/2011/03/31/education/31kipp.html?_r= 1&.

Goodnough, A. (1999, October 20). Structure and basics bring South Bronx school acclaim. *New York Times*. http://www.nytimes.com/1999/10/20/nyregion/structure-and-basics-bring-south-bronx-school-acclaim.html.

Grann, D. (1999, October 4). Back to basics in the Bronx. *New Republic*. https://www.cs.unm. edu/~sto/maunders/educate/grann.html.

Grannan, C. (2008, July 13). *Newsweek* recommends that Obama do a little teacher-bashing to win fans. *Examiner.com*. http://www.examiner.com/article/newsweek-recommends-that-obama-do-a-little-teacher-bashing-to-win-fans.

Henig, J. (2008). *What do we know about the outcomes of KIPP schools?* The Great Lakes Center for Education Research and Practice. East Lansing, MI: The Great Lakes Center for Education Research & Practice. http://greatlakescenter.org/docs/Policy_Briefs/Henig_Kipp. pdf.

KIPP Foundation. (2014a). *The promise of college completion: KIPP's early successes and challenges—Spring 2014 alumni data update*. http://www.kipp.org/files/dmfile/ 2013AlumniUpdateonCollegeCompletion.pdf.

Klein, J. (2014). *Lessons of hope: How to fix our schools*. New York: Harper.

Mathews, J. (2013, February 27). Biggest study ever shows KIPP gains substantial. *Washington Post*. http://www.washingtonpost.com/blogs/class-struggle/post/biggest-study-ever-says-kipp-gains-substantial/2013/02/26/ff149efa-7d50-11e2-9a75-dab0201670da_blog. html.

Mathews, J. (2009a). *Work hard, be nice: How two inspired teachers created the most promising schools in America*. New York: Algonquin Books.

Mathews, J. (2009b). Turmoil at two KIPP schools. [Blog post]. http://voices.washingtonpost. com/class-struggle/2009/03/turmoil_at_two_kipp_schools.html?wprss=rss_blog.

Mathews, J. (2008, November 7). The most promising schools in America. *Washington Post*. http://www.washingtonpost.com/wp-dyn/content/article/2008/11/07/AR2008110700861. html.

Monahan, R. (2014, November 11). Charter schools try to retain teachers with mom-friendly policies. *The Atlantic.* http://www.theatlantic.com/education/archive/2014/11/charter-schools-now-try-to-keep-teachers-with-mom-friendly-policies/382602/.

Nichols-Barrer, I., Gill, B., Gleason, P, & Tuttle, C. (2014). Does student attrition explain KIPP's success? *Education Next* 14 (4). http://educationnext.org/student-attrition-explain-kipps-success/.

PBS News Hour. (2015, January 8). *Can teaching kids to resist the marshmallow help pave the way to success?* [Transcript]. http://www.pbs.org/newshour/bb/can-teaching-kids-resist-marshmallow-pave-road-success/.

Rotherham, A. (2011, April 27). KIPP schools: A reform triumph, or disappointment? *Time.* http://content.time.com/time/nation/article/0,8599,2067941,00.html.

Smith, H. (2005a). *Making schools work.* [Transcript]. http://www.pbs.org/makingschoolswork/atp/transcript.html.

Somerby, B. (1999, September 24). Our current howler: Critique the children well. [Blog post]. http://www.dailyhowler.com/h092499_1.shtml.

Tuttle, C., Gill, B., Gleason, P., Knechtel, V., Nichols-Barrer, I., & Resch, A. (2013). *KIPP middle schools: Impacts on achievement and other outcomes.* Washington, DC: Mathematica Policy Research. http://www.kipp.org/files/dmfile/KIPP_Middle_Schools_Impact_on_Achievement_and_Other_Outcomes1.pdf.

Washington Post. (2013, March 1). KIPP doubters proven wrong in new study. *Washington Post.* http://www.washingtonpost.com/opinions/kipp-doubters-proved-wrong-in-new-study/2013/03/01/f003b95c-81ef-11e2-a350-49866afab584_story.html.

Wilgoren, J. (2000, August 2). The Republicans: The issues; for 2000, the G.O.P. sees education in a new light. *New York Times.* http://www.nytimes.com/2000/08/02/us/the-republicans-the-issues-for-2000-the-gop-sees-education-in-a-new-light.html.

Woodworth, K. R., David, J. L., Guha, R., Wang, H., & Lopez-Torkos, A. (2008). *San Francisco Bay Area KIPP schools: A study of early implementation and achievement. Final report.* Menlo Park, CA: SRI International.

Conclusion

None of the teachers interviewed for this book voiced any enthusiasm for sending their own children to a KIPP school, although one teacher said that she would consider a KIPP school if she had no other options other than a low-performing public school:

> If I was in [the public school district] and was not near a magnet school or a school that I liked, then I could see how KIPP would be a good alternative to a low performing school if those were my only options. But this is why suburbs exist because people move out there because they don't have to do that. They don't have to choose or think about worrying about getting their kids in a school where people have resources and they'll be motivated.

When I asked her why the suburbs were better, she said that in the suburbs, parents don't have to worry about quality because parents know their children are "going to be okay." Furthermore, she said, children of suburban parents are "going to have teachers that care and teachers that are going to try their best. You know that."

Another KIPP teacher said that KIPP did not fit her "philosophy of education" and that KIPP's "narrow view" minimizes student freedom and the opportunities for students to "express themselves and have opportunities to kind of explore and make mistakes and learn a wide variety of things." She continued:

> I have an insane amount of pressure and I am not even a reading [or math] teacher, and those teachers that have to have those tests, they have a huge, greater amount of pressure than I do because at the end of the year you also get a pay bonus based on how well your students do on the tests.

Another teacher elaborated on the responsibility-to-learn freedom that she recalled from her own experience as a middle school student, when she said that KIPP

> just didn't have the feeling. The kids had no freedom, you know? . . . I just remember being in middle school, and being able to walk around my campus, and I was responsible to get to class on time . . . part of my job was learning how to do that, and the kids [at KIPP] don't really seem to have that . . . they're restricted to a hallway. They don't have the run of the school to be moving around. So, no, I wouldn't send my children there.

Another teacher focused on the low level of learning, the lack of enrichment, and the lack of initiative that she found at KIPP, which represented what she did not want when she and her fiancé married and had children.

Two other teachers, both male, responded by relating incidents of humiliation and abuse that they had encountered, heard about, or participated in as the chief reasons for not wanting to send their own children to KIPP. The first teacher recounts his own yelling at students, and he recounts more intense yelling that he witnessed firsthand in situations in which a "mob mentality" among faculty dominated.

> Having worked at KIPP I've watched teachers cross that line from "we're disciplining you" into "we're tired and we're humiliating you out of anger." In terms of the humiliation, I know that I've seen it, I've slipped over, I've crossed that line, that's part of why I don't yell anymore. I've watched other teachers do it. I talked about that zeal, there's a bit of a mob mentality when you work for KIPP and it's different at different schools.
> Like in KIPP New York I've heard tales of teacher—if a kid bucks up, the teacher might push them a little bit, say hey, go against this wall—which would not be acceptable and probably is a fireable offense in a traditional public school, yet it works. But then when it crosses that line to you're just angry and a kid has gotten on your last nerve, I've seen teachers just yell at a kid in their face—full blown yell—the kind of thing that I would not want done to my daughter. I think KIPP long term will have to deal with that issue of short-term discipline that works with 5th and 6th graders versus longer-term stuff.

The second teacher who noted out-of-control disciplinary measures had also been personally involved with screaming at students. This former teacher had left teaching when he left KIPP. When asked if he would send his own child to KIPP, he replied: "Nope. And I live across the street from a KIPP school. I live in _____ and there are KIPP schools all over the place. I live literally across the street from one, and, no, I would not."

In responding to the follow-up "Why," this teacher recounted a story he had told me earlier about his low point at KIPP, which involved his losing control when dealing with a disciplinary situation.

> That was part of the real reflections I had when I thought about the kind of teacher that I felt I was becoming when I shared that story about T_____, that 7th grade girl who I got into a shouting match with, the kind of embarrassment and horror I felt was really related to this notion of, Lord's mercy, I didn't have this in 7th grade and I wouldn't send my kid to this kind of school. I still wouldn't. I know that life isn't fair and that some kids are born with more than others. I still believe very strongly that kids coming into 5th grade who are two years behind grade level are not gonna catch up unless they work hard and unless they have role models and inspiration and people to support them. I believe that goes along with probably an extended day, to some degree, depending on the activities of that extension, extended year, and depending upon the types of activities of that extension. But no, I wouldn't. I don't think I would send my children to a KIPP school.

Another former KIPP teacher discussed reasons for not sending her children to KIPP that involved treatment of children with special needs:

> They don't address students with learning disabilities in the right way. They didn't have a strong enough program for that. . . . Not to say that I would have a child with learning disabilities. But if you did, you wouldn't necessarily find out [that your child was not receiving adequate services]. You know, they would just go through the motions of, no, your child's not meeting the standard, no, you child's not following the rules, no, your child's not . . . You know, there was no [attempt to] investigate and find out more about why this child can't fit in.
>
> So you know, it was basically always the person's fault. If you can't be extremely successful on paper, it's your personal fault. That goes for teachers or students. And I don't want my child, my imaginary child . . . to be put in a situation, where they feel like they can't get out, and they're devalued if they have any kind of difficulty. Because it can be very difficult for people, for reasons that are maybe beyond their control.

During the twentieth anniversary KIPP Summit held in Houston, cofounders Mike Feinberg and David Levin responded to questions via Twitter from KIPP teachers at the Summit. Both Feinberg and Levin have young children, so it was natural, perhaps, that KIPP teachers would want to know what many of them already knew about their own preferences: Will Mike and Dave send their children to KIPP? Levin did not respond then or since, publicly, but Feinberg offered the following explanation. The transcript attempts to capture some of Feinberg's body language, but the video captures (KIPP Foundation, 2015e) what words cannot:

Feinberg: Gus and Abadit [Feinberg's two children] are not going to go to a
KIPP school [begins rubbing his face], and that's actually for—there are
several reasons for that. I mean, you get into, for, you know, with a 10
thousand kid waiting list, um, my kids have options, I don't want to take
away a seat from another [more beard rubbing] family that doesn't have
options, that's part of it, but at, with my parent hat, I want most for Gus and
Abadit. I would put them in a bunch of our primary schools in a heartbeat,
knowing what a great education they would get, how well they would get
taken care of. It would be unfair, I think, to Gus and Abadit, because in a
KIPP school, they wouldn't be Gus and Abadit, they would be Feinberg's
kids, and I don't want them—I want them to grow up, and being in a school,
being Gus and Abadit, and not be a fishbowl parent.

And I've seen this happen with other leaders' kids, where, ah, within five
minutes of being put in timeout, the school is talking about the kid being in
timeout. I just want them to have a chance to be Gus and Abadit and, as I
said, Gus, you know, he wants to be [begins scratching his face], to wear a
KIPP shirt, with, with pride, and he wants to be a KIPPster [starts rubbing his
hands together], he wants to come and tutor, and things like that, to find other
ways to get him plugged in to Team and Family [looks over to Levin with a
wan smile].

While it is true that KIPP has a number of oversubscribed schools, it has
many schools that have ample openings, where KIPP teachers are sent into
the neighborhoods to knock on doors with their clipboards to recruit new
students. It is likely that Feinberg could find one of those many underen-
rolled KIPP schools. Like most parents, whether KIPP or non-KIPP, Feinberg wants to protect the privacy of his children when they break the rules at
school. He and Levin are, nonetheless, codesigners of a high surveillance
system that uses KIPP paychecks to guarantee that every teacher knows
whether or not any KIPP child they come in contact with has been good or
bad by checking the paycheck that each KIPPster carries with him from class
to class.

We know, too, that public humiliation is common at KIPP, with individual students often called before a class or the entire school to confess their
offenses against KIPP. One of the former KIPP teachers who volunteered to
share her experiences at KIPP recounted a most egregious example of "public shaming" that involved a new fifth-grade boy who had only been at KIPP
for less than a month. This particular fifth-grade class had to cross a public
park to get to their PE class location, and like every new fifth-grade class,
they first had to learn to walk and to follow orders:

> They have this very rigid way they cross the street, single file. When they turn
> a corner, it's a choreographed thing that they practice and practice. They don't
> have gym class until they get it right. And one student, a little fifth-grade boy,

he had to go to the bathroom. And it was, you know, with kids that age, it was, like, urgent, right now. The teacher said, we're in the park now. You're going to have to wait. And the kid just couldn't wait, and so he relieved himself on a tree in the park.

And when they got back to school the next day, at the morning meeting, all the kids piled into the community room and the principal brought this kid to the front of everybody, you know, to stand in front of all of his peers and [be asked], "What did you do?" And so he had to say what he did. And he had to say that he was sorry he shamed the uniform and the school and everything that it stands for. And this was a fifth-grader in the second or third week of school.

Because the Feinberg children have real school choices, they will never have to worry about such indiscretions being shared publicly at their school. Yet Feinberg and the army of wealthy donors who support the KIPP Model want to make sure that the children of the poor have only a No Excuses option to the struggling public schools that have been publicly shamed with newspaper articles and "Needs Improvement" letters that are mandated for schools falling short of the fanciful No Child Left Behind testing targets.

Feinberg's floundering response to the Twitter question about what he will choose for his children reminds us of the uncomfortable and embarrassing disconnect between what the new paternalists demand for their own children as compared with what they accept for the children of others less privileged. Feinberg will choose twice, in fact: once for his children and a second time for all the parents who do not have a voice in KIPP school policies or regulations or what their segregated children must learn, how they should learn it, or how they prove that they do learn it. In the end, passing tests provides evidence for the Feinbergs and Levins that children of poverty are towing the line that has been drawn for them by the Fisher family and the other billionaire philanthropists' foundations that pump hundreds of millions of dollars into KIPP schools to make sure that the KIPP route is the most heavily traveled road on the forced march to self-improvement.

Feinberg's children will have to find other ways to become part of KIPP's "Team and Family." They can wear the KIPP shirt while off the street and inside the auditorium at the Summit, and they might be able to someday tutor a KIPPster and, perhaps, tell her some of the wonderful things they are learning out there in the educational world of real choices.

I conclude, finally, with remarks about KIPP from two parents, one whose daughter attended KIPP for four years in the Bronx, and the other who decided not to send her middle school son to KIPP when her Washington, D.C., community public school was closed. Both represent examples of resistance to the KIPP Model. The first remarks I would guess (she remains anonymous) are from a working-class mom, whose daughter attended a

Bronx KIPP middle school for four years before she and her child decided to cut their losses at the beginning of high school.

In a blog post that was published at Ed Notes Online in 2011 (Scott, 2011), this New York City parent notes that, during her daughter's four years at KIPP, she had been outspoken and committed to protecting her daughter from repeated cases of inappropriate and unfair treatment by KIPP teachers and school leaders, who offered the same response each time she presented concerns for her daughter's well-being at KIPP: "The principal always invited me to take my child out if I did not like it" (para. 8).

She notes that her daughter's friends captured the "true meaning" of KIPP when they described it as "Kids in Prison Program," and that she could substantiate her daughter's experiences because she "kept a log showing the hell the school put me through and the unethical behavior demonstrated towards my child and myself by the school for 4 years" (para. 4). In the concluding paragraph of her story that was published after her daughter graduated from the KIPP middle school, she said,

> I am happy that I did not allow her to go to the only KIPP high school [in New York City]. She begged me not to send her there and I know high school would probably have broken her down. She shared something very important with me that shocked me. She said, "Mom, when I was going to KIPP I always had a lot of pain in my body in the morning. But I don't have the pain any more." I always ask her if she is happy with the school she is at now. She says, "I love it." She is now attending a NYC public high school. (para. 13)

The final quoted excerpt is from writer and Washington, D.C., parent, Natalie Hopkinson, who published the following (Hopkinson, 2013) remarks at the *Washington Post* blog, *The Root DC Live*. In a most clear and incisive way, Hopkinson's commentary represents at least a partial answer to one of the questions posed in the preface of this book: When will black and white citizens, alike, demand what most former slave parents and their children asked for over a hundred years ago, which was an equal education in nonsegregated schools?

The obvious answer is that the "when" has already begun, and it seems likely that, given better information about No Excuses charter "chain gangs" to counter much of the corporate-sponsored promotional materials, more parents will come to share the views of Natalie Hopkinson, a middle-class African American mom who says that schools "should begin by building on what assets the community values and what their goals are for their children's future, not what the [KIPP] franchise decides are best practices" (para. 14).

As we know from the history of revolutions, it has most always been the members of the middle and upper classes—those who have not yet had their rage excised through dehumanization—who have touched off the "rebellions of the oppressed and downtrodden" (Arendt, 1969, p. 63). We may expect, perhaps, that urban parents and teachers of all income groups and ethnicities will come to share these parental views on the KIPP Model:

My family is among the unlucky Ward 5 residents whose neighborhood middle school has been closed. When we shopped for a middle school, my husband suggested we enroll our son in KIPP. A black friend, a lawyer who worked in education, warned against it: "That's like prison! They make those kids walk on lines like they're in the chain gang!" Although I know kids who have thrived there, it's a perception I've heard repeated by countless teachers, education policy folks and even school district leaders. An education consultant advising white middle class parents told The Post's Emma Brown that she tells her clients not be fooled by the high test scores—KIPP and its imitators would not be a "good fit." We have to ask ourselves why.

Wealthy and middle class schools are all about developing an independent voice and passions, exploring ideas and creativity. It treats children as individuals of innate value with powerful destinies to be realized. Many charters franchises . . . often emphasize compliance, repetition, "drill and kill." I am uncomfortable sending my child on that track. So how could I advocate it to other people's children who happen to look like mine? Why should we allow such policies to be applied to the whole traditional neighborhood system?

To apply this external mold on children, whether it is through standardized tests or a charter franchise, is to treat them as "gaps" to be bridged. It also creates awkward expectations for how black people should be treated. It's like when strange white men introduce themselves to my husband with a soul power grip instead of a handshake or white women address me (and maybe every other black woman) as "girlfriend." To have those assumptions about how urban minds work baked in the bread of how schools do business is dangerous. It also fuels and reifies racial and economic segregation.

For kids who are falling behind, extra interventions and classroom time are needed—and much appreciated. But certain types of interventions aren't always welcome. Fingerprinting systems at one charter that one 16-year-old said reminded her "of juvenile hall," many punitive disciplinary methods [that] show a contempt for the poor who lack the resources to defend themselves.

And, these interventions definitely don't come free. Right now, the price is being paid by idealistic young teachers who have the luxury of living as missionaries for a few years after college with their students calling their cell phones around the clock. And of course, it is heavily subsidized by corporate philanthropies eager to make a point about unions and private management.

At a certain point we have to start thinking of public education less as a charitable enterprise or for-profit business and more of a core value in our communities. Schools should begin by building on what assets the community values and what their goals are for their children's future, not what the [KIPP] franchise decides are best practices. Schools should be part of the ecosystem of a community, one that replenishes itself and stands on its own feet. (para. 9–14)

REFERENCES

Arendt, H. (1969). *On violence*. New York: Harcourt, Brace & World.

Hopkinson, N. (2013, June 7). Organic chemistry: Two tracks of schooling raise questions about class, race and community. *Washington Post*: *The Root DC Live*.http://www.washingtonpost.com/blogs/therootdc/post/organic-chemistry-two-tracks-of-schooling-raise-questions-about-class-race-and-community/2013/06/07/fd4706ec-cf78-11e2-9f1a-1a7cdee20287_blog.html?wprss=rss_therootdc.

KIPP Foundation. (2015e). KIPP school summit 2014. http://www.kipp.org/our-approach/sharing-and-collaboration/kipp-school-summit-2014.

Scott, N. (2011, April 14). An ex-KIPP Bronx parent speaks out. [Blog post]. http://ednotesonline.blogspot.com/2011/04/ex-kipp-bronx-parent-speaks-out.html.

References

Achievement First. (1999–2015). *Achievement First leadership team.* http://www.achievementfirst.org/about-us/leadership-team/ -ChiBio.

Allais, S. (2012). "Economics imperialism," education policy and educational theory. *Journal of Education Policy* 27 (2), 253–74.

Alter, J. (2010, September 20). Obama's class project. *Newsweek* 156 (12), 58.

Alter, J. (2008, July 11). Jonathan Alter on Obama and education. *Newsweek.* http://www.newsweek.com/jonathan-alter-obama-and-education-92615.

American Enterprise Institute. (2014, March 3). *From poverty to prosperity: A conversation with Bill Gates.* http://www.aei.org/files/2014/03/14/- bill-gates-event-transcript082217994272. pdf.

American Practitioner. (1912, September). Burbanking the human race. *The American Practitioner, 46,* 458.

American Statistical Association. (2014). *ASA statement on using value-added models for educational assessment.* https://www.amstat.org/policy/pdfs/ASA_VAM_Statement.pdf.

Anderson, J. (1988). *The education of Blacks in the South, 1860–1935.* Chapel Hill, NC: University of North Carolina Press.

Anderson, N. (2011, March 10). Most schools could face "failing" label under No Child Left Behind, Duncan says. *Washington Post.* http://www.washingtonpost.com/wp-dyn/content/article/2011/03/09/AR2011030903089.html.

Arendt, H. (1969). *On violence.* New York: Harcourt, Brace & World.

Ariely, D. (2013) *The (honest) truth about dishonesty: How we lie to everyone—especially ourselves.* New York: Harper Collins.

Ascend Learning. (2015). *The Ascend culture.* http://www.ascendlearning.com/about/culture/ .

Ascherman, R., & Li, K. (2014). "TFA truth tour" to expose the dark side of corporate education reform. United Students Against Sweatshops. http://usas.org/2014/03/23/tfa-truth-tour-to-expose-dark-side-of-corporate-education-reform/.

Asma, S. (2014, June 8). From China, with pragmatism. *New York Times.* http://opinionator.blogs.nytimes.com/2014/06/08/from-china-with-pragmatism/.

Bacon, A. (1986). *The Negro and the Atlanta Exposition.* Baltimore: Trustees of the John Slater Fund.

Baker, B. D., Libby, K., & Wiley, K. (2012). *Spending by the major charter management organizations: Comparing charter school and local public district financial resources in New York, Ohio, and Texas.* Boulder, CO: National Education Policy Center. http://nepc.colorado.edu/publication/spending-major-charter.

Banjo, S. (2009, November 11). *Dow Jones—"Getting personal: Gates Foundation invests in charter schools."* http://www.kipp.org/news/dow-jones-getting-personal-gates-foundation-invests-in-charter-schools-1.

Becker, G. (1993). *Human capital: A theoretical and empirical analysis, with special reference to education* (3rd ed.). Chicago: University of Chicago Press.

Bell, T. (1993). Reflections one decade after "A Nation at Risk." *The Phi Delta Kappan* 72 (8), 592–97.

Bell, T. (1988). *The thirteenth man: A Reagan cabinet memoir.* New York: Free Press.

Benjamin, M. (2010, October 14). "War on terror" psychologist gets giant no-bid contract. *Salon.* http://www.salon.com/2010/10/14/army_contract_seligman/.

Bennett, W. (1998). A nation still at risk. *Policy Review* 90, 23–29.

Berliner, D., & Biddle, B. (1995). *The manufactured crisis: Myths, fraud, and the attack on America's public schools.* Reading, MA: Addison-Wesley.

Bracey, G. (2003). April foolishness: The 20th anniversary of "A Nation at Risk." *Phi Delta Kappan* 84 (8), 616–21.

Brancaccio, D. (2007, June 22). *The report card and lending a hand.* NOW with David Brancaccio. http://www.pbs.org/now/transcript/325.html.

Brewer, J. (2014). Accelerated burnout: How Teach for America's academic impact model and theoretical culture of accountability can foster disillusionment among its corps members. *Educational Studies* 50 (3), 246–63.

Brookfield, S. (2004). *The power of critical theory: Liberating adult learning and teaching.* San Francisco: Jossey-Bass.

Brown, E. (2012, December 11). KIPP DC wins $10 million grant in Race to the Top competition. *Washington Post.* http://www.washingtonpost.com/local/education/kipp-dc-wins-10-million-grant-in-race-to-the-top-competition/2012/12/11/ad6a2802-43c3-11e2-8061-253bccfc7532_story.html.

Browne, L. W. (2009). *A character education approach to founding a KIPP college preparatory charter school.* (Doctoral dissertation). Retrieved from Dissertation and Theses database. (UMI No. 3344513).

Bush, G. W. (2000). *Bush for President announcement.* George W. Bush for President Website. http://www.4president.org/speeches/bush2000announcement.htm.

Carter, S. (2000). *No excuses: Lessons from 21 high-performing, high-poverty schools.* Washington, DC: Heritage Foundation.

Cartright, L. (2010, November 1). School big "bullies" kids. *New York Post.* http://nypost.com/2010/11/01/school-big-bullies-kids/ .

Cavanaugh, S. (2013). Amplify insight wins contract from common-core testing consortium. http://blogs.edweek.org/edweek/marketplacek12/2013/03/amplify_insight_wins_contract_from_common_core_testing_consortium.html?cmp=ENL-EU-NEWS2.

Center on Children and Families at Brookings. (2014). *Essay series on character and opportunity.* Washington, DC: The Character and Opportunity Project of the Brookings Institution. http://www.brookings.edu/~/media/multimedia/interactives/2014/ccf_characterseries/characterandopportunityessays.pdf.

Change.gov. (2008, December 16). *President-elect Obama nominates Arne Duncan as Secretary of Education.* http://change.gov/newsroom/entry/president_elect_obama_nominates_arne_duncan_as_secretary_of_education/.

Chernicoff, D. (2006, October 27). I want you, Yalie, to teach for America. *Yale Daily News.* http://yaledailynews.com/weekend/2006/10/27/i-want-you-yalie-to-teach-for-america/.

Choi, L. (2014, January 10). *For-profit colleges and the student debt crisis.* San Francisco: Federal Bank of San Francisco. http://www.frbsf.org/community-development/blog/for-profit-colleges-and-the-student-debt-crisis/.

Clarke, J. (2004). Dissolving the public realm? The logics and limits of neo-liberalism. *Journal of Social Policy* 33 (1), 27–48.

Cohen, D. K. (1996). Standards-based school reform: Policy, practice, and performance. In *Holding schools accountable.* Edited by H. F. Ladd. Washington, DC: The Brookings Institution.

Cohen, P. (2014, December 24). For recent black college graduates, a tougher road to employment. *New York Times.* http://www.nytimes.com/2014/12/25/business/for-recent-black-college-graduates-a-tougher-road-to-employment.html?_r=0.

Coleman, J. S., Campbell, E., Hobson, C., McPartland, J., Mood, A., Weinfeld, F., et al. (1966). *Equality of educational opportunity.* Washington, DC: U.S. Government Printing Office.

Collins, G. (1982, March 15). The psychology of the cult experience. *New York Times.* http://www.nytimes.com/1982/03/15/style/the-psychology-of-the-cult-experience.html?pagewanted=2&pagewanted=all.

DeBray-Pelot, E. (2006). *Politics, ideology, & education: Federal policy during the Clinton and Bush administrations.* New York: Teachers College Press.

DeBray-Pelot, E., & McGuinn, P. (2009). The new politics of education: Analyzing the federal education policy landscape in the post-NCLB era. *Educational Policy* 23 (1), 15–42.

Denning, L., Meisnere, M., & Warner, K. (Eds.). (2014). *Preventing psychological disorders in service members and their families: An assessment of programs.* Washington, DC: National Academies Press.

DeSilver, D. (2014, January 15). *College enrollment among low-income students still trails richer groups.* Pew Research Center. http://www.Pewresearch.org/fact-tank/2014/01/15/college-enrollment-among-low-income-students-still-trails-richer-groups/

DeSilver, D. (2013, December 19). *Global inequality: How the U.S. compares.* Pew Research Center. http://www.Pewresearch.org/fact-tank/2013/12/19/global-inequality-how-the-u-s-compares/.

Dewey, J. (1944). *Democracy and education.* Champaign, Ill.: Project Gutenberg.

Dewey, J. (1938/2007). *Experience and education.* New York: Simon & Schuster.

Dewey, J. (1897). *My pedagogic creed.* New York: E. L. Kellogg & Co. http://dewey.pragmatism.org/creed.htm.

Dillon, S. (2011a, September 6). Troubled schools try mimicking the charters. *New York Times.* http://www.nytimes.com/2011/09/06/education/06houston.html.

Dillon, S. (2011b, March 31). Study says charter network has financial advantages over public schools. *New York Times.* http://www.nytimes.com/2011/03/31/education/31kipp.html?_r=1&.

Dillon, S. (2010, August 5). Education Department deals out big awards. *New York Times.* http://www.nytimes.com/2010/08/05/education/05grants.html?_r=0.

Dobbie, W. (2011). Teacher characteristics and student achievement: Evidence from Teach for America. *Journal of Labor Economics* 9 (25), 95–135.

Dodd, D. (2011, August 15). KIPP schools' get-tough rules, lessons get results. *Atlanta Journal-Constitution.* http://www.ajc.com/news/news/local/kipp-schools-get-tough-rules-lessons-get-results/nQKYw/.

Doyle, D. (1993, April). American schools: Good, bad, or indifferent? *Phi Delta Kappan* 74 (8), 626–31.

Du Bois, W. E. B. (1903). *The souls of black folk.* Chicago: A. C. McClurg & Co.; Bartleby.com, 1999. www.bartleby.com/114/.

Duckworth, A., & Seligman, M. (2005). Self-discipline outdoes IQ in predicting academic performance of adolescents. *Psychological Science, 16* (12), 939-944.

Duxbury, S. (2008, July 18). Businesses invest in charter school innovation. *San Francisco Business Times.* http://www.kippbayarea.org/ files/ 2008_07_18_ SF%20Business%20Times. pdf.

Dweck, C. (2006). *Mindset: The new psychology of success.* New York: Ballantine.

Dweck, C., Walton, G., & Cohen, G. (2014). *Tenacity: Mindsets and skills that promote long-term learning.* The Bill and Melinda Gates Foundation. https://web.stanford.edu/~gwalton/home/Welcome_files/DweckWaltonCohen_2014.pdf.

Eccles, J. (1999, Fall). The development of children ages 6 to 14. *Future Child* 9 (2), 30–44.

Editorial Board, The Washington Post. (2013, March 1). KIPP doubters proven wrong. *The Washington Post.* http://www.washingtonpost.com/opinions/kipp-doubters-proved-wrong-in-new-study/2013/03/01/f003b95c-81ef-11e2-a350-49866afab584_print.html.

Education Week. (2014, January 3). State report cards. *Education Week* 33 (6). http://www.edweek.org/ew/qc/2014/state_report_cards.html.

Eichelberger, E. (2014, March/April). 10 poverty myths, busted. *Mother Jones.* http://www. motherjones.com/politics/2014/03/10-poverty-myths-busted.

Ellison, S. (2012a). From within the belly of the beast: Rethinking the concept of the "educational marketplace" in the popular discourse of education reform. *Educational Studies* 48 (2), 119–36.

Ellison, S. (2012b). It's in the name: A synthetic inquiry of the knowledge is power program [KIPP]. *Educational Studies* 48 (6), 550–75.

Farrington, C. A., Roderick, M., Allensworth, E., Nagaoka, J., Keyes, T. S., Johnson, D. W., & Beechum, N. (2012). *Teaching adolescents to become learners. The role of noncognitive factors in shaping school performance: A critical literature review.* Chicago: University of Chicago Consortium on Chicago School Research.

Faulkner, W. (1951). *Requiem for a nun.* New York: Random House.

Fernandez, J. (2010, September 16). How did 'Superman' fly with D.C. elite? *The Hollywood Reporter.* http://www.hollywoodreporter.com/news/how-did-superman-fly-dc-27963.

Finn, C. (1997). Paternalism goes to school. In *The new paternalism: Supervisory approaches to poverty*, 220–47). Edited by L. Mead. Washington, DC: Brookings Institution Press.

Finn, C., & Kanstoroom, M. (1998). Foreword. In D. Whitman, *Sweating the small stuff: Inner-city schools and the new paternalism*, ix–xvii. Washington, DC: Thomas B. Fordham Institute.

Fischer, B. (2013). Cashing in on kids: 139 ALEC bills in 2013 promote a private, for-profit education model. *Center for Media and Democracy's Special Report.* http://www.prwatch. org/node/12175.

Fletcher, M. (2007, November 13). Middle class dream eludes African American families. *Washington Post.* http://www.washingtonpost.com/wp-dyn/content/article/2007/11/12/ AR2007111201711_pf.html.

Flyvbjerg, B. (2001). *Making social science matter: Why social inquiry fails and how it can succeed again.* Cambridge: Cambridge University Press.

Foucault, M. (1977). *Discipline and punish: The birth of the prison.* New York: Vintage Books.

Foucault, M., & Lotringer, S. (2007). What is critique? In *The politics of truth*, 41–82. Los Angeles, CA: Semiotext(e).Fresno Unified School District. (2008, December 11). Notice to cure and correct violations. http://www.pdf-archive.com/2015/01/05/kipp-report-fresno/.

Foundation Center. (2014). Aggregate fiscal data for top 50 FC 1000 foundations awarding grants for education, 2011. http://data.foundationcenter.org/ -/fc1000/subject:education/all/ top:foundations/list/2011.

Foundation Center. (2008). Top 25 foundations awarding US focused grants for education. http://foundationcenter.org/focus/gdf/F_Educ_Dom_2007.pdf.

Fromm, E. (1956). *The art of loving.* New York: Harper & Row.

Fromm, E. (1955). *The sane society.* New York: Fawcett World Library.

Gabbard, D., & Atkinson, T. (2007). Stossel in America: A case study of the neoliberal/ neoconservative assault on public schools and teachers. *Teacher Education Quarterly* 34 (2), 85–109.

Gabriel, T., & Medina, J. (2010, May 9). Charter schools' new cheerleaders: Financiers. *New York Times.* http://www.nytimes.com/2010/05/10/nyregion/10charter.html?pagewanted=all.

Gilead, T. (2009). Human capital, education and the promotion of social cooperation: A philosophical critique. *Studies in Philosophy and Education* 28 (6), 555–67.

Gillham, J., et al. (2007). School-based prevention of depressive symptoms: A randomized controlled study of the effectiveness and specificity of the Penn Resiliency Program. *Journal of Consulting and Clinical Psychology* 75 (1), 9–19.

Gladwell, M. (2008). *Outliers: The story of success.* New York: Little, Brown and Company.

Golden, D. (2010, April 29). Homeless dropouts from high school lured by for-profit colleges. *Bloomberg.com.* http://www.bloomberg.com/news/2010-04-30/homeless-dropouts-from-high-school-lured-by-for-profit-colleges-with-cash.html.

Goldstein, D. (2010, September 1). Grading "Waiting for Superman." *The Nation.* http://www. thenation.com/article/154986/grading-waiting-superman.

Goodnough, A. (1999, October 20). Structure and basics bring South Bronx school acclaim. *New York Times.* http://www.nytimes.com/1999/10/20/nyregion/structure-and-basics-bring-south-bronx-school-acclaim.html.

GOV.UK. (2012, May 10). *Education secretary Michael Gove's speech to Brighton College.* https://www.gov.uk/government/speeches/education-secretary-michael-goves-speech-to-brighton-college.

Grann, D. (1999, October 4). Back to basics in the Bronx. *New Republic.* https://www.cs.unm.edu/~sto/maunders/educate/grann.html.

Grannan, C. (2008, July 13). *Newsweek* recommends that Obama do a little teacher-bashing to win fans. *Examiner.com.* http://www.examiner.com/article/newsweek-recommends-that-obama-do-a-little-teacher-bashing-to-win-fans.

Grant, G. (2009). *Hope and despair in the American city: Why there are no bad schools in Raleigh.* Cambridge, MA: Harvard University Press.

Green, E. (2011, February 14). A new graduate school of education, Relay, to open next fall. *Chalkbeat New York.* http://ny.chalkbeat.org/2011/02/14/a-new-graduate-school-of-education-relay-to-open-next-fall/ - .VLGzeyeTDOE.

Haas, E. (2007). False equivalency: Think tank references on education in the news media. *Peabody Journal of Education* 82 (1), 63–102.

Hanushek, E., & Kimko, D. (2000). Schooling, labor-force quality, and the growth of nations. *American Economic Review* 9 (5), 1184–1208.

Hartnett, K. (2012, May/June). Character's content. *The Pennsylvania Gazette*, 58–64. http://www.upenn.edu/gazette/0512/PennGaz0512_feature4.pdf.

Hayek, F. (1944). *The road to serfdom.* Chicago, IL: University of Chicago Press.

Haynes, V. (2005, August 25). Charter schools expand in several new directions. *Washington Post.*

Hedges, C. (2009). America is in need of a moral bailout. *Truthdig: Drilling beneath the headlines.* http://www.truthdig.com/report/print/20090323_america_is_in_need_of_a_moral_bailout/.

Hedges, C. (2010). *Empire of illusions: The end of literacy and the triumph of spectacle.* New York: Nation Books.

Henig, J. (2008). *What do we know about the outcomes of KIPP schools?* The Great Lakes Center for Education Research and Practice. East Lansing, MI: The Great Lakes Center for Education Research & Practice. http://greatlakescenter.org/docs/Policy_Briefs/Henig_Kipp.pdf.

Heyman, G., Dweck, C., & Cain, K. (1992). Young children's vulnerability to self-blame and helplessness: Relationship to beliefs about goodness. *Child Development* 63 (2), 401–15.

Holcombe, R. (2014, August 6). *Vermont's commitment to continuous improvement.* http://education.vermont.gov/documents/EDU-Letter_to_parents_and_caregivers_AOE_8_8_14.pdf.

Holton, G. (1984). A nation at risk revisited. *Daedalus* 113 (4), 1–27.

Hopkinson, N. (2013, June 7). Organic chemistry: Two tracks of schooling raise questions about class, race and community. *Washington Post: The Root DC Live.* http://www.washingtonpost.com/blogs/therootdc/post/organic-chemistry-two-tracks-of-schooling-raise-questions-about-class-race-and-community/2013/06/07/fd4706ec-cf78-11e2-9f1a-1a7cdee20287_blog.html?wprss=rss_therootdc.

Hoppe, H. (1994). F. A. Hayek on government and social evolution: A critique. *Review of Austrian Economics* 7 (1), 67–93.

Horn, J. (2014, December 15). The Fresno KIPP report that has been scrubbed from the web. [Blog post]. http://www.schoolsmatter.info/2014/12/the-fresno-kipp-report-that-has-been.html.

Horn, J. (2013, December 17). KIPP forces 5th graders to "earn" desks by sitting on the floor for a week. *Alternet.org.* http://www.alternet.org/education/kipp-forces-5th-graders-earn-desks-sitting-floor-week.

Horn, J. (2012, September 12). A former KIPP teacher shares her story. [Blog post]. http://www.schoolsmatter.info/2012/09/a-former-kipp-teacher-shares-her-story.html.

Horn, J. (2010a). Corporatism, KIPP, and cultural eugenics. In *The Bill Gates Foundation and the future of U.S. "public" schools*. Edited by P. Kovacs. New York: Routledge.

Horn, J. (2010b, March 15). The KIPP Fresno horror story that the national media won't tell: Part I. [Blog post]. http://www.schoolsmatter.info/2009/03/kipp-fresno-horror-story-that-national.html.

Horn, J. (2009, March 5). The KULT of KIPP: An essay review. *Education Review: A Journal of Book Reviews* 12 (3). http://www.edrev.info/essays/v12n3index.html.

Horn, J., & Libby, K. (2010). The giving business: The New Schools Venture Fund. In *The Bill Gates Foundation and the future of U.S. "public" schools*. New York: Routledge.

Horn, J., & Wilburn, D. (2013). *The mismeasure of education*. Charlotte, NC: Information Age.

Heyman, G., Dweck, C., & Cain, K. (1992). Young children's vulnerability to self-blame and helplessness: Relationship to beliefs about goodness, *Child Development* 63, 401–15.

Hunt, S., & Staton, A. (1996). The communication of educational reform. *Communication Education* 45 (4), 271–92.

Isaacs, J. B. (2007a). *Economic mobility of black and white families*. Washington, DC: Brookings Institution. http://www.brookings.edu/~/media/research/files/ papers/2007/11/black-white isaacs/11_blackwhite_isaacs. pdf.

Isaacs, J. B. (2007b). *Economic mobility of families across generations*. Washington, DC: Brookings Institution. http://www.brookings.edu/research/papers/2007/11/generations-isaacs.

Isaacs, J. B., & Sawhill, I. (2008). *Reaching for the prize: The limits on economic mobility*. Washington, DC: The Brookings Institution.

Jehlen, A. (2012). Boot camp for education CEO's: The Broad Foundation Superintendents Academy. *Rethinking Schools* 27 (1), 29–34.

Johnson, J. (2009, January 1). Gingrich, Sharpton, Duncan launch education tour in Philadelphia. http://www.ed.gov/blog/2009/10/al-sharpton-newt-gingrich-and-secretary-duncan-begin-education-tour-to-expose-challenges-and-highlight-reforms-in-philadelphia/.

Jones, S. E. (2004). *Studying "success" at an "effective" school: How a nationally recognized public school overcomes racial, ethnic and social boundaries and creates a culture of success*. (Doctoral dissertation). Retrieved from Dissertations and Theses database. (UMI No. 3145736)

Joseph, G. (2014). This is what happens when you criticize Teach for America. *The Nation*. http://www.thenation.com/article/186481/what-happens-when-you-criticize-teach-america.

Kamenetz, A. (2014). The end of neighborhood schools: New Orleans is home to the nation's first all-charter district. Is this the future of education? http://apps.npr.org/the-end-of-neighborhood-schools/.

Kelling, G., & Wilson, J. (1982, March). Broken windows: The police and neighborhood safety. *The Atlantic*. http://www.theatlantic.com/magazine/archive/1982/03/broken-windows/304465/?single_page=true.

KIPP Foundation School Leadership Program. (n.d). *KIPP school leadership programs: Overview of programs and services*. Retrieved from http://tntp.org/assets/tools/KSLP_Brochure_FINAL.pdf

KIPP Foundation. (2015a). *National partners*. http://www.kipp.org/about-kipp/the-kipp-foundation/national-partners.

KIPP Foundation. (2015b). Five pillars. http://www.kipp.org/our-approach/five-pillars.

KIPP Foundation. (2015c). *Character strengths and corresponding behaviors*. http://www.kipp.org/our-approach/strengths-and-behaviors.

KIPP Foundation. (2015d). *Frequently asked questions*. http://www.kipp.org/careers/application-resources/applicant-faqs#Candidate.

KIPP Foundation. (2015e). *KIPP school summit 2014*. http://www.kipp.org/our-approach/sharing-and-collaboration/kipp-school-summit-2014.

KIPP Foundation. (2014a). *The promise of college completion: KIPP's early successes and challenges—Spring 2014 alumni data update*. http://www.kipp.org/files/dmfile/2013AlumniUpdateonCollegeCompletion.pdf.

KIPP Foundation. (2014b). *Mike and Dave on Oprah April 2006*. [Video file]. http://vimeo.com/91438778.

KIPP Foundation. (2013). *KIPP: 2013 report card*. http://www.kipp.org/reportcard.

Klein, J. (2014). *Lessons of hope: How to fix our schools*. New York: Harper.

Kohn, A. (2001, January). Fighting the tests: A practical guide to rescuing our schools. *Phi Delta Kappan* 82 (5). http://www.alfiekohn.org/teaching/ftt.htm.

Kopp, W. (2003). *One day, all children . . . : The unlikely triumph of Teach for America and what I learned along the way*. New York: Public Affairs.

Kopp, W. & Farr, S. (2011). *A chance to make history: What works and what doesn't in providing an excellent education for all*. New York: Perseus Books Group.

Kovacs, P. E. (2006). Are public schools worth saving? If so, by whom? *Educational Policy Studies Dissertations*. http://scholarworks.gsu.edu/cgi/viewcontent.cgi?article=1005&context=ep s_diss.

Kovacs, P., & Boyles, D. (2005). Institutes, foundations and think tanks: Neoconservative influences on U.S. public schools. *Public Resistance* 1 (1), 1–18.

Kozol, J. (2007). The big enchilada. *Harpers Magazine*. http://harpers.org/archive/2007/08/the-big-enchilada/.

Kretchmar, K., Sondel, B., & Ferrare, J. (2014). Mapping the terrain: Teach for America, charter school reform, and corporate sponsorship. *Journal of Education Policy* 29 (6), 742–59.

Krugman, P. (2015a). Rip van skillsgap. *New York Times*. http://krugman.blogs.nytimes.com/2015/02/22/rip-van-skillsgap/?_r=0.

Krugman, P. (2015b). Knowledge isn't power. *New York Times*. http://www.nytimes.com/2015/02/23/opinion/paul-krugman-knowledge-isnt-power.html.

Lazear, E. (2000). Economic imperialism. *Quarterly Journal of Economics* 115 (1), 99–146.

Lemov, D. (2015). *Teach like a champion 2.0: 62 techniques that put students on the path to college*. San Francisco: Jossey Bass.

Lemov, D. (2010). *Teach like a champion: 49 techniques that put students on the path to college (K–12)*. San Francisco: Jossey-Bass.

Levenick, C. (2010, Winter). Closing the gap: The philanthropic legacy of Don Fisher. *Philanthropy Magazine*.

http://www.philanthropyroundtable.org/topic/excellence_in_philanthropy/closing_the_ gap.

Lewis, A. (1995, May). Schools and preparation for work. *Phi Delta Kappan* 76 (9), 660–61.

Lifton, R. (1961). *Thought reform and the psychology of totalism: A study of "brainwashing" in China*. New York: W. W. Norton.

Lubienski, C., Weitzel, P., & Lubienski, S. (2009). Is there a "consensus" on school choice and achievement?: Advocacy research and the emerging political economy of knowledge production. *Educational Policy* 23 (1), 161–93.

Lynam, D. et al. (1999). Project DARE: No effects at 10-year follow-up. *Journal of Consulting and Clinical Psychology* 67 (4), 590–93. http://homepage.psy.utexas.edu/HomePage/Class/Psy394Q/Behavior%20Therapy%20Class/Assigned%20Readings/Substance%20Abuse/DARE.pdf.

Lynch, M., Engle, J., & Cruz, J. (2011). *Priced out: How the wrong financial-aid policies hurt low-income students*. Washington, DC: Education Trust. https://edtrust.org/resource/priced-out-how-the-wrong-financial-aid-policies-hurt-low-income-students/.

Lyotard, J. F. (1991). *The inhuman: Reflections on time*. Stanford, CA: Stanford University Press.

Madison, J. (1900/1822). *The writings of James Madison*. Edited by Gaillard Hunt. New York: G. P. Putnam's Sons.

Main, T. (1997). Homeless men in New York City: Toward paternalism through privatization. In *The new paternalism: Supervisory approaches to poverty*, 161–81). Edited by L. Mead. Washington, DC: Brookings Institution Press.

Mathematica Policy Research. (2012). Charter-school management organizations: Diverse strategies and diverse student impacts. http://www.mathematica-mpr.com/publications/PDFs/Education/CMO_Final_updated.pdf.

Mathews, J. (2013, February 27). Biggest study ever shows KIPP gains substantial. *Washington Post.* http://www.washingtonpost.com/blogs/class-struggle/post/biggest-study-ever-says-kipp-gains-substantial/2013/02/26/ff149efa-7d50-11e2-9a75-dab0201670da_blog.html.

Mathews, J. (2009a). *Work hard, be nice: How two inspired teachers created the most promising schools in America.* New York: Algonquin Books.

Mathews, J. (2009b). Turmoil at two KIPP schools. [Blog post]. http://voices.washingtonpost.com/class-struggle/2009/03/turmoil_at_two_kipp_schools.html?wprss=rss_blog.

Mathews, J. (2008, November 7). The most promising schools in America. *Washington Post.* http://www.washingtonpost.com/wp-dyn/content/article/2008/11/07/AR2008110700861.html.

Mathews, J. (2008, Spring). Growing up fast: Will Houston's charter school expansionrevolutionize urban education? *Philanthropy Magazine.* http://www.philanthropyroundtable.org/topic/k_12_education/growing_up_fast.

Mayer, J. (2008a). *The dark side: The inside story of how the war on terror turned into a war on American ideals.* New York: Doubleday.

Mayer, J. (2008b, July 17). Mayer on Seligman. *The Atlantic.* http://www.theatlantic.com/daily-dish/archive/2008/07/mayer-on-seligman/214016/.

McDaniels, A. (2014, December 13). Collateral damage: Advocates aim to save Baltimore children from impact of violence. *Baltimore Sun.* http://www.baltimoresun.com/health/bs-md-health-violence-121114-story.html -page=1.

McDonald, L. (2013). Think tanks and the media: How the conservative movement gained entry into the education policy arena. *Educational Policy* 28 (6), 845–80.

McEvoy, A., & Welker, R. (2000). Antisocial behavior, academic failure, and school climate: A critical review. *Journal of Emotional and Behavioral Disorders* 8 (3), 130–40.

McGuinn, P. (2006). Swing issues and policy regimes: Federal education policy and the politics of policy change. *Journal of Policy History* 18 (2), 205–40.

Mead, L. (2012, March 19). James Q. Wilson: Another view. *Public Discourse.* http://www.thepublicdiscourse.com/2012/03/4991/.

Mead, L. (2009, Spring). Econs and humans. [Book review *Nudge: Improving decisions about health, wealth, and happiness*, by R. H. Thaler & C. R. Sunstein]. *Claremont Review of Books*, 18–19. http://www.aei.org/wp-content/uploads/2011/10/Econs and Humans.pdf.

Mead, L. (1997). *The new paternalism: Supervisory approaches to poverty.* Washington, DC: Brookings Institution Press.

Mead, L. (1993). *The new politics of poverty: The nonworking poor in America.* New York: Basic Books.

Mead, L. (1986). Beyond entitlement: The social obligations of citizenship. New York: Free Press.

Mehta, J. (2013). How paradigms create politics: The transformation of American educational policy, 1980–2001. *American Educational Research Journal* 50 (2), 285–324.

Milgram, S. (2009). *Obedience to authority: An experimental view.* New York: Harper Perennial Modern Classics. (Original work published 1974.)

Mindset Works, Inc. (2008–2012). *Mindset works: Spark learning.* http://www.mindsetworks.com/webnav/whatismindset.aspx.

Miron, G., Urschel, J., Mathis, W., & Tornquist, E. (2010). Schools without diversity: Educational management organizations, charter schools, and the demographic stratification of the American school system. East Lansing, MI: The Great Lakes Center for Educational Research and Practice. http://greatlakescenter.org/docs/Policy_Briefs/Miron_Diversity.pdf.

Miron, G., Urschel, J., & Saxton, N. (2011). *What makes KIPP work: Study of student characteristics, attrition, and school finance.* New York: National Center for the Study of Privatization in Education. http://www.ncspe.org/readrel.php?set=pub&cat=253.

Mischel, W. (2014). *The marshmallow test: Mastering self-control.* New York: Little, Brown.

Mischel, W., Shoda, Y., & Rodriguez, M. (1989). Delay of gratification in children. *Science* 244, 933–38.

Monahan, R. (2014, November 11). Charter schools try to retain teachers with mom-friendly policies. *The Atlantic*. http://www.theatlantic.com/education/archive/2014/11/charter-schools-now-try-to-keep-teachers-with-mom-friendly-policies/382602/.

Moore, C. (2006). *The development of commonsense psychology*. New York: Taylor and Francis.

Morris, R. (2011, September 15). KIPP co-founder: "We need to get rid of the government monopoly on education." *Uptown Messenger*. http://uptownmessenger.com/2011/09/founder-of-kipp-schools-speaks-at-tulane-university/ -comment-4836.

National Center on Education and the Economy. (2007). *Tough choices or tough times: The report of the New Commission on the Skills of the American Workforce*. San Francisco: Jossey-Bass.

National Commission on Excellence in Education. (1983, April). *A nation at risk: The imperative for educational reform*. Washington, DC: U.S. Federal Department of Education.

New Jersey Department of Education. (2004). *District Factor Groups for school districts*. http://www.state.nj.us/education/finance/rda/dfg.shtml.

New York Times. (1999, September 3). Excerpts from Bush's speech on improving education. http://www.nytimes.com/1999/09/03/us/excerpts-from-bush-s-speech-on-improving-education.html.

New York Times. (1898, November 14). To aid Hampton Institute: Dr. Frissell, the principal, explains the work for colored people and Indians at a church meeting. http://timesmachine.nytimes.com/timesmachine/1898/11/14/102127757.html?pageNumber=2.

Nichols-Barrer, I., Gill, B., Gleason, P, & Tuttle, C. (2014). Does student attrition explain KIPP's success? *Education Next* 14 (4). http://educationnext.org/student-attrition-explain-kipps-success/.

Nichols-Barrer, I., Gill, B., Gleason, P, & Tuttle, C. (2012). *Student selection, attrition, and replacement in KIPP middle schools* (updated edition). http://www.mathematica-mpr.com/~/media/publications/PDFs/education/KIPP_middle_schools_wp.pdf.

Nolen, J. (2014). Learned helplessness. *Encyclopedia Britannica*. http://www.britannica.com/EBchecked/topic/1380861/learned-helplessness.

Obama, B. (2011, January 1). Remarks by the president on No Child Left Behind flexibility. http://www.whitehouse.gov/the-press-office/2012/02/09/remarks-president-no-child-left-behind-flexibility.

Orfield, G. (2001). *Schools more separate: Consequences of a decade of resegregation*. Cambridge, MA: Harvard University Civil Rights Project. http://la.utexas.edu/users/hcleaver/330T/330TPEEOrfieldSchoolsMoreSeparate.pdf.

Orfield, G., & Yun, J. (1999). *Resegregation in American schools*. Cambridge, MA: Harvard University Civil Rights Project. http://escholarship.org/uc/item/6d01084.

Orlich, D. (2007, March 27). Poverty, ethnicity, and high stakes tests: A challenge for social and educational justice. Washington State Children's Justice Conference, Seattle, WA March 27, 2007

Orlich, D., & Gifford, G. (2006, October 20). *Test scores, poverty, and ethnicity: The new American dilemma*. Phi Delta Kappa Summit on Public Education, Washington, DC October 20, 2006. http://macaulay.cuny.edu/eportfolios/liufall2013/ files/2013/10/Highstakes-testing_poverty_ethnicity. pdf.

Padilla, R. (2011). HyperQualLite version 1.0. Computer software. Boerne, TX: Author. https://sites.google.com/site/hyperqual.

PBS News Hour. (2015, January 8). *Can teaching kids to resist the marshmallow help pave the way to success?* [Transcript]. http://www.pbs.org/newshour/bb/can-teaching-kids-resist-marshmallow-pave-road-success/.

PBS News Hour. (2010, December 7). *Secretary Duncan: Schools must become centers of communities*. [Transcript]. http://www.pbs.org/newshour/bb/education-july-dec10-duncan_12-07/.

Peters, M. (2011). *Neoliberalism and after?: Education, social policy, and the crisis of Western capitalism*. New York: Peter Lang.

Peterson, C., & Seligman, M. (2004). *Character strengths and virtues: A handbook and classification*. New York: APA/Oxford University Press.

Pew Charitable Trusts. (2013a, November). *Moving on up: Why do some Americans leave the bottom of the economic ladder, but not others?* Washington, DC: The Pew Charitable Trusts.

Pew Charitable Trusts. (2013b, December). *Mobility and the metropolis: How communities factor into economic mobility.* Washington, DC: The Pew Charitable Trusts.

Pew Charitable Trusts. (2012, July). *Pursuing the American dream: Economic mobility across generations.* Washington, DC: The Pew Charitable Trusts. http://www.Pewtrusts.org/~/media/legacy/uploadedfiles/pcs_assets/2012/PursuingAmericanDreampdf.pdf.

Philanthropy News Digest. (2009, August 21). *Richard Barth, Chief Executive Officer, KIPP Foundation.* http://philanthropynewsdigest.org/newsmakers/richard-barth-chief-executive-officer-kipp-foundation.

PR Newswire. (2010). *Paramount Vantage acquires worldwide rights to a new film by Oscar winning documentarian Davis Guggenheim and Participant Media.* http://www.prnewswire.com/news-releases/paramount-vantage-acquires-worldwide-rights-to-the-new-film-by-oscarr-winning-documentarian-davis-guggenheim-and-participant-media-82294712.html.

Quazzo, D. H., Cohn, M., Horne, J., & Moe, M. (2012). *Fall of the wall: Capital flows to education innovation: GSV Advisors' white paper.*

Rampell, M. (2009, August 27). SAT scores and family income. *New York Times.* http://economix.blogs.nytimes.com/2009/08/27/sat-scores-and-family-income/.

Rawls, K. (2013, May 8). Who is profiting from charters? The big bucks behind charter school secrecy, financial scandal and corruption. *Alternet.* http://www.alternet.org/education/who-profiting-charters-big-bucks-behind-charter-school-secrecy-financial-scandal-and.

Reckhow, S. (2013). *Follow the money: How foundation dollars change public school politics.* New York: Oxford University Press.

Rich, A. (2004). *Think Tanks, public policy, and the politics of expertise.* Cambridge, UK: Cambridge University Press.

Rich, M. (2013, August 26). At charter schools, short careers by choice. *New York Times.* http://www.nytimes.com/2013/08/27/education/at-charter-schools-short-careers-by-choice.html.

Risen, J. (2015, April 30). American Psychological Association bolstered CIA torture program, report says. *New York Times.* http://www.nytimes.com/2015/05/01/us/report-says-american-psychological-association-collaborated-on-torture-justification.html?ref=topics&_r=0.

Roeser, R., Eccles, J., & Sameroff, A. (1998). Academic and emotional functioning in early adolescence: Longitudinal relations, patterns, and prediction by experience in middle school. *Development and Psychopathology* 10, 321–52.

Rose, M. (2014, October 22). *Character education: A cautionary note.* Washington, DC: The Brookings Institution. http://www.brookings.edu/research/papers/2014/10/22-character-education-cautionary-note-rose.

Rotherham, A. (2011, April 27). KIPP schools: A reform triumph, or disappointment? *Time.* http://content.time.com/time/nation/article/0,8599,2067941,00.html.

Rothstein, R. (2004). *Class and schools: Using social, economic, and educational reform to close the black-white achievement gap.* Washington, DC: Economic Policy Institute.

Rumberger, R., & Palardy, G. (2005). Does segregation still matter? The impact of student composition on academic achievement in high school. *Teachers College Record* 107 (9), 1999–2045.

Sahlberg, P. (2011). *Finnish lesson: What can the world learn from educational change in Finland?* New York: Teachers College Press.

Saltman, K. J., & Gabbard, D. (2003). *Education as enforcement: The militarization and corporatization of schools.* New York: RoutledgeFalmer.

Sawhill, I., & Morton, J. (2007, May). *Economic mobility: Is the American dream alive and well?* Washington, DC: Brookings Institution.

Schein, E. (1961). *Coercive persuasion: A socio-psychological analysis of the "brainwashing" of American civilian prisoners by the Chinese Communists.* New York: W. W. Norton.

Schram, S. (1999). The new paternalism. [Review of the book *The new paternalism: Supervisory approaches to poverty*, by Lawrence M. Mead]. *Journal of Public Administration Research and Theory: P-PART* 9 (4), 667–72.

Scott, E., & Steinberg, L. (2008, Fall). Adolescent development and the regulation of youth crime. *Future Child* 18 (2), 15–33.

Scott, J. (2009). The politics of venture philanthropy in charter school policy and advocacy. *Educational Policy* 23 (1), 106–36.

Scott, J., Lubienski, C., & DeBray-Pelot, E. (2009). The politics of advocacy in education. *Educational Policy* 23 (1), 3–14.

Scott, N. (2011, April 14). An ex-KIPP Bronx parent speaks out. [Blog post]. http://ednotesonline.blogspot.com/2011/04/ex-kipp-bronx-parent-speaks-out.html.

Sharkey, P. (2009). *Neighborhoods and the black-white mobility gap*. The Economic Mobility Project. Washington, DC: Economic Mobility Project of the Pew Charitable Trusts.

Sharkey, P., & Graham, B. (2013). *Mobility and the metropolis: How communities factor into economic mobility*. Washington, DC: Economic Mobility Project of the Pew Charitable Trusts.

Simon, S. (2013). Teach for America rises as a political powerhouse. *Politico*. http://www.politico.com/story/2013/10/teach-for-america-rises-as-political-powerhouse-98586.html.

Singal, J. (2014, December 9). Meet the psychologists who helped the CIA torture. *New York Times Magazine*. http://nymag.com/sciencofus/2014/12/meet-the-shrinks-who-helped-the-cia-torture.html.

Sleeter, C. (2008). Equity, democracy, and neoliberal assaults on teacher education. *Teaching and Teacher Education* 24 (8), 1947–57.

Smith, H. (2005a). *Making schools work*. [Transcript]. http://www.pbs.org/makingschoolswork/atp/transcript.html.

Smith, H. (2005b). *School-by-school reform: Interview with Mike Feinberg*. Headrick Smith Productions. http://www.pbs.org/makingschoolswork/sbs/kipp/feinberg.html.

Socol, I. (2010, September 1). Irrepressible ed blogger beats me up, again. http://voices.washingtonpost.com/class-struggle/2010/09/irrepessible_ed_blogger_beats.html.

Soldz, S., Raymond, N., Reisner, S., Allen, S., Baker, I., & Keller, A. (2015). *All the president's psychologists: The American Psychological Association's secret complicity with the White House and US intelligence community in support to the CIA's "enhanced" interrogation program*. http://www.nytimes.com/interactive/2015/05/01/us/document-report.html.

Somerby, B. (1999, September 24). Our current howler: Critique the children well. [Blog post]. http://www.dailyhowler.com/h092499_1.shtml.

Sondel, B. (2014). My many voices. *Critical Educators for Social Justice*. http://www.cesjsig.org/blog/my-many-voices-by-beth-sondel.

Soros, G. (2010). *The Soros lectures at the Central European University*. New York: Public Affairs.

St. HOPE Public Schools. (n.d). *Five pillars*. http://sthopepublicschools.org/five-pillars/.

Steinberg, L. (2014). *Age of opportunity: Lesson from the new science of adolescence*. New York: Dolan/Houghton Mifflin Harcourt.

Strauss, V. (2014, September 19). Why *"no excuses" charter schools mold "very submissive" students—starting in kindergarten*. [Blog post]. http://www.washingtonpost.com/blogs/answer-sheet/wp/2014/09/19/why-no-excuses-charter-schools-mold-very-submissive-students-starting-in-kindergarten/.

Stuit, D., & Smith, T. (2009). *Teacher turnover in charter schools*. Nashville, TN: Vanderbilt University. http://www.vanderbilt.edu/schoolchoice/documents/stuit_smith_ncspe.pdf.

Sullivan, C. (2012, July 11). *The J-factor*. [Blog post]. http://www.newschools.org/blog/the-j-factor.

Sweet, L. (2009, July 16). Obama's NAACP speech, New York, July 16, 2009. [Transcript]. *Chicago Sun-Times*. http://blogs.suntimes.com/sweet/2009/07/obamas_naacp_speech.html.

Taylor, D. (2010). Testimony regarding Seattle education. *Seattle Education*. http://seattleeducation2010.wordpress.com/2010/11/08/testimony-regarding-teach-for-america/.

Taylor, K. (2015, April 6). At Success Academy Charter Schools, high scores and polarizing tactics. *New York Times*. http://www.nytimes.com/2015/04/07/nyregion/at-success-academy-charter-schools-polarizing-methods-and-superior-results.html?_r=1.

Teach for America (2014). Teach for America welcomes most diverse talent in 25-year history. www.teachforamerica.org/press-room/press-releases/2014.

Teach for America. (2007). *2007 annual report: Teach for America.* Retrieved from http://www.teachforamerica.org/assets/documents/TeachForAmerica_Annual_Report_2007_000.pdf

Teach for Us. (2012). Has Teach for America's philosophy shifted? http://abcde.teachforus.org/2012/03/10/wendy-kopp-visits-hgse-has-tfas-philosophy-shifted/.

Thernstrom, S., & Thernstrom, A. (2003). *No excuses: Closing the racial gap in learning.* New York: Simon and Schuster.

Toch, T. (2009). Charter-management organizations: Expansion, survival, and impact. *Education Week* 29 (9), 26–27, 32.

Tomlinson, T. (1987). A nation at risk: Towards excellence for all. *Annals of the New York Academy of Sciences* 517 (1), 7–27.

Tough, P. (2012). *How children succeed: Grit, curiosity, and the hidden power of character.* New York: Houghton Mifflin Harcourt.

Tough, P. (2011, July 7). No, seriously: No excuses. *New York Times.* http://www.nytimes.com/2011/07/10/magazine/reforming-the-school-reformers.html?pagewanted=all&_r=1&.

Tough, P. (2006, November 26). What it takes to make a student. *New York Times Magazine.* http://www.nytimes.com/2006/11/26/magazine/26tough.html?pagewanted=all.

Tschang, C. (2000, January 8). *Confessions of a twenty-something single Asian male.* [Blogpost]. http://chi.blogspot.com/2001_01_07_archive.html -1898968.

Tuttle, C., Gill, B., Gleason, P., Knechtel, V., Nichols-Barrer, I., & Resch, A. (2013). *KIPP middle schools: Impacts on achievement and other outcomes.* Washington, DC: Mathematica Policy Research. http://www.kipp.org/files/dmfile/KIPP_Middle_Schools_Impact_on_Achievement_and_Other_Outcomes1.pdf .

U.S. Department of Education. (2012, November 8). *Remarks of U. S. Secretary of Education Arne Duncan at the Education Trust conference.* http://www.ed.gov/news/speeches/remarks-us-secretary-education-arne-duncan-he-education-trust-conference.

U.S. Department of Education. (2011, September 28). *U. S. Department of Education announces grants for $25 million to charter school management organizations.* Retrieved from http://www.ed.gov/news/press-releases/us-department-education-announces-grants-25-million-charter-school-management-or.

U.S. Department of Education. (2004). Successful charter schools. http://www.p12.nysed.gov/psc/documents/USDOESuccessfulCharterSchoolsreport.pdf.

U.S. Government Accounting Office. (2010, August 4). *For-profit colleges: Undercover testing finds colleges encouraged fraud and engaged in deceptive and questionable marketing practices.* Washington, DC: U.S. Government Accounting Office. http://www.gao.gov/new.items/d10948t.pdf.

Veltri, B. (2015). Voices of revitalization: Challenging the singularity of Teach for America's echo chamber. In *Teach for America counter-narratives: Alumni speak up and speak out.* Edited by T. Jameson Brewer and Kathleen deMarrais. New York: Peter Lang Publications.

Veltri, B. T. (2010). *Learning on other people's kids: Becoming a Teach for America teacher.* New York: Information Age Publishers.

Vogell, H. (2009, March 22). Charter school faces withdrawals over punishment. *Atlanta Journal-Constitution.* http://charterschoolscandals.blogspot.com/2010/05/kipp-south-fulton-academy.html.

Warne, L. (2013, July 18). Business behind charter schools. http://educationblog.ncpa.org/business-behind-charter-schools/.

Washington Post. (2013, March 1). KIPP doubters proven wrong in new study. *Washington Post.* http://www.washingtonpost.com/opinions/kipp-doubters-proved-wrong-in-new-study/2013/03/01/f003b95c-81ef-11e2-a350-49866afab584_story.html.

Weber, M., & Rubin, J. (2014). *New Jersey charter schools: A data-driven view, part 1.* Rutgers Graduate School of Education. http://www.saveourschoolsnj.org/save/corefiles/wp-content/uploads/2014/10/NJ-Charter-School-Report_10.29.2014.pdf.

White, T. (2015). Beyond dupes, disciples, and dilettantes: Ideological struggles of Teach for America corps members. In *Teach for America counter-narratives: Alumni speak up and speak out.* Edited by T. Jameson Brewer and Kathleen deMarrais. New York: Peter Lang Publications.

White, T. (2013). *Teach for America (TFA) and the "endangerment" of communities: Counterstories from TFA teachers of color.* Paper presented at the American Educational Research Association Annual Meeting, San Francisco, CA.

Wieder, B. (2012). Teach for America alums take aim at state office. *Pew Charitable Trusts.* http://www.Pewstates.org/projects/stateline/headlines/teach-for-america-alums-take-aim-at-state-office-85899401348.

Wilgoren, J. (2000, August 2). The Republicans: The issues; for 2000, the G.O.P. sees education in a new light. *New York Times.* http://www.nytimes.com/2000/08/02/us/the-republicans-the-issues-for-2000-the-gop-sees-education-in-a-new-light.html.

Woodworth, K. R., David, J. L., Guha, R., Wang, H., & Lopez-Torkos, A. (2008). *San Francisco Bay Area KIPP schools: A study of early implementation and achievement. Final report.* Menlo Park, CA: SRI International.

Zwilling, M. (2012, November 17). 6 right times to be a ready-fire-aim entrepreneur. *Forbes.* http://www.forbes.com/sites/martinzwilling/2012/11/17/6-right-times-to-be-a-ready-fire-aim-entrepreneur/.

Index